MANAGING THE GLOBALIZED ENVIRONMENT

Managing the Globalized Environment

Local strategies to secure livelihoods

edited by
TIIARIITTA GRANFELT

IT PUBLICATIONS 1999

Intermediate Technology Publications Ltd,
103-105 Southampton Row, London WC1B 4HH, UK

© the individual authors; this collection IT Publications 1999

A CIP record for this book is available from the British Library

ISBN 1 85339 4513

Typeset by J&L Composition Ltd, Filey, N. Yorks
Printed by Cromwell Press, Trowbridge

Contents

Preface

THE ENVIRONMENT AND sustainable development have grown into one of the most urgent concerns for humanity. During the last decade they have been highlighted in many ways. The United Nations Conference on Environment and Development, UNCED, held in Rio de Janeiro in 1992, became a milestone for global awareness of linkages between environment and development. It built further on the Brundtland Commission, which had focused attention on sustainability in the long term, seen from the point of view of poor people, by defining sustainable development as concerning both environment and development.

Applying the UNCED recommendations expressed in Agenda 21 requires the investigation of the local impact of global structures. A combined perspective is needed, integrating the local with the global, and this follows from globally recognized threats to the environment and people's livelihoods.

One of the themes receiving attention after UNCED is environmental coping strategies under conditions of scarcity as a precondition for secure livelihoods. Security becomes a central aspect in resource utilization; the potential for conflict stems not only from the control of resources, but also from different ways of perceiving the resource base and its proper use as a prerequisite for social and environmental security. People's relationship to the environment is always more than purely biological and rational: socio-cultural systems encompass different perceptions of the environment and influence the patterns and choices in its management.

The focus of this volume is on understanding resource management as a socio-cultural concept. The challenge this concept has brought to environmental research facing today's problems lies in integrating different areas of knowledge and combining several approaches at different levels. Improved understanding of various human management systems and their potential to adaptation and change is an urgent research need to secure people's livelihoods for the twenty-first century.

The framework for understanding the complexity in upholding secure livelihoods through sustainable resource management is outlined by Hjort-af-Ornäs and Lundqvist in their background essay. They highlight the areas of difference in understanding and capacity between local cultural systems and wider levels of societies and nations. Conflict can in many cases arise because of the range of perceptions and interests of the actors at separate levels involved in resource management.

A comprehensive discussion of security is provided in another chapter by Hydén, who traces the evolving discourse on the concept in the 1990s. The notion of security has been widened from the fast-moving variables such as military intervention or economic crashes to those operating on a longer time scale, like land degradation, population growth and climate change, all affecting the security of resource use and subsistence livelihoods. Hydén calls for integrating security at various levels—local, national and global—since different situations need and create various policy alternatives applicable in different settings.

Ibeanu presents an example of the growing incidence of conflicts arising from environmental pollution. In the Nigerian case, the source of conflict lies in political and economic power over a profitable natural resource—oil—a power ignoring the ecological and social security of local people. The idea of conflicts arising from different actors' varying definitions of resources leading to different kinds of resource management regimes is further developed in the Tanzanian setting by Rogers et al. and Boesen et al. In the former essay, we see a process of conflict finally expanding to international level between groups with entirely different world views and needs, competing over the management of a land area. In the latter one, institutional aspects of resource management and the dynamics of developing resource management mechanisms related to changing resource utilization and livelihood strategies are discussed as a means of avoiding conflict.

These essays on environmental conflict reveal the crucial role of the world view in environmental management. The discussion on sustainable livelihoods should therefore be inseparable from the cultural and political framing of how different actors perceive the world. Understanding the cultural variation in environmental management should include the consideration of the different perceptions of nature and the world, both profane and sacred, as argued by Svedin in his essay, which outlines a cultural framework for environmental management. He emphasizes, however, that there is both independence and dependence between culture and the natural world, and that the normative, value-related aspects of resource management are constantly developing in the interplay between humans and nature.

This two-way relationship between world view and nature is elaborated in Follér's historical review of the actors from different 'worlds' utilizing the tropical rain forest in Peru. Here the uneven power relations between the actors have led to a partial destruction of socio-cultural structures in parallel with natural resources depletion. She shows the continuum from the Western view of indigenous groups in the days of Columbus to that of natural resources utilization in the twentieth century: the European world view plays a central role in the globalization and modernization process with long-term impact on both local land use and people in Latin America. Follér's view on the survival of traditional management systems in the globalized environment offers some small hope in the form of growing global awareness in the 1990s.

Brondízio's study in the same geographical area presents quite a different case of traditional Amazon peasants increasing their management levels in response to growing demand for the products of the forest by urban dwellers. He examines the distinct ways in which the peasants manage flood plain forest by changing its species composition, without significantly changing its structural and functional characteristics, to meet growing demand for fruits from native species. This form of intensification of resource use has, according to him, had minimal impact on the landscape, and is an instructive example of how to intensify resource use without bringing about resource degradation and deforestation.

Norström gives another example of a local group managing a situation of environmental and social change induced by outsiders. His study reveals that this group of hunter-gatherers in South India took new subsistence opportunities in order to protect and uphold its own socio-economic structure. Norström criticizes studies analysing the influence of the globalized economy on local societies' subsistence structures. According to him, interpretations of development situations have mainly been made within a macro perspective and using an 'outside-in' angle, focusing on the economic level of society, and resulting in a too-generalized evaluation of the social processes taking place. The lack of a micro perspective often leads to an underestimation of local people's ability to deal with the outside forces, and neglects the capacity of their cultural systems to incorporate or adjust to new economic pursuits.

One more case which criticizes taking too narrow a view on complicated problems in environmental management is presented in the European context by Anderberg. He analyses the much-used material-flow perspective, and shows its limitations in focusing on single elements and in lacking connections to social changes related to economic and technological development and power relations. Anderberg calls for additional perspectives and a wider context to handle the temporal and spatial aspects of material flows, including their physical, economic and social frameworks .

The main issue of this volume, that secure livelihoods relate to sustainable resource management in a complex manner, is highlighted from different perspectives. The connecting issues of how security should be seen in this context and how environmental management varies with culture, further accentuate the interconnectedness of local and global activities. The selection of essays is intended to illustrate this complexity of local–global interaction in environmental management. The message that stands out is the urgent need to combine different perspectives, both at different levels and from separate traditions and disciplines, as well as cultural and organizational experiences.

The contributions to this volume are based on presentations at the conference on 'Livelihoods from resource flows: Awareness and contextual analysis of environmental conflict', held on 19–22 August 1996 in Linköping in Sweden and organized by The Research Programme on Environmental Policy and Society, EPOS, together with the Department of Water and Environmental Studies at the Tema Institute at Linköping University in Sweden. The conference was arranged as an Inter-Congress of the International Union of Anthropological and Ethnological Sciences, IUAES, and with participation from the International Geographical Union, IGU. The following essays were selected from among 80 contributions in order to illustrate from different angles and geographical areas the relationship of human societies to resource management and security. The rest of the contributions presented at the conference are available electronically at http://www.tema.liu.se/epos/l_h.htm. The conference and the editing of this book were made possible through grants from The Swedish Council for Planning and Coordination of Research (FRN), The Swedish International Development Cooperation Agency (Sida), UNESCO, Swedish Society for Anthropology and Geography (SSAG), Swedish Council for Research in the Humanities and Social Sciences (HSFR), The Swedish Institute, The Bank of Sweden Tercentenary Foundation and Linköping University.

The planning of the subject matter of the conference was initiated by Professor Anders Hjort-af-Ornäs, Director of EPOS. I owe him and Professor Eric Sunderland, the Secretary-General of IUAES, special thanks for their intellectual and organizational support.

TIIARIITTA GRANFELT
Editor

Contributors

STEFAN ANDERBERG, International Institute of Applied Systems Analysis (IIASA), Austria and Institute of Geography, Copenhagen University, Denmark

JANNIK BOESEN, Centre for Development Research, Copenhagen, Denmark

D. BROCKINGTON, Geography Department, Cambridge University, London, UK

EDUARDO S. BRONDÍZIO, Department of Anthropology and the Anthropological Center for Training and Research on the Human Dimensions of Global Environmental Change, Indiana University, USA

MAJ-LIS FOLLÉR, Section of Human Ecology, Göteborg University, Sweden

TIIARIITTA GRANFELT, EPOS, Research Programme on Environmental Policy and Society, Tema Institute, Linköping University, Sweden

ANDERS HJORT-AF-ORNÄS, Department of Water and Environmental Studies, Tema Institute, Linköping University, Sweden and EPOS, Research Programme on Environmental Policy and Society

K. HOMEWOOD, Anthropology Department, University College, London, UK

GÖRAN HYDÉN, Department of Political Science, University of Florida, USA

O. OKECHUKWU IBEANU, Centre for Advanced Social Science, Port Harcourt Nigeria

H. KIWASILA, Institute of Resource Assessment, University of Dar es Salaam, Tanzania

JAN LUNDQVIST, Department of Water and Environmental Studies, Tema Institute, Linköping University, Sweden

FAUSTIN MAGANGA, Institute of Resource Assessment, University of Dar es Salaam, Tanzania

CHRISTER NORSTRÖM, Department of Social Anthropology, University of Stockholm, Sweden

RIE ODGAARD, Centre for Development Research, Copenhagen, Denmark

PETER J. ROGERS, Department of Government and International Studies, Berry College, Rome, GA, USA

UNO SVEDIN, Professor, Swedish Council for Planning and Coordination of Research and Tema Institute, Linköping University, Sweden

Life, livelihood, resources and security— Links, and a call for a new order

ANDERS HJORT-AF-ORNÄS and JAN LUNDQVIST

HUMAN ACTIVITIES ARE a strong force in re-shaping the face of the earth, for better but also for worse. This volume addresses the complexities in the relations between humans and nature. It suggests that focusing on livelihood and resource flows is a suitable mode for approaching the issues. While accepting that human life and livelihoods impact on the biological and physical world in a complex manner, the point of departure is sufficiently specific for locating key principles for the earth's reshaping. At least three main outlooks can be identified, all of which concern the interplay between humans and nature and thus have a bearing on securing livelihoods. One is the fact that the physical world forms the source for meeting our basic biological needs: food, water, shelter and various services arising from ecosystems and the landscape. The second outlook refers to the aftermath of human intervention in the landscape, including the use of it as a sink for used products and various kinds of waste. The third one is of another character: it encompasses the conceptualizing of the environment; the models which form a context for human intervention in nature in space and time. The complexity is derived from the fact that all three outlooks combine for a very specific issue: upholding security in the new world called for at the Rio Summit.

The physical dimension

A significant feature of the interactions between humans and nature is an interference in the flows that occur in nature and transformations of natural capital into socially and politically desirable goods and services. Apart from benefiting from renewable resources, i.e. those resources that are regenerated through biological and hydrological cycles, humans mobilize natural capital that otherwise would have been affected only through geological processes. Most of the natural capital is returned to the landscape after use, but not in the same form. The actual form of what remains reflects on the quality of human resource management.

Any use of land, water, minerals, energy or other physical assets necessarily results in alterations in the resource set-up, as well as in the generation of by-products and waste. Some of the most essential resources are renewable and it is in this category that we find the major current challenges. If extraction and use are higher than rates of regeneration of natural capital, then fuelwood may be less easy to collect, wells may run dry, and so on. Access to physical resources becomes socially and geographically stratified. Increased consumption by more consumers suggests an intensified exploitation of both renewable and non-renewable natural resources. Paradoxically, however, access to resources on *a global scale* has never been as 'easy' as it is today (cf. Fogel, 1994). But for the poor, such figures and information are of no

1

avail. There is no comfort in watching others having access to resources while being deprived of them yourself. For the poor, access or entitlement to resources—be they food, water, or shelter—is as problematic as it used to be. The real challenge as regards decent livelihood and sustainability is to make them real—not only to some, but to all people.

By-products and waste end up in various sites; they disturb processes in a landscape and cause environmental impacts. Unwanted changes in the areas where people live and work, as well as in ecosystems, are frequently reported. Many of these changes are negative and may, for example, result in health hazards. Links between morbidity and mortality and environmental changes are, however, extremely difficult to verify. Nonetheless, the pollution of environments increases human exposure to risk. The important and partly new situation is that it is not only the immediate neighbourhood of human habitations and places where pollution occurs that is at risk. Long-distance transfer of pollutants is well documented. Harmful substances, many of which unfortunately are persistent and/or soluble and/or 'foot-loose', will reach and hit humans through air and water, food chains and consumer items, far outside the site where they are generated. Moreover, the effects of emissions are not confined to narrow time periods. Rather, the problem can be described as a lingering worry or a time bomb with widening geographical and social configuration of impacts.

The cultural and social dimension

The paradox regarding a combined increase in and hampered access to natural resources, referred to above, lies in the fact that global resources are more accessible for those who have the economic, political, technological and cultural power to control their extraction, distribution and use, while the individual or community may experience increased insecurity over resource control. Moreover, more diversified land-use patterns lead to new resource perceptions. Traditional social and cultural institutions for addressing natural resource use, for example regulating pasture access, may prove inefficient when confronted with new situations. Also, new knowledge changes the possibilities of establishing societal security by introducing increased competence, a wider resource base, and so on.

Interaction between humans and the landscape is to a large extent expressed in values and symbols, ranging from identity and solidarity to property control and power relations. Values and norm systems are significant features of the management of resource flows and have an important impact on life and livelihood. The importance of values and ethics should therefore be duly considered in discussions about sustainable development, in environmental negotiations and for the success of governance at all levels of society. Property control and power relations are crucial determinants for access to resources and, of course, to goods and services that emanate from natural resources. To be more precise, it is the access to the flow of resources from natural capital and their conversion through technology to the required goods and services, that constitute the basic life-support and conditions for livelihoods in all communities. Cultural systems (knowledge systems) and institutions provide the means to identify and deal with the interface between the environment and development. Failure to achieve the goals outlined in Agenda 21 leads to security problems. Indeed, poor access to vital resources is common in the midst of plenty, and conspicuous consumption is often a neighbour to hunger and overt destitution.

Recent thinking about development goes far beyond conventional economic growth thinking. The possibilities of supporting life and livelihoods and ensuring ecological and social sustainability are some of the significant dimensions emphasized in the current debate. Equity issues in terms of entitlement and empowerment are significant determinants in resource use. The extraction of goods and services essential for living from the natural resource base, is largely dependent on the existence of an effective demand and entitlement. A mixture of technological applications and institutional arrangements formed by the culturally determined knowledge is the very means which is required in order to withdraw resources from their natural state, distribute them and regulate their use in society.

Links between environmental sustainability and security

There are some pertinent questions which relate to the points brought up above and which underlie much of the current concern for achieving sustainability in social and political terms *if* environmental sustainability is at risk. In agreement with the notions mentioned above on the relations between humans and the physical and biological world, two issues may be identified. One refers to the carrying capacities of various resource bases. How much food and biomass, for instance, can be produced on a sustained basis, given certain constraints like, for example, finite and vulnerable water resources? On top of this physical dimension comes the qualitative one, with specific social systems and (power-based) norms for resource access. To what extent can produced food remain palatable in terms of nutritional value, and social and cultural acceptance, if pollution and environmental degradation continue unabated?

Food security could thus be addressed both in terms of overall production and how it is distributed, and in terms of food quality and its relation to environmental changes. Concerning overall production, views differ significantly. According to Sen (1994), for instance, human ingenuity, translated into technological and social progress, has brought about a situation where food output per capita has steadily increased since the days of Malthus. Sen's calculations suggest that the average per capita availability in terms of production was about 14 per cent better at the beginning of the 1990s as compared to the situation a decade earlier and 6 per cent better if the comparison refers to the situation in the mid-1970s (ibid.: 56). Also the price of food in real terms has continued to decrease (a key argument in Sen's analysis is that the purchasing power of the consumer will largely determine the level of production or increases in production). Similar analyses, although with more reservations, have been presented by, for instance, IFPRI (1995). A very different picture is provided by Brown and Kane (1994), who argue that per capita production world-wide has started to decline since the early 1990s. There is no consensus on trends in overall productivity of key resource systems and obviously no common understanding of environmental sustainability either.

Environmental sustainability may be thought of as a condition which guarantees that the functioning of ecosystems is not impaired, and that the quality of the goods and services that emanate from the natural capital is not reduced or changed so as to increase the risk for human life and well-being. An ecosystem may change in terms of composition and appearance without this having any negative impact on the life and livelihoods of those who depend on it. Change and succession is a natural feature of most of the basic resources on which humans depend. Static landscapes do not exist, even in the absence of humans. If a new set of goods and services satisfies human needs to the same degree as a previous state, there is no degradation of the resource base in terms of its potential to sustain life and livelihoods. Goods and services derived from natural capital may not be, and indeed cannot be, 'identical' over time. Changes in landscape may fit in with new human preferences. They may be perceived as undesirable from a social and cultural point of view, but not necessarily from a purely health and nutritional point of view.

There are other processes of change in the resource base that may be classified more objectively as negative. The well-known processes of desertification and desiccation are examples of such changes. Situations where resources are depleted or the productive capacity of natural capital is reduced or eliminated may be temporary, like water-logging and salinization, while others are irreversible, like the mining of fossil energy sources. Changes in ecosystems can also take place without affecting productivity in terms of yields or output, but the extractable goods and services may cause health hazards. Regardless of perception, such a change reduces security for life and livelihoods. Crops may grow very well in highly polluted soils, as the aftermath of the Chernobyl blast illustrates. Less dramatic but much more common problems arise from the use of persistent organic compounds. Pesticides and other chemicals are used widely and, as a consequence, harmful substances are bioaccumulated and spread through food chains. In most cases of this kind, the exposure is not visible and is hard to detect, while the risk of contracting diseases is significant. The sustainability of ecosystems is thus different from the sustainability of human security.

Environmental sustainability and various aspects of security are likely to be major issues when a new world order is unfolding. The agenda of the United Nations Conference on Environment and Development (UNCED) demonstrated that this awareness has permeated into the highest political level. But there are many unresolved issues in terms of how the control and management of resource flows should be designed in order to avert the threat of resource depletion and environmental degradation on the one hand, and to meet the needs and wants of a steadily growing world population on the other hand. One of the crucial issues is how to deal with the results of resource-related conflicts. Another one refers to the challenge to change and transcend the top-heavy and sectorized governance structure for the management of resources and the environment. These and other challenging issues relate to environmental awareness among the public and to political structures, norms and value systems, institutional matters, entitlement and empowerment, and, of course, to technology. These issues are dealt with in the contributions to this book. Below are a few remarks on some of the cross-cutting questions.

4

A new world order?

Conflicts and tension arise for various reasons. Mainstream Western-influenced academics tend to give them cultural, economic, political and social prefixes. This is unfortunate, since notions building upon experiences from the past tend to have limited relevance in the current situation. In many cases it is more convincing to seek deeper-lying factors behind conflicts than the socio-cultural-political. Homer-Dixon et al. (1993), for example, register a worry over a growing scarcity of renewable resources, which may spill over into social instability and civil strife. In his often-quoted article, Kaplan (1994) portrays a grim picture of how resource scarcity, among other things, could destroy the social fabric of our planet.

As already indicated, scarcity can be the outcome of insufficient availability ('absolute' scarcity) or deprived access to resources (resources in this context could refer to natural ones, but also to such assets as know-how and information). Access could be deprived through a lack of technological capacity or through socio-political barriers. There is evidence of a general polarization between those who are increasingly marginalized and those who produce or have access to produced goods and benefits (cf. UNDP, 1994, 1995). In addition, many poor 'produce', but they nevertheless have low or little access to the flow of goods and services in society, nor do they have any political influence. Child labour is an illuminating example of this.

The attention to a development which is not only interpreted in conventional growth parameters, but seen in the context of environmental support capacity and sustainability, has brought into focus new dimensions and driving forces behind stress and insecurity. Even if this did not appear centrally on the UNCED agenda (Vaillancourt, 1993), the attention to political and conflict dimensions of environment and development has been given within other global fora (such as the Global Change Programme and the NGO Global Forum).

Military relations between states are no longer at the forefront of discussions about security and political stability (cf. Hjort-af-Ornäs and Lodgaard, 1992). Instead, relations between the state and communities are given primacy, and questions of ecology dominate over, or combine with, those of economics. At the international level, natural resource sustainability has become so pertinent that it no longer makes sense to discuss international economic, political and security relations without ascribing environmental issues a central place. The struggle for (environmental) sustainability will stand out on international agenda after the ideological struggle of the Cold War period has ended. The forms of interaction will be radically different from the striving for global ideological hegemony.

One of the consequences of this new context is that diplomacy should deal more with environmental security than with military security if a new world order is to be safe. Political influence and improvements in livelihoods will increasingly emanate from environmental consideration and sound economic leadership, and less from military power. Confidence building in the twenty-first century must depart from the environmental and natural resource challenges: this is a common task which transcends national, political, ethnic, and other boundaries and which has a truly inter-generational validity.

5

Different perceptions of environmental problems at local, national and global levels

The inclusion of environmental issues in negotiations and agreements between nations and in global fora is a challenging task for two major reasons. One is that the kind of 'environmental consciousness' that has emerged so far still needs to develop a firm scientific basis of support, founded on sufficient empirical information. A distinct environmental policy for long-term sustainability is therefore difficult to formulate and execute. Environmental issues do not often lend themselves to quick and concise analysis. The myriad interlocking webs of causes and effects simply do not permit a firm interpretation of relationships between the state of the environment and secure livelihoods. This should not be an excuse and argument for doing nothing. The guiding principle should be an established political dictum that calls for action and measures to reduce the likelihood of environmental degradation.

Another major reason for inclusion is that a concern for the environment tends to look differently at various levels of aggregation and, notably, in different parts of the world. Local, national and global perceptions, for instance, differ because the problems are of different magnitudes at different levels of aggregation. Global warming may prove a serious (potential) threat for people residing in low-lying areas of the world, while it is not a direct problem for nations without a coast.

Environmental problems are not confined to administrative units. An environmental degradation process does not stop at political boundaries. Seen in this context, the nation-state and other administrative and jurisdictional entities represent rather arbitrary outcomes mainly of political and military aspirations and behaviour. Most of them have nothing to do with the kind of resource and environmental issues which now increasingly occupy national leaders and, indeed, people at large. Linking environmental security and national security too closely together may therefore be questioned. But nations are the main units and framework for policy-making through formal political and economic activities. The dissolution of nation states and their international networks is hardly a worthwhile proposition. Rather, the challenge is to define the role of these political and administrative units in the new world order (cf. Hydén in this volume).

Local perceptions about the environment are, of course, coloured by the existing needs and wants within communities. While local decisions are taken continuously, they have contextual constraints, not least in powerful economic and political or bureaucratic interests (cf. Desai, 1992: 626). This is also the issue for much of the Third World and NGO criticism of UNCED: that big business and other heavy economic interests have had a great influence through compliant national systems.

The local conceptualization of 'development' or 'livelihood' refers to a composite set of factors where natural resource management is only a part, although it could be a crucial one. There is usually a more profound difference between local conceptualizations and those representing values and approaches at higher levels in society. At the aggregate, policy-making level, problems are not experienced personally, but are 'approached' through professional obligations and interests. This is, of course, fundamentally different from the perception of people who are directly affected. Moreover, it is ironic that problems which constitute concrete threats and worries at one level, offer jobs and career opportunities at another level.

Who should be responsible for improved resource management?

Scarcity of resources and a lack of entitlement and empowerment raise the question of responsibility for improvements of life and livelihood security. Should the responsibility rest with the people who are currently deprived of access to goods and services from resource flows, or should it rest with external agencies, i.e., the state and its affiliations, together with 'professionals'? What is the role of NGOs and other organizations outside the state, including the private sector?

One possible starting point for approaching the responsibility issue is to argue that the knowledge, skills and ideas among resource users themselves—not the competence and visions among governments and external 'development agents'—must form the basis of strategies to improve resource management. This is in line with the increased activity level of NGOs and the emphasis on a 'people-first' perspective. A significant argument supporting this view is that dependence on external support has proven to be a cumbersome and tricky way out of poverty. And perhaps more crucially: cultural systems, competence and strategies may be overthrown by external interventions. Respect for indigenous values and norms is important according to this view. The importance does not only refer to its intrinsic values, however: unless the prevailing value system and the associated human resources are duly considered, it may be hard to understand a development process, so that any development intention, formulated through external agents, might give unexpected results.

It is important to distinguish between indigenous knowledge and local knowledge. Indigenous knowledge is culturally based and is of stored experiences, while local knowledge can comprise new local trials based on external experience. The argument that indigenous knowledge and capacities are the most appropriate, if not the best, approach for arresting environmental degradation and conserving the productivity of life-support systems needs to be challenged, not least since its validity is of significant relevance in the design of entitlement and empowerment strategies. Entitlement and empowerment are of limited significance if people are hindered or in other ways incapable of fully benefiting from such strategies. The establishment of new formal rules gives people titles, for instance, to land, water and other resources. The creation of an 'enabling environment', where the new social order might develop into a desirable and acceptable development, presupposes the generation of new knowledge.

Popular participation in natural resource management has been dealt with extensively, and increasingly so after UNCED. Attention is rightly given to the interplay between central and community planning and between traditional and modern knowledge systems. The conclusion regarding balance is not obvious. An analysis of environment and development with a paradigmatic shift towards 'people first' does not necessarily mean that development recommendations should exclusively be expressed in local or community terms. While local competence and entitlement to natural resources may be a necessary condition for food security and improvement in livelihoods, it is seldom sufficient or satisfactory for the desired development.

What is lacking, according to the current study, is systematic attention to the interplay between the ways resources flow into society and the ways these resources are perceived and dealt with through local institutions and local knowledge. The new order after UNCED is to progress towards, globally and locally, a sustainable existence. This goal is achieved through a mixture of initiatives at policy level in both local communities and within the state, as well as globally. The way to the new paradigm may be turbulent and the goal must be well outlined. What will sustain progress in the long run is the degree of harmony between the approaches and the effectiveness of maintaining the vision in a transient period.

Ogoni—Oil, resource flow and conflict in rural Nigeria

O. OKECHUKWU IBEANU

Introduction

THE OGONI OF Nigeria, a minority ethnic group of about 500 000 people inhabiting the oil-rich Niger delta, have become the symbol of militant resistance by rural oil-producing communities to the environmental degradation and economic ruin resulting from crude oil production.

In fact, the Ogoni situation typifies what has been happening in other rural communities of the Niger delta: oil pollution, state violence and militant resistance by local communities. In 1990, when the Ogoni resistance began, there were 75 recorded incidents of oil spillage in the area, involving over 10 000 barrels of crude oil (Ezeanozie, 1991:43). In July 1981, 10 000 villagers in Rukpokwu blocked the routes to 50 Shell oil wells, while the inhabitants of three villages in Egbema seized Agip installations at Ebocha. In October 1989, oil-drilling equipment worth N10 million (approx. US $1 million) belonging to Elf was destroyed by angry villagers in Oboburu. Two expatriate engineers were among 22 persons seriously injured. And on 1 November 1990, over 20 villagers from Umuechem were massacred by the paramilitary forces for protesting against the multinational oil giant, Shell.

There is a paucity of research literature on environmental conflicts in Africa. The few existing studies are theoretically and methodologically inadequate, though not necessarily wrong. Researchers have mostly focused attention on the negative impact of armed conflicts on the environment, and how 'wrong' environmental policy choices by African governments have resulted in conflicts. What has been most seriously neglected is how environmental pollution and degradation generate conflicts. Yet such clashes are becoming a common feature of life in many rural communities in Africa. For instance, the felling of trees for firewood and other uses has been a potent source of strife in the Sahel region. Land degradation from soil erosion has also been an important cause of communal conflict in south-eastern Nigeria (Ibeanu, 1992).

Moreover, apart from a few studies, among them some contributions to the volume edited by Hjort-af-Ornäs and Salih (1989), existing studies are also too descriptive to meet the academic necessity of explaining the link between environmental pollution and conflicts. As such, the dynamics by which pollution results in conflicts, especially in rural Africa, have been seldom delimited, conceptualized and empirically studied.

This chapter examines the logic of the growing incidence of conflicts arising from the pollution of the environment in crude-oil producing communities of rural Nigeria. Specifically, by using the Ogoni experience it explores the increasingly antagonistic relations between the Nigerian state and petrobusiness on the one hand, and local communities from which crude oil is extracted on the other. (By 'petro-business' we mean dominant social groups in Nigeria that are the beneficiaries of the oil industry, as well as multinational oil corporations. These include oil contractors, consultants, marketers, bunkerers, etc.) Repeatedly at issue in such conflicts are two things: the tremendous damage that oil production inflicts on the local environment and the requisite compensation for the afflicted communities. As Hjort-af-Ornäs (1992:5) has rightly pointed out, particular issues of concern in man's exploitation of nature today are how justice, participation and security are presented both to individuals and to countries. Indeed, security is the key concept in understanding environmental conflicts in rural Nigeria.

Rethinking security—a theoretical perspective

Predominantly, studies of security have been by Western scholars, and have tended to derive from the experiences of the West. In their self-referent construction of meaning, security is portrayed essentially as a political issue relating to power relations among states. Early on, studies were rooted in the realist tradition of international relations with its state-centric and power-focused heritage. For realists, security is an adjunct of national interest and national power. It is the capacity of a nation state to protect its internal values from external threats (Berkowitz and Bock, 1968:40). For Lippman, this capacity exists when a state '. . . does not have to sacrifice its legitimate interests to avoid war, and is able, if challenged, to maintain them by war' (quoted in Wolfers, 1952). Wolfers suggests that security is a continuum ranging from complete insecurity to almost complete security, and encompasses both objective and subjective conditions. According to him:

> . . . security, in an objective sense, measures the absence of threats to acquired values, in a subjective sense, the absence of fear that such values will be attacked. In both aspects a nation's security can run a wide gamut from almost complete insecurity or sense of insecurity at one pole, to almost complete security or absence of fear at the other (Wolfers, 1952:485).

What came to be known as the integrationist school goes one step further to link the security of states to international security. The integrationist argument is that any increase in the security of one nation may be dependent on an increase in the security of other nations, and that the concept of international security may well be as relevant as that of national security (Berkowitz and Bock, 1968; Bock and Berkowitz, 1966; Freedman, 1992).

For the past five decades, the realist perspective has dominated thinking on security in the West in spite of recent globalizing trends, particularly since the end of the Cold War. These trends are threatening the ideal of national sovereignty and the organization of the world into nation states, the very basis of the realist conception of security. As Ake et al. (n.d.) have rightly argued, globalization is itself unleashing conditions of insecurity in both the North and South:

> . . . many citizens of the North are puzzled to find themselves powerless, unemployed, poor and deprived. This perplexity often leads to paranoia, irredentism, xenophobia and aggressiveness.

In the South, the end of the Cold War has exacerbated the multiple crisis of security, economy and identity and engendered a surge of ethnic consciousness (Ake et al., n.d.:1–2).

In addition, by predicating security on the state, this conception of security legitimizes the state politically and morally. Any 'threats' to security conjure fears which are projected on to social groups which, for one reason or another, are seen as threatening security. This serves the convenience of the political élite, who then misrepresent their own security as state security (Ake et al., n.d.). Related to this, the realist view of security over-reifies the state, thereby masking the class and other regional interests that define its security. In other words, state security cannot be understood apart from the interests of social forces in struggle.

What is clear, therefore, is that all social groups desire security. Because these groups have different, often conflicting, interests, however, they place a priority on different conditions of security. As such, what is important is not state security but negotiating consensus (Ake et al., n.d.:7–8). De-emphasizing state security means that a premium is put on social security, that is security from poverty, disease, ignorance, arbitrary power, etc., both for groups and individuals or households (Ake et al., n.d.; Hjort-af-Ornäs and Salih, 1989:9; Hjort-af-Ornäs, 1989:67).

Hydén (in this volume) aptly summarizes the evolving discourse on security in recent years. The trend, as he sees it, is to rethink security both laterally (what security?) and horizontally (whose security?). In both cases, the realist focus on military power and the state is contested. The emerging lateral and vertical extension of the definition of security yields four current schools on security, namely realist, liberal, moralist and populist schools.

Security defined

Security, as we shall try to understand the concept, has two related meanings. First, it has a strictly political meaning that refers to the capacity of a ruling group to protect its interests or values (internally and externally located) from external threats, and to maintain order internally with minimal use of violence. It is in this regard that we could speak of weak and strong states. Externally, ruling groups of weak states show a low capacity to protect their interests; and internally, force or violence characterize the state's transactions with civil society. Although the use of violence and the emasculation of civil society make such states appear strong internally, it is only an illusion because they are in fact weak states (Amin, 1987:3–5).

Second, security has to do with relations of the labour process. In this sense, it designates two organically connected relations. First is the relation between members of a society and the natural environment in which they live. Security here refers to the carrying capacity of the biophysical environment. In other words, security measures the capacity of the natural environment to sustain the physical needs of man. In this sense, two issues are important in measuring the security of a society: the extent to which members of the society understand the laws of nature (science) and use this understanding to create tools (technology), thereby enhancing their capacity to derive their physical needs from nature (Rodney, 1982); and their capacity to exploit nature *efficiently*. By this we mean the sustainable exploitation of nature, that is striking a balance between the exploitation of nature for man's immediate physical needs on the one hand, and its protection for his future needs on the other. This is what is now widely termed sustainable development.

The second relation of the labour process to which security appertains is the relation among members of a society. The relation between humans and nature always manifests itself in a historically determined social form. It involves certain relations of production (Poulantzas, 1975:18), usually expressed in social structures and institutions. Here, security means the capacity of groups (and individuals as their agents) to provide their physical and psycho-social needs and livelihoods. This means a progressive elimination of objective conditions that limit this capacity, as well as a reduction of fears and anxieties about people's abilities to meet these needs. In this sense, security has to do with protection from poverty, exploitation, disease, injustice and the like. The issue here is the control of resource flows. In modern societies, social relations are invariably antagonistic as all groups strive to maximize their security, given finite resources. The foregoing points also mean that all groups desire security. The problem is that different people have different perceptions and want different conditions of security (Ake et al., n.d.:7).

A primal role of the state is to mediate these opposing relations and conditions of security in order to keep them 'within the bounds of order' (Engels, 1978). To accomplish this role requires that the state should 'rise above' social contradictions and opposing conditions of security and appear as an impartial arbiter, always striving for consensus. By that position, it becomes possible increasingly to eliminate the use of force in managing social antagonism. It is this issue that has been variously posed in the literature as the problematique of state autonomy, Bonapartism, the national popular state, etc. (Gramsci, 1971; Poulantzas, 1978; Alavi, 1972; Leys, 1976; Ake, 1985; Ekekwe, 1986; Ibeanu, 1993a).

An examination of the Nigerian state shows, however, that it has been unable to become 'popular-national'. This has been attributed to the history of its constitution (Ibeanu, 1993a). We find that instead of appearing as the representation of the general interests of the people-nation, the Nigerian state is 'privatized' (Ake et al., n.d.), 'parcelled-out' (Ibeanu, 1993a), 'prebendal' (Joseph, 1987) and a 'means of production' (Ekekwe, 1986) used in the name of regional, ethnic, religious, class and other special interests. As a result, the Nigerian state has been clearly embroiled in social struggles and has been most ineffective in mediating them.

This has had profound consequences for conflict and security. First of all, social relations are particularly violent as a privatized state becomes the instrument of groups in prosecuting social struggles. Second, state violence becomes a principal variable in social conflicts. Thus it would be argued by some observers that what is happening in Nigeria is not conflict, but state violence through militarism, even though resistance to this state violence is always defined as relations between social groups. This is only an illusion, however, because it is actually the repression of the privatized state which is the cause of conflicts (Ake et al., n.d.:9). Third, since the Nigerian state has become essentially a repertory of violence used against specific groups, instead of a repository of all the interests of the people-nation, the violence it vents in clashes is devastating in terms of social cost. Finally, state violence makes conflict resolution very difficult.

All these factors also impact on security (both state and social security) in a number of ways:

o The state being privatized and parcelled out to groups and interests, the security of private individuals and groups becomes increasingly deflected as the security of the state.
o The internal security of the state, which, as we have argued, was thought to consist in the elimination of force and violence in the maintenance of internal order, by contrast becomes an unending cycle of conflict and violence as state violence leads to resistance by targeted groups, resulting in more state violence and more resistance.
o The insecurity of the state against external aggression and insecurity felt by victims of state violence increase tremendously. We also see an increasing possibility that external threat will lead to civil strife (Rosenau, 1964).
o Security of the environment also decreases. For one thing, we find that the ability of people to protect the natural environment declines as a result of growing social stress and violence by the state. In fact, there is a positive correlation between environmental stress and social stress. For instance, where entire villages are sacked by the military and people are impoverished, environmental protection will be the least of their concerns. For another thing, state violence fuels the inefficient exploitation of nature as groups that control the state use it to justify and perpetuate their unsustainable use of natural resources and the degradation of the environment.

It is within the above theoretical perspective that the Ogoni 'story' here is situated. The first empirical deduction from our theoretical perspective is that conflicting conditions of security are canvassed by Ogonis on the one hand, and petro-business and state officials on the other (Figure 1). For the latter, security means an uninterrupted production of crude oil at 'competitive' (low) prices. Informed by a pro-growth ideology, their concern is the production of petroleum to satisfy their interest (cf. Stockdale, 1989; Underwood and King, 1989; Colby, 1991; Folke and Jansson, 1992). This is paramount, irrespective of the impact on the local inhabitants and environment or the economic irrationality of the process. For example, one of the paradoxes of oil exploitation in Ogoniland is that renewable natural resources, such as arable land and aquifers, are destroyed for the extraction of a non-renewable, finite resource like crude oil.

The continued extraction of oil in the face of opposition from oil-producing communities benefits from the support of an authoritarian political regime. The maintenance of Nigeria's military regime is linked to the uninterrupted production of crude oil. It is not difficult to see that a democratic government will be more sympathetic to the conditions of local communities and the local environment. Of course, maintaining the military government means containing the growing local and international pressures over its draconian policies, especially regarding human rights and the opening up of political

	Conditions of security	
Relations of the labour process	State officials and petro-business	Ogoni people
Relation I— man and nature	• Uninterrupted production of crude oil	• Maintenance of the carrying capacity of the environment: sustainable use of both renewable and non-renewable resources
Relation II— social relations	• Control of crude oil reserves in Ogoni and production at low prices • Maintenance of the military regime • Containment of local and international pressures on the military regime arising from its policies • Preventing the spread of Ogoni-type disaffection and strategies to other oil-producing communities	• Exercise of control over local resources, including crude oil • Eliminating the sense of deprivation • Eco-consciousness: protection of the environment from degradation by petro-business • Mass mobilization and political awareness

Figure 1. *Different conditions of security: Petro-business/state officials and Ogoni people*

space. Consequently, the security of state officials and petro-business means securing the military regime.

At another level, the struggles of oil-producing communities tend to have a demonstration effect: there is always the possibility that grievances will spread quickly from one community to another. If they are isolated, however, it becomes easier for the repressive apparatus of the state to snuff them out. Therefore, state officials seek to prevent a link-up and escalation of the struggles of oil-producing communities. This is done in two ways: by repressing single communities and by setting the oil-producing communities against one another.

On the part of the Ogoni, the condition for group security is the maintenance of the carrying capacity of the environment. It is the realization that an unsustainable exploitation of crude oil, with its devastation of farm land and fishing waters, threatens resource flows and livelihoods. As a result, protection of the environment is invariably linked with their perception of security.

When livelihoods are threatened, a feeling of deprivation ensues. People who feel deprived also feel anxious about their livelihoods. Such people are insecure. Therefore, a condition of security for the Ogoni is the elimination of deprivation, especially because of the known amount of wealth that accrues to Nigeria from crude oil. Partly therefore, the issue is justice in the distribution of resources, which, for the Ogoni, means that a fair part of the wealth generated from their land should return to them.

Finally, for the Ogoni, security is not possible without effective mobilization of the people. Most Ogonis are rural dwellers. Although the level of education has been rising across Nigeria's rural communities since independence, a great majority of the people still lack a basic education. Certainly, getting people to understand their plight and to do something about it requires effective mobilization through grassroots organizations, which are usually led by the petty bourgeoisie. This was effectively provided, at least for some time, by the Movement for the Survival of Ogoni People (MOSOP).

One historic role of the petty bourgeoisie in Africa has been the mobilization of the people into mass movements for political goals. Sometimes these movements are progressive, serving the interests of the masses of the continent. For instance, anti-colonial and independence movements fall within this category. At other times, these movements have tended to be reactionary, serving only the interests of the petty bourgeoisie, or to begin as progressive and in time degenerate into reactionary anti-people organizations. Ethnic organizations, which in many cases were active in independence struggles but in the post-independence era have been the catalysts of undemocratic policies, fall into the last group.

The tragedy of most mass movements led by the petty-bourgeoisie is that they have a high propensity to disintegrate under the weight of the selfish, anti-people interests of individuals. This is a strong indication of the inherent anti-democratic character of the African petty bourgeoisie.

The second empirical deduction that we draw from our theoretical perspective is that the Ogoni have become a target of state violence, as a result of the conflict between their conditions of security and those of the state and petro-business. The Ogoni have, in turn, mobilized themselves and tried to resist state violence, hence the spiral of violence in Ogoniland. The rest of the chapter will attempt to demonstrate these hypothetical empirical deductions derived from our theory.

Oil and a dependent political economy

Petroleum exploration in Nigeria dates back to the first few years of this century. Organized marketing and distribution were started around 1907 by a German Company, Nigerian Bitumen Corporation. In 1956, the Anglo-Dutch group Shell D'Archy discovered oil in commercial quantities at Oloibiri, a town in the Niger delta. By February 1958, Nigeria had become an oil exporter with a production level of 6000 barrels per day. Other multinational oil companies have since joined Shell (now Shell Petroleum Development

15

Company of Nigeria, SPDC), and at peak production in the 1970s, Nigeria's output was two million barrels of crude oil per day.

Today, crude oil is produced in eight states of the country, namely Rivers, Delta, Edo, Imo, Abia, Akwa-Ibom, Cross-River and Ondo. Rivers State, which is where the Ogoni and a number of other minority ethnic groups live, accounts for over half the total crude oil production in Nigeria. Shell remains the largest producer in Nigeria. Recently, the company reported that it had 94 oil fields in all, covering an area of 31 000 square kilometres in the Niger delta, from which nearly one million barrels of oil were produced daily (Shell, 1995:1).

Oil was discovered in commercial quantities in Ogoniland in 1958 (Bomu oil field). Since then, other oil fields have been established in Bodo West, Tai, Korokoro, Yorla, Lubara Creek and Lekuma. Shell, together with its joint-venture partners—Nigerian National Petroleum Corporation, Elf and Agip—runs five major oil fields in the Ogoni area. These are made up of 96 wells hooked up to five flow stations in Bomu, Korokoro, Yorla, Bodo West and Ebubu. The fields have a production potential of 28 000 barrels daily (Shell, 1995:2).

After 38 years of political independence from Britain, the Nigerian economy is one that continues to pursue essentially the colonial project of export of primary products and import of finished ones, especially consumer goods. Even the import substitution industrialization of the 1970s, which only served to deepen Nigeria's external economic dependence, has virtually collapsed, heralding a return to the very pure form of the colonial economic scheme. At the centre of this dependent economy is crude oil. Today, crude oil exports account for between 90 and 95 per cent of Nigeria's external earnings, and, with the level of domestic economic activities dwindling day by day, accounts for over 80 per cent of all national wealth.

It is not surprising that crude oil has been particularly important to the ruling groups in Nigeria. Being basically unproductive groups, they have depended profoundly on state resources. Contracts awarded through government agencies have been the main conduit for creaming off state funds generated from crude oil sales. For instance, it was recently revealed that in the last 25 years about N50 billion had gone into parastatals, with very little to show for it. The government has promised to bring to book all those who milked these agencies, although many Nigerians see this as another frantic search for legitimacy. Another case is that of the Oil Minerals Producing Areas Development Corporation (OMPADEC), which was established in 1992 as a development agency for the oil-producing communities. The agency received a take-off grant of N3 billion, and since then has almost single-handedly disbursed through contracts the 3 per cent of national revenue allocated to oil-producing communities, amounting to billions of dollars. By August 1993, only about a year after it was established, OMPADEC said that it had executed projects worth N7.5 billion in oil-producing communities. Still, most of these communities wear a depressed look. Not surprisingly, Ken Saro-Wiwa, the late Ogoni rights' crusader, described OMPADEC as an insult. In addition, the government established a Petroleum Trust Fund through which contracts worth billions of naira are being awarded.

16

As it is for state officials, so it is for petro-business. In fact, the interests of both are so interlocked that separating them is perhaps only conjectural. According to SPDC's own figures, about 634 million barrels of oil have been taken so far from Ogoniland alone. If we take an average price of $20 per barrel, we would be talking about more than $12 billion worth of crude oil. And according to Shell, this represents only 3 per cent of its crude oil production in Nigeria.

Oil is clearly a matter of life and death for Nigeria's ruling groups, especially petro-business. Their concern is to continue to produce oil at a very cheap cost. In this the environment and local communities feature very little. Obviously, environmental protection and the welfare of local communities will only feature in their calculations if their operations are threatened. It is this fact that oil-producing communities have realized and are using increasingly.

To be sure, oil production is also important to local communities. It is an irony, for instance, that the Kalabari and Nembe, two other ethnic minorities in the Niger delta, were killing each other over Shell compensation, each claiming ownership of the land on which the company struck oil in the area. On 3 February 1994, 14 Nembe people were killed by gunmen wearing military fatigues. Among the dead was a former minister and traditional ruler, Chief A.T. Spiff. At issue were Shell oil wells located on the disputed land. Five months later, on 16 July 1994, a retaliatory attack by the Nembe saw the thriving Kalabari town of Elem Sagbama levelled, with loss of lives and displacement of hundreds of Kalabaris (*The Guardian*, 1994:3:28). In the town of Finnima, inhabitants fought openly with machetes and other dangerous weapons over N20 million compensation paid by Shell (*African Concord*, 1994:4:11). These events took place at the same time as the Ogoni were crying out against Shell's environmental atrocities.

The benefits of crude oil to oil-producing communities, however meagre, have come both through OMPADEC and oil companies. OMPADEC has been engaged in all sorts of projects, including roads, electrification, water, shore protection, health, the construction of markets and schools, and housing. For its part, Shell insists that between 1987 and 1992 it spent about $2 million in Ogoniland, and since 1986 it has provided five water schemes, seven school blocks, one hospital, 17 sets of school furniture and 11 sets of science equipment to about 82 Ogoni communities, with a population of 500 000 (Shell, 1995:3–4). However, the communities insist that these are insufficient, and, more importantly, that what has been given does not vitiate the devastating ecological damage caused by crude oil production.

Environmental pollution and material deprivation in Ogoniland

The negative environmental impact of crude oil mining and refining is very well known. The pollution arising from oil spillages destroys marine life and crops, makes water unsuitable for fishing and renders many hectares of farm land unusable. Brine from oil fields contaminates water formations and streams, making them unfit as sources of drinking water. At the same time, gas flaring in the vicinity of human dwellings and high pressure oil pipelines that form a mesh across farmlands are conducive to acid rain, deforestation and the destruction of wildlife.

In addition, the dumping of toxic, non-biodegradable by-products of oil refining is dangerous to both flora and fauna, including man. For instance, metals that at high concentrations are known to cause metabolic malfunctions in human beings, such as cadmium, chromium, mercury and lead, are contained in refinery effluents constantly discharged into fresh water and farmland. They enter the food chain both by direct intake via food and drinking water, and indirectly. For example, fish are known to be able to store mercury in their brains without metabolizing it. People could in turn eat such contaminated fish (Nwankwo and Irrechukwu, n.d.).

Specifically in Ogoniland, it is recorded that 30 million barrels of crude oil were spilled in the area in 1970 (Earth Action, 1994). According to Shell, this was a result of sabotage by the Biafran Army following their defeat in the civil war (1967–70) (Shell, 1995:8). Shell figures also claim that 'in Ogoni from 1985 up to the beginning of 1993, when we withdrew our staff from the area, 5352 barrels of oil were spilled in 87 incidents'. However, other independent sources give much higher figures. According to Earth Action (1994) there were more than 2500 minor and major oil spills in Ogoniland between 1986 and 1991, including a major one in which Shell dallied for 40 days before patching a ruptured pipeline.

The tendency has been for state officials and oil companies to blame the problem on sabotage by local communities. For instance, Shell claims that out of 87 oil spill incidents in Ogoniland between 1985 and 1993, 60 (about 70 per cent) were sabotage, 44 using hacksaws. This agrees with the picture the government wants to paint. According to the Rivers State Ministry of Petroleum Resources, 8 out of 11 incidents in Ogoniland in 1990, or 73 per cent, were sabotage.

Ecological damage engendered by the petroleum industry has gone hand-in-hand with resource scarcity in oil-producing areas. Consequently, local communities have come to associate the two, sometimes unjustifiably. For instance, there is no doubt that the general economic situation in Nigeria has deteriorated tremendously in the last decade. Inflation has risen in leaps and bounds and the value of the naira has fallen dramatically from about $1 = N3 in 1986, to $1 = N80 in 1996. Under an IMF-imposed Structural Adjustment Programme (SAP), public spending has been widely cut, subsidies to mass consumption goods such as petrol have been withdrawn (the pump price of petrol has risen from N0.75/litre in 1986 to N11/litre in 1996), and a total freeze has been placed on employment. These strategies have drastically affected the standard of living and resource availability across the country, including in oil-producing communities. It is not surprising that resentment in oil-producing communities of rural Nigeria has escalated during these years of SAP. Evidence shows clearly that although there were conflicts before 1980, the situation worsened in the second half of the 1980s and into the 1990s.

However, because oil exploration by multinational oil corporations has dominated the lives and livelihoods of people in oil-producing areas for four decades, and being increasingly aware of the contrast in wealth between themselves on the one hand, and petro-business and people in government on the other, local communities hold the oil companies and government responsible for their deprivation. This is demonstrated in the demands that

18

are being made: roads, schools, hospitals, employment, support for farming, indeed everything to improve their livelihoods. Oil companies and government insist that these claims are exaggerated. The point is, however, that they reflect the strong feeling of deprivation in oil-producing communities.

The Bill of Right which the Ogoni presented to the government and people of Nigeria in October 1990 claims that their land has provided Nigeria with $30 billion dollars in oil money since 1958. In return, Ogoni people have nothing: no representation whatsoever in any institution of the Federal Government of Nigeria, no pipe-borne water, no electricity, no job opportunities in federal, state, public sector or private sector companies, and no socio-economic projects of the federal government. The Bill of Rights further insists that:

> . . . the Ogoni languages of Gokana and Khana are underdeveloped and are about to disappear, whereas other Nigerian languages are being forced on us.
> . . . That the Shell Petroleum Development Company of Nigeria Limited does not employ Ogoni people at a meaningful or any level at all, in defiance of the federal government's regulations. That the search for oil has caused severe land and food shortages in Ogoni, one of the most densely populated areas of Africa. . . . That Ogoni people lack education, health and other social facilities. That it is intolerable that one of the richest areas of Nigeria should wallow in abject poverty and destitution (MOSOP, 1992:10–11).

Some of these claims have been challenged by Shell, the government and even neighbouring oil-producing communities like Asa-Ndoki (Shell, 1995; *Daily Champion*, 1994:8:24; *AM News*, 1985:10:12). However, it is the sense of relative deprivation, the gap between expectation and actualization, concealed in these claims that is important, for it is that which makes men rebel (Gurr, 1974). It is also this sense of deprivation that is sucking more and more oil-producing communities into the whirlpool of conflict with the state and oil companies in Nigeria.

The spread of grievances

Possibly the most serious concern that the Ogoni impasse poses to the Nigerian state and its petro-business ally is the increasing probability that the Ogoni demands and strategies will have a knock-on effect and spread to other oil-producing communities. It is this fact that makes the Ogoni issue a matter that has to be solved quickly and by every possible means. Already, the shutting down of operations in Ogoniland since 1993 is hurting. Going by Shell's own figures of 28 000 barrels daily, the government and oil interests may well be losing over half a million dollars daily. For a cash-strapped, non-elected government in a decaying society, which is desirous to legitimize itself, that is an enormous loss.

Certainly, the question of legitimacy must feature strongly in the calculations of the government. The present military regime, which most Nigerians believe is little more than an extension or parody of the infamous Babangida regime, has hardly endeared itself to Nigerians. The lingering problem of the annulment of the 1993 presidential election, the continued incarceration of

19

the winner, Chief M.K.O. Abiola (who later died in jail), the yet unresolved murder of his wife, who was a leader of the pro-democracy movement, the continued harassment of democratic organizations, a transition to a civil rule programme that looks like a dress rehearsal of the Babangida one, and an inability to improve the economic conditions of Nigerians, have meant popular disaffection towards the regime. From abroad, sanctions have been imposed by the United States, European Community and the Commonwealth. On 6 May 1994, the Congressional Human Rights Caucus of the U.S. House of Representatives wrote to General Sani Abacha informing him of their concerns about human rights violations in Ogoniland, and asked him to do everything to end such violations. At home, in spite of the teetering pro-democracy movement, popular resistance, especially in the oil-producing areas, continues to keep the government on its toes. These pressures have created an urgent need to contain the Ogoni problem before it spreads irretrievably to other communities.

As far back as November 1990, about one month after the Ogoni Bill of Rights was issued, the Ogoni experience already appeared to be pointing to the future relationship between the state/petro-business and the local communities from which crude oil is exploited. The Umuechem case, in which over 20 persons were murdered in 1990 after Shell officials called in the paramilitary mobile police force to deal with demonstrating villagers, is already well publicized. More recently, *Human Rights Watch/Africa* has documented the cases of four other communities in the Niger delta: Obagi, Brass, Nembe Creek and Rumuobiokani (Human Rights Watch, 1995:34–8).

The situation is, however, that the entire oil belt of Nigeria is restive. Communities are claiming all manner of reparation from the state and oil companies. What we are witnessing is 'the politics of sharing' the national wealth, and demands for group security. What makes matters worse is that most of the oil-producing communities are ethnic minorities. As a result, 'the politics of sharing' is grafted onto the politics of ethnic majorities and minorities, giving a recipe for an inferno. In Nigeria, revenue allocation is high politics. It has remained one of the most contested political issues since the 1950s. The shift in the mid-1960s from strong regions to a strong central government was accompanied by a de-emphasis on derivation as a revenue allocation principle. Royalties for mining paid to the regions (and later to the states) fell from 50 per cent in 1963 to 20 per cent in 1975. With the promulgation of the Land Use Decree in 1978 and a new constitution in 1979, the states lost such royalties completely. The decree and the constitution vested control and ownership of all land and minerals, mineral oils and natural gas under it in the Federal Government. The result of this has been that people inhabiting areas generating the bulk of the national revenue, incidentally belonging to minority ethnic groups, feel cheated. The Ogoni are scapegoats because their strategy, which centres on the effective use of the media to create bad press for the government and petro-business, seems to be bearing fruit, especially regarding the intervention of the international community. The fear is that other communities will adopt the same means. Ken Saro-Wiwa personified this strategy.

In April 1993, Saro-Wiwa travelled to Warri in Delta State to address the National Association of Itsekiri Students. The Itsekiri are another minority, oil-rich ethnic group. On arrival, he was apprehended by 20 armed policemen. He was temporarily detained and later taken to the Patani Bridge which links Delta and Rivers States and asked not to return to Delta State (*The News*, 93:5:17). The reason for this illegal act by the police was that the authorities feared that his address would incite the students to action. Saro-Wiwa had this to say about how the other oil-producing communities were relating to the Ogoni struggle:

> They are getting interested. They have been coming to me for advice as to how they can organize their fight. . . There is no way you can take 30 billion dollars out of a territory and put nothing back. It is immoral. By the time I finish, Nigeria is going to be ashamed standing before the council of the world (*The News*, 93:5:17).

By 1993, Ken Saro-Wiwa and the Ogoni had become serious threats to the position of both state officials and petro-business. They had to be stopped, by violence if necessary.

State violence and popular resistance in Ogoniland

Ake et al. have suggested that what is happening in Africa for the most part is violent aggression by the state, rather than conflict. This is because:

> Those who are aggressed—communities, ethnic groups, minorities, religious groups, peasants, the poor, counter élite—are often not in any dispute or even systematic interaction with the people who aggress them. The aggression often occurs in the routine business of projecting power, carrying out policies without consultation or negotiation with other parties or spreading terror to sustain domination (Ake et al., n.d.:8–9).

We agree that state aggression is very important in understanding African conflicts and particularly so in the Ogoni experience. However, we do not accept that aggressors have to be the direct users of the instruments of violence for conflict to be said to exist. All they have to exercise is control, that is, the capacity to call those instruments of violence into use. Thus, when Shell called in the Second Amphibious Brigade (or caused them to be called in) to shoot unarmed villagers of Biara protesting the destruction of their crops by Shell contractors, Wilbros, it was not the soldiers who were the aggressors but Shell and government officials. It is Shell and government decision-makers with whom the villagers have been in conflict and systematic interaction.

Our thinking is that state violence is an important aspect of African conflicts, perhaps a special characteristic of it. This characteristic exists because of the private appropriation of the state in Africa. As a result, the coercive means of the state, which should be above the specific interests of conflicting parties and employed sparingly to maintain internal security, are in Africa used brazenly to aggress, repress and suppress opponents.

In Ogoniland, state violence has taken three major forms. First, it has taken the form of the harassment of Ogoni leaders through arrests, detention, surveillance, and so on. Since the Ogoni campaign began in earnest in 1991, their leaders have become regular victims of the state's security and intelligence agencies. On many occasions, the then leaders of MOSOP, like G.B. Leton,

Kobani and Saro-Wiwa, were detained and questioned. In January 1993, they were arrested in Lagos. In April of the same year, Saro-Wiwa was arrested twice. Again, on 21 June 1993 he was arrested with two other MOSOP activists, N. Dube and K. Nwile. On 13 July, criminal charges were brought against them (Ibeanu, 1993b:9; Human Rights Watch, 1995). In December 1993, Ledum Mitee, another MOSOP leader, was arrested and detained without charge. Between May and June 1994, following the murders of four Ogoni leaders, several hundred people were arrested in Ogoniland (Human Rights Watch, 1995).

Second, state violence has been used against the Ogoni by encouraging violent conflict between the Ogoni and their neighbours, and using this as a pretext to repress the Ogoni. The government readily proclaims such clashes to be purely ethnic clashes, but the frequency of such clashes among erstwhile peaceful neighbours, the extent of devastation and the sophistication of the weapons employed have convinced some independent observers that '. . . broader forces might have been interested in perhaps putting the Ogonis under pressure, probably to derail their agenda' (Claude Ake, quoted in Human Rights Watch, 1995:12). Between July 1993 and April 1994, there were at least three such conflicts between the Ogoni and their neighbours, involving the destruction of many villages, loss of life and refugees: the Andoni in July 1993, the Okrika in December 1993 and the Ndoki in April 1994. In each case, the Ogoni were blamed by the security forces.

Finally, state violence has been direct violence using the armed forces and police. Extra-judicial killings, flogging, torture, rape, looting and extortion by the security forces against the Ogoni have been widely reported. In fact, following the situation in Ogoniland, the Rivers State government established an Internal Security Task Force under Major (later Lt. Col.) Okuntimo. His job has been the systematic use of violence against the Ogoni. Indeed, Okuntimo bragged on prime-time national television that the army had taught him 204 ways of killing people, but he had used only three on the Ogoni. It is not surprising that since 21 May 1994, when four Ogoni leaders were killed in the town of Giokoo, at least 50 Ogonis have been executed by the security forces (Human Rights Watch, 1995:17). Earlier, in April 1993, in what has become known as the Wilbros Affair, at least 11 Ogonis, among them a woman, were shot at Biara by a detachment of the Second Amphibious Brigade based in Bori. They were protesting against the laying of a pipeline from Rumuekpe to Bori. Major U. Braimah of the Brigade claimed that his men were carrying out duties directed by the Federal Government (*The News*, 93:5:17).

To give legal backing to some of these acts, the military government of Babangida made a catch-all decree against treason on 4 May 1993. The decree, among other things, stipulates the death penalty for anybody who organizes war against Nigeria, attempts to intimidate the president or state governor, utters any word or publishes anything capable of breaking up Nigeria, or flies flags and does anything suggesting the creation of a new state, local government or country.

On their part, the Ogoni have reacted by way of increased mobilization and a media campaign against the state and oil companies, and sometimes through violent demonstrations, spearheaded by the Movement for the Survival of Ogoni People (MOSOP). It is the last strategy that provided the immediate cause of the division within MOSOP. A weakened MOSOP in turn meant the intensification of state violence and the death knell of the Ogoni struggle.

The implosion of the Ogoni resistance

The involution and implosion of MOSOP which culminated in the killing of four Ogoni leaders by their own people on 21 May 1994 did not surprise many. From early 1993, internal wrangling among the leaders of the movement was so great that the events of 21 May, in which Chief Edward Kobani, a former Commissioner in the Rivers State government, Chief Albert Badey, a former Secretary to the state government, Chief Samuel Orage and Chief Theophilus Orage lost their lives, were predictable.

Following the Wilbros Affair in April 1993 some leaders of MOSOP were accused of selling-out to the government. The rancour generated by that had hardly died down when a controversial decision by MOSOP led to the boycott of the 12 June presidential election that year. It was obvious that the leadership of the movement had been split into two. One group, led by Dr Leton, president of the movement, Albert Badey, Dr Birabi, Chief Kobani and the Orages, believed that the decision negated an undertaking that MOSOP had given to the Babangida Government during negotiations going on at the time. Subsequently, both Leton and Kobani resigned their positions as president and vice-president of the movement. They accused Saro-Wiwa of being brash, confrontational and authoritarian, claiming that he created the National Youth Council of Ogoni People (NYCOP) as a private army for intimidating and eliminating his enemies. They also accused him of planning to kill 13 Ogoni leaders, among them some of those who later died on 21 May 1994.

On 21 June 1993 Ken Saro-Wiwa was arrested in connection with the boycott of the election. In reaction, Ogoni youths, probably members of NYCOP, went on the rampage. Their demonstration was later seized on by their neighbours, the Andoni, to attack some Ogoni villages like Kaa in August 1994. A subsequent peace accord brokered by the Rivers State government was rejected by the Saro-Wiwa faction of MOSOP. Exchanges of angry letters among leaders of the movement followed until Gokana, one of the five clans that make up the Ogoni ethnic group, repudiated MOSOP and Saro-Wiwa in the so-called Giokoo Accord of March 1994. At that point the involution of MOSOP was completed and the struggle became Ogoni against Ogoni.

The popular view in Nigeria is that the division within the Ogoni leadership was an ideological one between moderates led by Leton and militants led by Saro-Wiwa. The author believes it to be much more than that. Without doubt, the mass of Ogoni people joined MOSOP basically to protect their livelihoods, but their leaders were essentially interested in personal power and money. The Nigerian petty bourgeoisie are not given to ideological fidelity: they are simply power fetishists. In any case, they lack the discipline and strength of character to pursue any ideological line consistently. What is always overriding is power: the power of money. Moderates could become militants and militants moderates in a short period.

The tragedy of popular movements in Nigeria is the inability of the rank and file to impose their interests on the leadership. Unless such control exists, popular movements led by the petty bourgeoisie easily degenerate into authoritarianism. The tendency of this class is to concentrate power in themselves, first as leaders of the people and then as individuals. Collective leadership is not natural to the petty bourgeoisie. The signs are always clear: internal bickering and self-seeking manoeuvres for power and money. Moderation and militancy are only strategies, not philosophies. In short, a successful mass movement like MOSOP was destined to implode and crumble as a result of leadership in-fighting, especially because of the money and power that was at stake.

Conclusions

The Ogoni story forcefully illustrates the strong link between security, resource flows and livelihoods. For one thing, livelihoods are intricately linked to patterns of resource flows, both locally and internationally. Greater control of resources by groups is a guarantee for better livelihoods. The converse is also the case. Again, resources constitute the material basis of security, however defined.

The Ogoni struggle demonstrates three things. First, the dominant state-centric, military-focused conception of security by the realist school needs to be seriously rethought, given the need to secure access to resources and protect the livelihoods of individuals and groups at both the domestic and international levels. As Hydén (in this volume) correctly argues, the post-Cold War world has given rise to 'new political interests in principles of security, notably how the security of individuals, groups and communities other than the state, can be objects of international policy'.

Second, in concrete social situations different groups perceive security differently and favour different conditions of security. The role of the state is to reconcile the different and often contradictory perceptions and conditions of security. Where the state fails to do this because it has become too partisan in favour of some groups and regional interests, violent conflicts result. Because of its bias, state violence against disfavoured groups also becomes a characteristic of conflicts. Then, the resistance of oppressed groups and victims of state violence completes what becomes a spiralling cycle of violence.

Finally, the persistence of violence distorts and destroys resource flows, thereby threatening livelihoods and the security of groups. Persistent violence also further erodes the ability of the state to reconcile the contradictory perceptions and conditions of security of different social groups. This is because the addition of state violence to social conflicts escalates violence and engenders widespread distrust of the state. Under such conditions, the 'internal security' of the state declines tremendously. At the same time, the internal weakness of the state, which arises from its inability to keep social conflicts within the bounds of order, reduces its ability to achieve the national (read: ruling groups') interests externally. In the end, the security of all groups, including the state, which is the incarnation of the dynamic interaction of the interests of all groups, is profoundly imperilled. Therefore, the Ogoni story does suggest that even though it means different conditions to different groups, the security of a nation remains an organic issue and constitutes a dialectical unity.

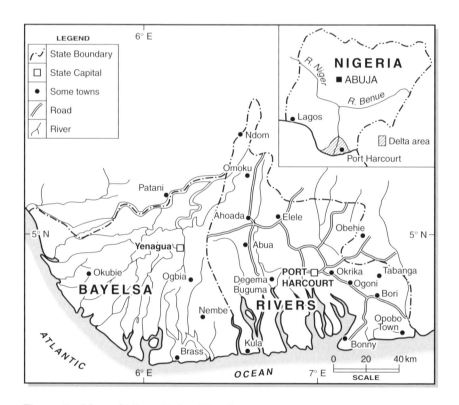

Figure 2. *Map of Niger Delta, Nigeria*

Environmental awareness and conflict genesis—People versus parks in Mkomazi game reserve, Tanzania

PETER J. ROGERS, D. BROCKINGTON, H. KIWASILA
and K. HOMEWOOD

Introduction

RESOURCES ARE DEFINED in the context of human use and their values to human communities. As a result, conflicts over resources can arise when several groups see differently resources in the same natural system. These conflicts are often exacerbated by the fact that different definitions of resources are usually accompanied by a variety of resource management regimes. In these cases, two or more groups are not only competing for resources from the same natural system, they are also attempting to impose often radically different notions of resource management upon such a system. Conflicts of this sort over resource definition and management regime in the contemporary world are likely to take place at many sites and on many scales, as the contending parties bring to bear their respective political and economic capabilities in the venues where they feel they will have the greatest success.

An excellent example of this process can be seen in the case of the Mkomazi Game Reserve (MGR), located in north-eastern Tanzania along the border with Kenya (see Figure 4 on page 50). MGR was gazetted in 1951, but grazing by local communities was allowed until 1988. At that point, pastoralists were evicted to protect the area from environmental degradation and restore the integrity of the reserve.

This chapter first explores the theoretical issues of environmental security at play in MGR: the definitions of resource, threat and security and the levels of conflict involved. Then a detailed examination of the evolution of these issues is given, tracing the changing nature of concern over resources and the escalation and internationalization of conflict. Finally an attempt is made to discuss how such conflict may be mitigated.

Theoretical issues

From a theoretical point of view, this chapter seeks to make two points. The first concerns what is understood by 'natural resources' and how such resources, seen as a subset of the more general category of 'goods', are defined as security issues. The second has to do with the multiple levels and sites of conflict and co-operation where issues of resource management and security are contested, and also the variety and number of actors who stake claims to resource definition and use. The general nature of the contemporary international system and the particular vulnerability of developing countries such as Tanzania to transnational forces mean that what might once have been local conflicts over access to resources have now often become internationalized.

26

Natural resources as social constructs and implications

Natural resources are commonly seen as those elements of the natural environment which human communities require and utilize for their survival and development. This definition emphasizes that natural resources are not independent of human needs and desires. Natural resources are as much a construction of people as they are of natural processes. Pre-industrial societies viewed surface deposits of petroleum as a moderately useful lubricant and waterproofing agent, but not as critical to their continued survival; petroleum was not seen as a security concern. Today, petroleum is the key energy source for the global economy and is commonly viewed as the most important natural resource from a security perspective. Petroleum reserves and processing facilities have been the focus of numerous, bloody military campaigns during the twentieth century, most recently the 1990 Gulf War against Iraq.

A different situation provides a similar example: the case of the African hunting dog (also known as the African wild dog) in the MGR. During the colonial era, game management authorities regarded these animals as threats to both wildlife and domestic livestock. No provisions were made for the conservation of the African hunting dogs, and their elimination was officially sanctioned. Now, however, because of their endangered state and the contemporary international values of biodiversity and aesthetics, the African hunting dog is being reintroduced to the MGR (Fitzjohn and Ellis, 1992a:6; Mduma, 1988:18; Fitzjohn, 1993:4).[1] The African hunting dog is the same animal today as it was in the 1950s. Only now, a certain human community values its existence, and it has become an important resource.

An area like the MGR contains numerous biotic and abiotic elements, all of which have the potential to be valued as natural resources by one or more groups. Pastoralists, among them the Maasai and Parakuyo (also known as the Wakwavi), value the MGR for its grazing potential, as do agropastoralists such as the Pare and Sambaa (sometimes referred to as the Shambaa). Tanzanian economic and political élites see the area's wildlife as a potential source of wealth through hunting or tourism. Conservationists, both expatriate and Tanzanian, regard the MGR highly on account of the values of biodiversity and aesthetics noted above in the example of the African hunting dog. Each of these social groups thus constructs a different MGR and a different set of natural resources, depending on how they perceive and value the different elements of the natural system.[2]

It is but a short step from the idea that natural resources are social constructs to concerns about the security of natural resources. When a social group defines and values a resource, then it will want to retain access to this resource over time. It will want to ensure natural resource security. There are

---

[1] It should be noted that the re-introduction currently underway is questioned by some conservationists due to a lack of veterinary protocols and the unknown impact of African hunting dog relocation upon the areas from where they have been obtained (Jo Driessen, pers. comm., 22 April 1996).

[2] Social construction does not mean that these groups in any sense necessarily materially alter the natural system, though material alteration may result from differing strategies of resource use. Rather, it refers to the way social groups create mental and perceptual constructs of material objects, including other social groups (see Berger and Luckmann, 1967; Schneider and Ingram, 1993).

two steps to achieving such security: first, identifying threats to the resource; and second, devising strategies to counter such threats. In the context of natural resources, these strategies are often natural resource management regimes.

For the pastoralists of northern Tanzania, a primary threat to their grazing resources has always been the over-use of resources at inappropriate times. The semi-arid savannas inhabited by pastoralists, of which the MGR is a prime example, are dynamic, unstable natural environments with a great degree of intra- and inter-year variation (see, for example, Behnke et al., 1993; Scoones, 1994). Survival of both people and their livestock requires that certain range areas be conserved until the dry season, in order that range resources are available throughout the year and in times of drought.

Pastoralists have thus developed a system of common property resource management that limits the use of certain range areas out of season and allows for the mobility and flexibility essential for the efficient utilization of the available forage and water. The reservation of areas for dry season grazing is a central feature of much pastoral management, well documented in other studies (Potnanski, 1994; Bekure et al., 1991). Calves and sick animals are unable to walk far to water and so must have grazing close to water sources, thus these dry-season reserved grazing areas (called *ololilii* or *ololopoli* in Maasai, and *mlimbiko* in Chasu, the Pare language) are frequently located near water sources. (In this chapter they will be referred to as *mlimbiko*.)

Through such management, pastoralists have attempted to achieve natural resource security. Threats to this management regime can be crudely categorized into two groups: internal threats, which arise from the misuse and abuse of reserved areas by pastoralists themselves or from visiting pastoralists of other ethnic groups (Potnanski, 1994; Charnley, 1994; Bekure et al., 1991); and external threats, those from non-pastoral interests who seek to use the land in different ways, such as for large-scale or subsistence agriculture (see, for example, Arhem, 1985; Homewood and Rodgers, 1991; Lane, 1991; Campbell, 1993; James Igoe, pers. comm.).

Ironically, the very success of the pre-colonial Maasai common property resource management regime has proved to be its undoing during the colonial and post-colonial periods when external threats have increased. A key element of pre-colonial times was the common, rather than private, ownership of land. The common ownership and regulation of access to land allows pastoralists to make use of widely scattered grazing resources that appear and disappear seasonally and from year to year. However, groups have often not been able to counter the threat posed by land alienation and private or state ownership in more recent times (see, for example, Lane, 1991; Campbell, 1993; Galaty, 1994). Lacking a concept of private land ownership, they are often unaware of the implications of land alienation by outsiders until it is too late (Fr Benedict, pers. comm., 7 March 1996; James Igoe, pers. comm., 3 April 1996).[3]

---

[3] Father Benedict was the Director of the Arusha Diocesan Development Office (ADDO) of the Catholic Church from 1986 to 1993. One of the initiatives sponsored by ADDO during his tenure was a pastoralist village registration programme designed to protect pastoralist land from alienation. Father Benedict, himself a Maasai, said that one of the main

However, conservation interests have generally been quite clear on the threats faced by wildlife, and conservationists have made attempts to ensure the security of their valued natural resources. A particularly powerful international social construction apparent in the case of the MGR, is the notion of 'nature' as wilderness or something apart from humanity, at least from modern human populations. A common theme found in a number of conservationist writings on the MGR is the image of 'a forgotten wilderness' or a 'little-known wilderness [enjoying] years of peace after the graziers have gone' (George Adamson Wildlife Preservation Trust, 1994 2; Watson, 1991:14–15). This human/nature dualism has a long history in Western thought, and though often under attack by both philosophy and science, it continues to play an important role in modern constructions of natural resources (see Evernden, 1992).

A constant theme in conservation has thus been the threat posed to 'nature', most often in the form of wildlife, by human activity.[4] This idea and its policy implications have a long history in Tanzania, going back to 1911 and the creation by the German administration of a wildlife reserve in the Serengeti/Ngorongoro area. In 1959, under British colonial rule, this protection was strengthened and all human habitation and activity, other than for research and tourism, was forbidden in the Serengeti. These policies have continued since independence and were officially sanctioned by the then President Julius Nyerere in the Arusha Manifesto of 1961 (Neumann, 1995). The expulsion of pastoralists from the MGR in the late 1980s was the latest in a long series of moves designed to separate humans from nature for the protection of the latter.[5]

Thus pastoralists and conservationists have historically not only made different social constructs out of the natural resources of areas such as the MGR, but out of these constructs have flowed varied, and often incompatible, concepts of management, threat, and natural resource security. These differences arise not only out of competing material needs (range for livestock as opposed to range for wildlife), but also out of radically different cultural and historical traditions. Because of these basic value differences, the resolution of such conflicts is often difficult. Even new and seemingly progressive conservation initiatives such as 'eco-development' and 'community-based conservation' are often viewed suspiciously by now wary pastoralist communities (Neumann, ibid.).

Natural resources as goods

Natural resources, be they endangered species or wet-season grazing for livestock, are only a part of the total basket of 'goods' sought after by social

---

problems faced by ADDO was the Maasai's lack of understanding of land ownership. There were not even words in the Maasai language to express this concept. Eventually, ADDO settled on the phrase 'branding the land' to describe village land registration, drawing parallels between the ownership of land and the ownership of cattle.

[4] For a discussion of these ideas in Africa more generally, see Anderson and Grove 1987,

[5] As a Game Reserve, Mkomazi occupies an ambiguous position in the hierarchy of protected areas in the Tanzanian legal code. Unlike a National Park, such as Serengeti, human use and settlement is not prohibited outright. Instead, in a Game Reserve, the Tanzanian Government has the right to determine what sorts of human activity are allowed. This can range from limited settlement and resource extraction, as in the Ugalla Game Reserve and Mkomazi prior to 1988, to a total ban on all but scientific and tourist uses, in effect making a Game Reserve a quasi-national park.

groups (Olson, 1965). Where attempts to secure or maintain access to such goods interact with the social construction and management of natural resources, they become relevant to this chapter.

One of the goods desired by the Tanzanian state is respect for its legitimacy and authority by both the citizens of Tanzania and international actors. This is a basic desire of all states, embodied in the concepts of national sovereignty and national security.[6] The breakdown of the MGR residence and grazing permit system in the 1970s (detailed later) was seen not merely as a threat to the MGR's natural resources, however they were defined, but also as a threat to the authority of the Tanzanian state. The decision to expel the residents of the MGR and to withdraw grazing permits thus not only served to secure the conservationist construction of natural resources, but it also had implications for state authority. The permitting system had proven to be vulnerable to corruption and manipulation, and its continued existence only served to highlight the vulnerability of state authority. Whatever the ecological outcomes of a blanket expulsion, the MGR evictions did provide the Tanzanian state with a situation that was easier to administer and an opportunity to reassert authority previously brought into question.

Non-natural resource goods can also be used to secure access to natural resources, and vice versa. Currently there are several court cases taking place against the Tanzanian Government by local people. At Vumari, in Same District, Pare agropastoralists are fighting to regain access to land and farms from which they were evicted in 1992. The other major case is that of the Maasai/Parakuyo who have taken the Tanzanian Government to court over their expulsion from the MGR. A major element of the Maasai legal argument is that the evictions violated the basic human and constitutional rights of the Maasai to live and subsist in an area to which they have a historical claim (Juma, 1996).[7] The Maasai are thus pursuing the goods of human rights in order to regain their lost natural resources. It is thus important to remember that conflicts over natural resources do not occur in isolation from the pursuit of other goods.

Internationalization and levels of conflict

One of the intriguing dimensions of the controversy over the MGR, and similar areas elsewhere in Africa and around the globe, is the degree to which it has become internationalized, often through the activities of non-governmental, rather than the more traditional state, actors (see McCormick, 1993; Haas et al., 1993). The debate over the future of the MGR is not just being conducted in the regions of Kilimanjaro and Tanga, but also in the Tanzanian capital of Dar es Salaam, as well as elsewhere around the world. All sides on the ground in Mkomazi seek allies and support from outside

---

[6] Over an almost 30-year period, comparative politics has moved from the study of 'order' to the role of 'civil society' in developing countries such as Tanzania (see, for example, Huntington, 1968; Hyden, 1980; Wunsch and Oluwu, 1990; Harbeson et al., 1994). However, in all of these works there has always been at least an implicit focus on state legitimacy and authority.

[7] Ibrahim Juma is a member of the University of Dar es Salaam Legal Aid Committee and a lawyer for Ilaramatak Lolkonerei, a Maasai NGO.

sources, with the aim of making their case to the Tanzanian state and relevant international organizations.

Three significant levels or sites of conflict can be identified: the international, national, and local.[8] At the international level, all sides seek to shape the discourse on conservation in their favour and to obtain resources, financial and otherwise, which will enable them to pursue their own constructions of natural resources, management regimes, and security strategies. Conservation, as it is currently practised in Tanzania and elsewhere in Africa, is to a great degree the product of external, non-African initiatives and interventions beginning in the colonial era (see Bonner, 1993; Parkipuny, 1989). Though currently Tanzanians occupy all the administrative positions in the country's conservation authorities, the ideas and values which drive conservation policies are still primarily of non-African origin (see Neumann, 1995). While Tanzanian conservation officials have enthusiastically adopted and acted upon these values and policies, at a more practical level, the funding of conservation programmes in Tanzania is very much dependent on external sources, either through direct grants or revenue from international tourism.

The extent of international influence and the dependence of African conservation upon Western thought and money is clearly demonstrated by The George Adamson Wildlife Preservation Trust. In addition to basing their constructions of natural resources on Western ideas about the separation of nature and humanity, conservation groups such as The George Adamson Wildlife Preservation Trust have done extensive fund-raising in the United States and Europe. This has even included an event sponsored by the Polo Ralph Lauren Beverly Hills store, which featured the introduction of Safari Perfume for men (Fitzjohn and Ellis, 1992b:9). This sort of activity allows internationalist conservation organizations to tap into popular stereotypes of Africa for their own financial benefit, while at the same time strengthening the images they manipulate to collect these funds (see Appadurai, 1994 for a general discussion of 'the global cultural economy', and Lutz and Collins, 1993 for the more specific example of *National Geographic* magazine).

African communities have been slower off the mark to enlist international allies, but this has recently begun to change. A number of pastoralist non-governmental organizations (NGOs) have been formed in Tanzania over the last five years with the aid of external donors. The Maasai NGO Ilaramatak Lolkonerei has been heavily involved in legal attempts to overturn the 1987 withdrawal of residence and grazing permits for the MGR. Its efforts have been funded by the Dutch donor NOVIB with the support of the Canadian NGO Canadian University Service Overseas (CUSO) (Saning'o and Heidenreich, 1996:2). Ilaramatak Lolkonerei has also received technical assistance and analytical support for its position from the UK-based International Institute for Environment and Development (Mustafa, 1995). In part, the recent emphasis on the goods of human rights by pastoralist groups reflects their links to, and the influence of, these international organizations. Appeals based on the human rights of 'indigenous peoples' are more

---

[8] Rosenau (1990) and Kiser and Ostrom (1982) provide slightly different views of the role of levels in political processes, with the former emphasizing the 'turbulent' nature of contemporary global politics and the latter taking a more hierarchical approach.

likely to be met with support than narrow arguments on the technical causes and impacts of overgrazing (MS-Danish Association for International Co-operation, 1996:9–10). As with conservation organizations, ideas and funds have been imported from the West into Tanzania.

It is also at the international level that the enterprise of science is conducted. Haas (1989) has suggested the existence of 'epistemic communities', informal organizations of scientists and technical experts who guide the policies of states and international organizations. However, unlike Haas's case of the Mediterranean Action Plan, a consensus has not yet been reached on many environmental issues facing the MGR, and various scientific assertions have been put forward to justify different resource management strategies. It is our hope that this epistemic conflict can give way to the more systematic testing of various hypotheses in order to gain a better understanding of what actually is happening on the ground in Mkomazi.

Despite the historical and continuing importance of the international level as a source of conservation values, it is the Tanzanian state that has ultimate authority over the use of resources in the territory under its jurisdiction. However, it is critical not to reify the state and see it as an actor in its own right. Rather the state is one more site of conflict in struggles over the construction of natural resources and resulting management strategies. Also, as was noted above, it is at the level of the state that various other goods will often make their presence felt, affecting conflicts over natural resources.

Instead of a single monolithic state, a better view is of the state as a collection of semi-autonomous actors, either organizations or individuals, with their own values, interests, and goods (see, for example, Nordlinger, 1987; March and Olson, 1989). The contrasting objectives and actions of officials at the Department of Wildlife and party leaders of *Chama cha Mapinduzi* (CCM) during the period prior to the 1987 withdrawal of permits is instructive on this count.[9] The Tanzanian Department of Wildlife began to push for the eviction of pastoralists and other residents from the MGR in the 1970s. However, it faced opposition from CCM, which was less interested in the goods of wildlife and wilderness, and more interested in the goods of popular support which might be endangered by mass expulsions (Mangubulli, 1992).

Tanzanian state actors do not operate in a vacuum at either the national or local levels. The role of non-state social groups and their relationship with the state and with each other is an important factor in any considerations of conflicts over natural resources. One key problem here is the often-stated dilemma of the weak state in Africa (see Migdal, 1988; Rothchild and Chazan, 1988). Social groups are often able to penetrate the state and advance their own agendas at the expense of official government policies and/or the interests of other communities (Bayart, 1993).

Social penetration of the state can occur both by élites and grassroots communities. An example of the former is the introduction of commercial tourist

---

[9] Prior to 1992, Tanzania was constitutionally a one-party state. As such CCM, and its pre-1977 predecessor the Tanganyika African National Union (TANU), should be viewed as integral elements of the Tanzanian state during the period in question (Msekwa, 1977; Okumu and Holmquist, 1984).

hunting in the MGR following the 1988 evictions. It was probably not the aim of the Tanzanian Department of Wildlife and its allies in international conservation organizations to remove the pastoralist 'threat' to the MGR's wildlife in order to allow the killing of this wildlife by expatriate sportsmen. However, élites in and out of the state were able to use their access to the organs of government to obtain hunting blocks in the MGR and, until 1995, to obtain substantial personal revenue from this activity, thus bringing new meaning to the notion of the 'predatory state' (Fatton, 1992). The penetration of the state by local pastoralists and agropastoralists and the impact on the MGR permitting system prior to 1987 will be discussed later.

A new element has recently been introduced into state–society relations and natural resource conflicts in Tanzania. This is the decision of pastoralist NGOs to seek redress through the judicial system, and is part of the ongoing process of political liberalization initiated in Tanzania in the late 1980s.[10] At the moment, it is not yet clear if this strategy will be effective, but it does indicate that yet another arena of conflict has been opened in the struggle for the control over and definition of natural resources. However, to the degree that the judiciary is able to make binding decisions and to have its legitimacy respected by all parties, then this might also become an avenue for conflict resolution.[11]

The local level involves not only the sort of state–society interactions described above, but also conflicts both between and inside social groups. In terms of state–society relations, it is at the local level that the MGR's protected status is actually enforced. It is also at the local level where the Department of Wildlife, in co-operation with The George Adamson Wildlife Preservation Trust, has been engaged in The Mkomazi Game Reserve Outreach Programme to supplement the 'sticks' of law enforcement with the 'carrots' of community conservation. Ultimately, the success or failure of the MGR will be determined by the effectiveness of local-level governance (see Lewis and Carter, 1993, and Western and Wright, 1994, for a recognition of this issue by active conservationists).

Another dimension of local-level conflict over natural resources is the way in which different social groups compete for the same resources. Four different ethnic groups can be found in the area of the MGR, with many individuals from each group permitted to live inside the MGR. The conflicts between these groups can be divided into two phases. During the period when residence and grazing were allowed inside the MGR, one of the factors which

---

[10] The first pastoralist legal challenge to Tanzanian state alienation of land came in 1981 when the Barabaig pastoralists of Hanang District filed suit against the National Agriculture and Food Corporation (NAFCO) over the seizure of grazing land for a Canadian-funded wheat scheme. While the Barabaig won the first round of the case, they later lost when NAFCO appealed the initial ruling in 1985 (Mwaikusa, 1993).

[11] Prof. Ringo Tenga of the University of Dar es Salaam Legal Aid Committee, an organization which has been very active is supporting pastoralist legal initiatives, feels that political considerations still play an important role in the Tanzanian judicial system, and this works against pastoralist communities which generally lack political clout. Tenga, himself a non-pastoralist, explicitly sees his legal work with pastoralists as part of the large process of political liberalization now underway in Tanzania (Tenga, pers. comm., 14 February 1996).

hastened the collapse of the permitting system was inter-group competition, often involving penetration of the state to secure grazing permits.[12]

After the 1988 evictions, the conflict shifted to the already settled areas surrounding Mkomazi, as the reserve's pastoralist inhabitants grazed livestock illegally in farmed areas, incurring fines for themselves and causing general acrimony. Since the evictions, many pastoralists and their livestock have moved far away from the MGR in all directions — from Pangani to Chalinze, Handeni, Simanjiro, and Moshi, and even as far as Monduli. In a sense, then, the problems perceived by conservationists in the MGR have been displaced to other parts of Tanzania.[13] Lastly, while many groups have been affected by the evictions from the MGR, the focus of most protests and legal action has been on the plight of the Maasai. This has angered other affected communities and led to resentment against the Maasai and the international organizations supporting them.

The final dimension of local-level conflict to be considered here is that of intra-social group conflicts, specifically between the Maasai and their NGOs. The most notable example of this has been the conflict between Ilaramatak Lolkonerei and Inyuat e-Maa, another Maasai NGO, over which one should be responsible for organizing and leading legal action against the 1987–8 evictions from the MGR. Kiondo (1994) has noted how the retreat of the state in Tanzania has opened up opportunities for local élites to use NGOs, and foreign donors to these NGOs, as vehicles for class formation and élite accumulation. Inside the Maasai community, competition between NGOs is often intense as the various organizations jockey for position and attempt to portray themselves as the legitimate leader of the community. These élites and NGOs are thus not only pursuing the goods of recovering the lost natural resources of the MGR for the Maasai community as a whole, but they are also each pursuing the narrower goods of legitimacy as leaders of the Maasai community in the eyes of both the Maasai of Tanzania and international donor organizations. (See Lemarchand, 1972 for a discussion of the link between patronage and ethnicity.)

The history of the Mkomazi Game Reserve

It is necessary now to make a more detailed examination of the history of MGR, to consider how the concerns for natural resource security outlined above have developed, and to give context to the issues outlined above. The account below focuses exclusively on the pastoral interests in the area. It is based on interviews with elders in the area, archival records, 'grey' literature and published articles.

Overview

For over 35 years, from 1951 to the late 1980s, large parts of MGR were effectively a joint-use management scheme. People and wildlife used the area

---

[12] Ironically, it was often the colonial state that played an important role in solidifying these ethnic identities (see Lemarchand, 1972; Young, 1986).

[13] Dryzek (1987) discusses the problem of 'displacement' as an all too common solution to environmental problems, rather than actual elimination or reduction of an environmental threat.

together. The end of joint use, with the eviction of pastoralists in the late 1980s, has aroused considerable national and international interest, but this sudden attention follows a long history of negotiation and conflict between pastoralists and government.

The issues at stake have not remained constant. They originated as concerns for the integrity of the state's laws and for pastoralists' needs from the gazetted area. They have changed to become the goods of, on the one hand, ensuring state sovereignty, safeguarding the environment and protecting rare and endangered species, to, on the other hand, preserving pastoral livelihoods and culture. The changing concerns reflect partly the changing context of conservation in Africa. Alarm has grown at the fate of some species and the perceived pressures of population on the few remaining areas of wild habitat. Equally, pastoralist claims are intensified by the diminishing area of lands to which they have access.

As the issues have altered, so have the participants involved. The sites of conflict have escalated from local and regional government and pastoralists to national government and international pressure groups. The dividing lines between interest groups have varied. Debates over resource definition and management have not been solely between the state and the pastoralists, for, as emphasized above, there are different viewpoints in the state and both state agents and pastoralists have been divided amongst themselves. Pastoralists have expressed concern over degradation by other pastoralists and have altered their management of the area to meet the resulting threats. Agents of the state have not always opposed pastoralists and have tried to influence and modify pastoral management. Sometimes pastoralists have had to cope with the state adding to the numbers of pastoralists in the reserve. Within the state there have been conflicting opinions as to the best use of MGR. These the pastoralists exploited, and an alliance between state agents and institutions was necessary before pastoralists were removed.

The present entrenched positions are separated not only by definitions of resources and their management, but also by a paucity of means available to negotiate the compatibility or otherwise of these concerns. In addition, entrenched positions have been adopted over the reserve as a whole, treating it as one block. It can be shown, however, that there are different histories of resource use, management, degradation and concern over degradation within MGR.

The creation of the Mkomazi Game Reserve

Early British interest in what is now MGR is recorded in 1924. Then a District Commissioner's report (Tanzania National Archives [TNA] File 1733 [28]) refers to a great waterless wilderness north of the Usambara mountains that was the domain of Wakamba people hunting rhino and elephant. This illicit traffic, organized by Arab traders, was the first international impact on the area (cf. Kimambo, 1996).

Pastoralism has a long history in the area. There is a number of records of pastoralists here in the last century, although they may have moved following the rinderpest epizootic of the early 1890s. Oral records date the current

Date	Event
1951	MGR established by British colonial authorities to replace the Ruvu Game Reserve which was thought too degraded for wildlife.
1952	List of Parakuyo pastoralists allowed to live in the area compiled in accordance with the Faunal Conservation Ordinance.
1957	Boundaries altered: Kalimawe area excised from MGR to allow grazing and cultivation. Dindira dam built.
1965	Boundaries altered: Igoma area excised for grazing and cultivation.
1967	Kavateta and Ngurunga dams complete.
1968	List of legal residents increased.
1970	Western half of the reserve opened up for grazing.
1974	Wildlife Conservation Act passed. Legal basis for residence inside reserves is altered[14]. First attempts to remove pastoralists from the western half of the game reserve fails.
1976	Further attempts to remove pastoralists fail.
1977	District level meeting advocates the removal of pastoralists.
1987	Kilimanjaro regional authorities write to cancel all previous permits for pastoralists and order them to leave the area.
1989	Eviction efforts largely complete. Further operations will be mounted as pastoralists re-enter the area repeatedly. Rehabilitation work and anti-pastoral patrols by the George Adamson Wildlife Preservation Trust begins.

Figure 3. *Table showing the history of Mkomazi Game Reserve*

Parakuyo in the area to the early 1900s (Interview: VC 26/11/1995)[15]. Records of the presence of Parakuyo pastoralists at this time are also available from mission documents of the Lutheran church (Kiel, pers. comm.). The pastoralism practised was trans-human, with people moving extensively if necessary to find pasture. This long-range movement would be from a central area, or base, to which stock returned when possible. At the base a more permanent homestead existed. Smallstock, calves and sick cows unable to move far would graze in the special grazing reserves (the *mlimbiko*) kept aside for the dry season and located close to water (Interviews: KK 10/5/1996; MK 29/4/1996). Officials in the colonial government were concerned with the extent of such movement. Regulations required permission to be sought for

---

[14] Resistance to the eviction of pastoralists in the Tanzanian courts centres on the legality of such a change and on the proper interpretation of the new powers afforded by the Wildlife Conservation Act.

[15] Interviews were conducted by D. Brockington as part of his PhD research.

inter-district movement, and crossing international borders was technically forbidden. Local geography compounded the problem. At the end of the long dry season the rains in Lushoto District fell earlier than in Same District. Pas-toralists in Same District wanted to move into Lushoto District as soon as rains made grazing available after the long dry season (Interview: Kwemkwazu 22/5/1996). Records are full of attempts to regulate the movement, especially in the interests of disease control, but it was recognized to be difficult.

MGR was gazetted in 1951.[16] David Anstey, the Game Warden of Tanga Region, reported (Anstey, 1955) that it was gazetted after a new reserve was requested 'in a stretch of country as yet uninhabited'. MGR was a replacement for the de-gazetted and degraded Ruvu Game Reserve (Parker and Archer, 1970; Mangubulli, 1992). In 1952 a report by Anstey described in detail the western half of the reserve up to the border with Lushoto (TNA File 6/1/vol. III). He recorded abundant wildlife populations and found that game increased quickly and markedly in size and visibility with the protection afforded by the reserve. He also noted the presence of 20–30 000 livestock and a few hundred inhabitants east of the Kambaga river and west of the Pare–Lushoto border. This area was de-gazetted in 1957. Additionally he found 15–20 000 cattle watering at the Katamboi waterholes. These animals belonged to Maasai pastoralists whom authorities later tried to remove from the area. Finally, Anstey found Parakuyo families further east in Lushoto District itself. These he allowed to stay, writing their names on a special list in accordance with the terms of the Faunal Conservation Ordinance. He did this because they had a long history of residence in the area and also because he thought they had a beneficial effect on the environment and deterred poachers (Anstey pers. comm.). Length of residence in the area was crucial. He rejected a claim of the Pare cattle people to grazing around the Maji Kununua area (the north-westernmost part of the reserve), saying that they had 'no traditional claim on the region at all' (1953 report, TNA File 6/1/vol. III).

It is important to note that residence in the reserve was restricted to a few families in a specific area in the Lushoto half of the reserve alone. In the western half of the game reserve, in areas of what was to become Same District, there were few pastoralists. Pastoralism here was restricted to the fringes of the mountains. Although it was expanding, as the Pare people's request indicates, the western half of the reserve remained broadly free of livestock and pastoralists until the end of the 1960s (cf. Parker and Archer, 1970).

Pastoralists in Lushoto District were noted for their strong grazing man-agement. Dry-season calf pastures were set up and policed with strict fines of a goat or a cow that would be slaughtered and eaten by all users of the calf pasture, or else sold and the money spent on beer. Parakuyo pastoralists cursed their pastures and believed that those who flouted the regulations would suffer death of stock to lions or snake bites (Interviews: MzK 15/5/1996; KK 18/5/1996; MK 21/5/1996). Cases of deliberate breaking of

---

[16] When originally founded, MGR was part of Tanga Region and fell across the Districts of Pare and Lushoto. Since it has been gazetted, administrative changes have seen the cre-ation of Kilimanjaro Region in 1963, of which Pare District was a part, and the splitting up of Pare District into Same and Mwanga Districts, both still in Kilimanjaro Region, in 1978. MGR now stretches across two regions and three districts.

the law were few, happening only once every two to three years. Residents of the area are unanimous that outsiders did follow the pasture regulations. Outsiders were not sufficiently numerous, and the calf pastures were too well established and well known for there to be trouble (KK 18/5/1996). Access to them was largely determined by residence, with people using the pastures to which they were nearest.

Management of pastures in the Lushoto portion of the reserve was generally determined by the availability of water, the main permanent source of which was the Umba River. *Mlimbiko* would be established close to water where calves, smallstock and sick cattle would not have to travel far in order to get both water and grazing. The use of areas far from the Umba River was restricted by lack of water. Grazing could only be used there in the wet season when natural depressions, such as Katamboi, filled with water. These were public water sources with access allowed to anyone. In Lushoto District the only water sources beyond the River Umba were privately controlled wells at Kamkota, discovered in the early years of this century. Access to these was restricted to the members of the finder's family. *Mlimbiko* were established around these wells, which sufficed for people, smallstock and calves, but not for adult cattle. Outsiders were allowed temporary access to water, but not on a regular basis, only when they were moving their stock past the area on long journeys (Interviews: MK 29/4/1996; LK 9/5/1996; YK 16/5/1996).

Early pastoral pressures on the reserve

Whilst pastoralism was allowed in some parts of MGR, the existence of a list of residents constituted official interference with pastoral management. Pastoralism in such semi-arid areas depends on widespread cattle movements. As animals follow the rains, so it is necessary to move beyond the present base into other people's grazing areas; it is also necessary sometimes to welcome 'outsiders'. Such reciprocal grazing rights depend upon mutual access to each other's resources. To draw up a list of legal residents is an attempt to remove such residents from this mutual access system. MGR provided highly valued and relatively disease-free grazing and there was pressure to gain access to the area. Game department records are full of concern about the immigration pressure and the consequences for residents and the environment of the influx of outsiders. Conversely, pastoralists trying to get in, and their friends and relatives who were trying to receive them, had to cope with this threat to the management of their resources and their security. They tried a mixture of opposition to the state, appeal to it, penetration of it and subterfuge.

When MGR was first gazetted, the area was already experiencing a considerable influx of Maasai pastoralists from Toloha (south-east of Lake Jipe), some of whom had been evicted from the Tsavo National Park (Mangubulli, 1992). Anstey referred to them in his early reports, complaining of some 20 000 cattle finishing up the water in the Kasigovi–Katamboi water holes, which are found just inside the Kenyan border, north of Mnazi (1952 report TNA File 6/1/vol. III). The District Commissioner (DC) of Lushoto was also concerned with the Toloha Maasai. He noted that there were many pastoralists and few game in this eastern half of the reserve (TNA File 962–1953). These pastoralists were the Parakuyo whom Anstey permitted to stay, and the

Toloha Maasai whom the DC wanted to remove. The archives record that he thought the Toloha Maasai were a nuisance and, in 1952, in accordance with a decision made at Same by Kenyan and Tanganyikan officials, began to remove them from the area (TNA File 62/6 vol. III).

The Parakuyo families (referred to as Wakwavi in government files of the period), who were already resident in the area, appear to have been highly influential in the DC's objection to the Maasai presence. There was a long history of enmity between the two groups and the Maasai were bitterly resisted when they first appeared in 1949. There was conflict on the ground, and the Parakuyo leaders also went to Lushoto to complain of the Maasai presence and to get them evicted. The DC's attempts to do so were only partly successful in 1953, when drought made it difficult to move animals long distances (TNA File 962-1953). In 1954, though, it was reported that all Maasai had left the area and that the search was continuing for as yet undiscovered households (TNA File 4/962/1954). However, this 'success' mainly reflects Parakuyo acceptance of the Maasai presence and improved relations between them. They stopped complaining and the two groups formed close relationships[17]. Intermarriage and stock friendships strengthened co-operation. Maasai men also asked for, and were given, the names of dead Parakuyo in order that they might be included on the list of legal residents (URT TA/GD/ G10/22/193; Interviews: VC Nov. 1995; MM Nov. 1995; KK 10/5/1996). Immigration of Maasai from Toloha and the Ruvu continued until the end of the 1960s, when it tailed off.

A second pressure was the descent of livestock from the Usambara mountains to the plains, instigated by the government as part of the Usambara Mountain Development Scheme. This increased the cattle populations on the reserve periphery, though probably not as much as periodically occurred when larger plains herders temporarily immigrated, following good rains. Nevertheless, it did contribute another vocal group desiring to use the reserve. At one stage, these people hired a lawyer in their bid to obtain grazing rights (Tanga Regional Archives [TRA] V.10/10 no. 169 and 182). Although they were not successful, it is clear that, where direct means failed, pastoralists were able to succeed by other methods. Maasai were not the only pastoralists to gain unofficial access. Sambaa and Pare pastoralists were able, in the 1960s, to use the reserve on a daily basis, keeping their stock near their farms outside the reserve area. Later, they were able to buy official permits from Tanga sanctioning this activity. The permits were not cheap, worth the equivalent of a large cow, some TSh100 000 at today's prices (Interview: Antakaye 20/5/1996). Pastoralists of all groups were able to penetrate the state to secure their resources.

---

[17] An extract from an interview with a Kwavi elder neatly summarizes what happened: 'Well, when they starting coming here in large numbers, we're just human, you know. We talked together, we understood each other. We understood each other, married into each other's families, we exchanged cattle. We kept quiet, we did not raise the alarm any more, we did not complain to the government. We just left it: we all lived here together'. (KK 5/10/1996).

The growth of state concern for the environment
Officials in the 1950s and 1960s were principally concerned with the effects of overgrazing and the need to balance pastoralist and wildlife needs. Anstey noted in 1953 (TNA File 962-1953) that there was probably cause to de-gazette the overgrazed area east of Kambuga.[18] This was done later, and the excised area is currently part of the Kalimawe Game Controlled Area (GCA). The DC of Lushoto, also in 1954, referred to the pastoralist-occupied area as heavily overgrazed (TRA File 4/962/1954). The government concerns were for protection of the wild environment from the damage of cattle; poaching concerns were not mentioned. (Indeed, by way of comparison with today's concerns, elephant and some 10–14 rhino were regularly shot each year for farm raiding. Also, in the mid-1950s Anstey wrote that there were too many wild dogs in the area [Anstey, 1955.]) The wildlife resources were not seen to benefit under pastoral resource management, however the latter were recognized as having some right to the area by virtue of their residence. In 1953 the DC of Lushoto wrote that: 'There is no objection to the continued existence of the reserve if it is felt to be worthwhile, provided that the existing human interest within the reserve (except the Maasai)[19] are not prejudiced' (TNA File 962 Lushoto District Annual Report, p. 14).

Anstey was prepared to set in motion the excision of the Kalimawe Game Controlled Area to meet pastoral needs and to establish a list of Parakuyo who were to be legal residents in the remaining part of the game reserve. Thus environmental security and the security of pastoral livelihoods were both official concerns, with pastoralists' rights governed by tradition of residence. The balancing occurred only in the east of the reserve. The western half, in Same District, still had few pastoralists at this time. In Lushoto District, concerns over the number of pastoralists in the area intensified in the 1960s, both because of the perceived impact of pastoralism on the environment and also because of threats to state sovereignty caused by the flouting of the permit system which the game wardens realized was occurring. Three investigations followed from these concerns, but with opposite conclusions.

In April 1966 an ecological study of the Kalimawe Game Controlled Area found that this periphery of the reserve was 15–20 times overstocked with cattle (TRA TA4, Box 12 G.1). A passionate letter by the game warden, sent to all the top officials in Tanga, Arusha, Moshi and Dar es Salaam, linked the damage in Kalimawe with problems in the reserve and called for strong action (TRA Box 12 G.1 1966:7:22). Nothing, however, appears to have been done. In 1967 an investigation into the value of MGR as a reserve concluded that turning it over to human use would just result in the destruction of the environment (Anderson, 1967). In March 1968 a further study in the Umba River area overturned findings of an investigation of 1960 and concluded that the area was 16 times overstocked. Once again it was recommended that all Maasai leave the area. Indeed the game warden went further, calling for the

---

[18] 'De-gazette' means removing a particular area of land the status of a 'game reserve'. A GCA has restrictions neither on human residence nor use of land and resources. In a game reserve both can be forbidden.
[19] 'Maasai' in this context quite clearly means the Toloha Maasai and not the Parakuyo.

Parakuyo to 'go back' to Maasai land and be incorporated into Maasai Range Development. As before, those recommendations were also sent to top government officials (URT TA/GD/G.10/16/22/19).

Exactly one month after this letter was written, a meeting decided to extend the residence permits of the existing Parakuyo and also to include a larger number of people. This meeting followed the efforts of a deputy game warden, Mussa Maimu, to deal with the many illegal occupants of the reserve. Appointed in 1963, he came across many pastoralists inside MGR who were not listed on the official register of those allowed to stay in the reserve. He had difficulty evicting them, as they claimed that they were the children of legitimate occupants who had been omitted from the original lists. A long-running dispute followed, as pastoralists without permits, with false permits, and with permits but who had moved outside of the game reserve, were all encountered by the warden as he tried to establish who was legally present. The dispute culminated in the drawing up of a new list on 17 April 1968 which comprehensively included all dependents of authorized household heads and all people whose claims were being debated. Residents were required to report to the reserve authorities any additions to their family (URT TA/GD/G10/22/193).

The record of the game department's concerns at the meeting is interesting. First, the state was not a monolithic entity attempting to control illegal immigration into the area. The game warden complained of intercession on the pastoralists' behalf by government officials who had not properly investigated the issue. Second, the warden was hardly concerned about degradation issues at all. He mentioned once that pastoralists should limit the amount of wood they cut for building, surely a minor concern as there were only 445 men, women and children recorded present at all. Instead, the issues at stake were those of state integrity—the need for the nation's laws to be obeyed. Pastoral resource management would continue so long as the state was sovereign over it.

Some explicit attempts to regulate pastoral resource management were made. There were demands for social change and nation building, with pastoralists urged to sell their animals and bank their money and contribute to national development. More significantly, pastoralists were warned not to move beyond the reserve, as it would give those without permits an opportunity to move into the reserve with the returnees' stock. The requirements of a list, strengthened this time by movement controls, both anathema to pastoralism, were reasserted. Finally, pastoral residence was also controlled by pastoralists being limited to one dry and one wet season *boma* compound.

Clearly, the requests of those concerned about rangeland degradation were refused. The changes requested were too great. Moreover, the process of sorting out permitted residents from illegal immigrants, which happened from 1963 and 1968, had clearly stirred the waters. The request of the conservationists fell on the ears of officials who were probably already deafened by the complaints of pastoralists. Mr Mwaimu specifically complained of government interference, and past behaviour by pastoralists indicates that they were immediately ready to approach the highest levels of government if their herds were threatened. Their lobbying in the 1960s was simply more successful than that of the conservationists.

Immigration into the Same section of the reserve in the 1970s and its consequences

All these debates concerned the eastern half of the game reserve and its periphery. In the west, in Same District, the area was managed for wildlife alone, although tourism never reached significant levels[20]. The main developments here were the building of three dams at Dindira, Ngurunga and Kavateta in the 1950s and 1960s. These provided a previously dry area with water points that could last much of, if not all, the dry season.

In 1969, following a severe drought, pastoralists petitioned the government to be allowed to use the western half of the game reserve. This signalled the start of a rapid and significant rise in livestock numbers in this western half, which rose from several thousand animals before 1970 to some 40 000 cattle, 18 000 goats and 11 000 sheep according to the 1978 census (Same District Livestock Office). The census is probably an underestimate, and did not mark the peak of livestock numbers. A rinderpest campaign in 1983 vaccinated over 50 000 cattle in the Same side of the reserve, 10 000 more than those found in the census of the following year (KWL). In 1986 a collection for a new water source was conducted, with pastoralists contributing 1 shilling for each head of cattle. Over TSh80 000 was raised (Interview EK 16/4/1996).

As in Lushoto District, areas of MGR within Same District provided excellent grazing. However, the rate of immigration experienced in Same District from 1970 onwards was much higher than that experienced in Lushoto District in the 1950s and 1960s. There are several reasons for this. The grazing in the west was probably even better than in the east. It combined sweet nutritious grasses with salty, mineral-rich species found on black cotton soils which are ideal for livestock. Herders would practise a two-day rotation, alternating between sweet grass and salty grass. The new water sources built by the Department of Wildlife were regarded as public resources, *maji ya mungu* ('God's water'), equal in status to natural pools and rivers (Interviews: MK 29/4/1996; MM 10/5/1996; KK 10/5/1996; MzK, LK 15/5/1996; YK 16/5/1996 and cf. Potnanski, 1994). Their presence improved access to pastures otherwise only reached in the wet season. Whereas in Lushoto District the only water sources far from the river were the privately owned wells of Kamakota, the water in the dams was an open access resource and use of it was not regulated. Also, these new areas of Same District were closer to the Ruvu and Toloha, which had been the source of immigrants to Lushoto District. The western half of the reserve was easier to get to for many people. Moreover, it was extremely easy to buy permits, giving unlimited access to the reserve. Finally, with few pastoralists to begin with, this area provided abundant grazing and it rapidly acquired a good reputation.

It is possible that grazing management was weaker in the west than in the east. In areas of Lushoto District there were well-established pastoral populations and management of grazing. Permission had to be sought from them to use wells and calf pastures. In Same District such controls were weaker in some places and could be overridden by the weight of immigrants' numbers. Throughout the 1970s, but especially after 1974 until the mid-1980s, there

---

[20] Visitors to MGR rarely exceeded 1000 each year in the 1960s and 1970s, of whom less than 50 might be overseas visitors (Turner, 1970; Ibeun, 1976).

was a remarkable rate of immigration into the reserve. The immigration was concentrated in Same District. Lushoto District experienced largely seasonal influxes in accordance with its earlier rains, but otherwise was not the focus of immigration. Indeed some pastoralists left Lushoto District to move to Same District. Immigration into Same District was further swelled by Pare pastoralists descending from the hills and starting to herd on the plains. Immigrants thus tended to be of two types: those who bought permits and resided inside the reserve; and those who just came anyway and who tended to reside around the edge of the reserve, entering and leaving on a daily basis as opportunity provided.

As a result of the immigration of the 1970s and 1980s, there was increasing concern from pastoralists and government alike about certain forms of natural resource degradation in the western half of the game reserve. The two groups were concerned with slightly different issues: the reserve authorities were concerned about the safety of wildlife and about the state of the environment, the pastoralists about overgrazing.

On the government side, it was decided, in June 1972, that no more permits were to be given because of the considerable illegal immigration that accompanied them and also because of an increase in poaching contingent upon the presence of pastoralists (URT DSG/F/40/1/77). Despite the 1972 decision, however, permits to use the game reserve continued to be issued by regional authorities. There was also immigration without state endorsement, and altogether cattle numbers rose. Unsuccessful attempts were made to evict pastoralists in 1974 and 1976. The action of 1976 provoked such uproar as to cause a general meeting between pastoralists and government officials, again the latter all local to Same District. The report of the meeting (URT DSG/F/40/1/77) reveals that the action was taken as a result of a build-up of concerns over the reserve's integrity and of degradation consequent upon immigration by pastoralists. There was also concern for the illegality of pastoral moves after some legal residents of the eastern half of the game reserve moved into the western half in the mid-1970s. The impression from the report of the meeting is that pastoral management *per se* was not thought bad, but that too much pastoralism was. The reserve authorities had to be able to control pastoralism, and pastoralists' disobedience was a threat to the legitimacy and authority of the state. The 1976 meeting resolved that all illegal residents must seek proper permission before being allowed to stay in the area.

Some pastoralists struggled to cope with the influx of livestock. A letter from the Kiswani Ward to the Same District Secretary in January 1976 (KWL File 5/1/1976) complained of illegal entry by Maasai and their herds from Ngujuka, Makonga and Makanye. It requested help to expel these herders. In September 1977 (KWL 8/9/1977) the Pare people of Igoma village, following up an earlier request, complained that outsiders were using up their grazing and then leaving the area in search of fresh pastures. The villagers requested help to survey the land and so determine a suitable stocking rate. In the following month an angry letter written by Parakuyo leaders (KWL 28/7/1977) complained of immigrants from Ngujuka bribing their way into the area and damaging the grazing; the letter claimed that long-term residents were being threatened with eviction, whilst the reserve management knew very well who the recent immigrants were. The final written word on overgrazing comes in early 1980 (KWL 20/2/1980) when the leader of the Parakuyo and Maasai pastoralists in the area, Yafuna Oseki, called a meeting of all pastoralists which announced the establishment of *vitunga*, reserved grazing areas, to which access was forbidden from 1 January to 25 August each year. These reserved grazing areas are not the same as *mlimbiko*, for they applied to all cattle, young and old, and, when open, could be used by all stock. This step was necessary because of the numbers of cattle that had been brought into the area and because of the extremely wet years at the end of the 1970s which had greatly swelled resident livestock populations. When rains lessened in the early 1980s, stockholders had trouble providing for such an abundance of animals, as grazing was finished early in the dry season. For this reason the dry-season grazing was set aside.

Grazing management was generally weaker in parts of Same District than in Lushoto District. For example, the disruption of reserved grazing areas occurred as a direct consequence of state-sanctioned immigration by pastoralists. It happened in the mid-1970s when the Pare pastoralists' *mlimbiko* near Kisiwani village were grazed out of season by Maasai and Parakuyo immigrants coming into the area in large numbers from the eastern half of the game reserve (Interviews FRM 15/2/1996; IRM 4/7/1996). Continued state-sanctioned and illegal immigration did not help matters. Interviews suggest that *mlimbiko* in the western half of the reserve were under more pressure than those in Lushoto District (Interviews ML 24/6/1996; EK 16/4/1996). Despite this, some remained strong, either because of the strength of the people governing them or because the areas they served did not experience such high immigration pressure. Areas that did experience pressure were on the borders of the reserve. Here interviewees report that much damage was also done by pastoralists without permits. These people would live around the edge of the game reserve with their herds (Interviews FRM 15/4/1996; MN 1/4/1996; MM 10/5/1996). They were afraid to graze deep inside the reserve lest they were caught and fined, and, in waiting at the edge they grazed the dry-season grazing areas that the pastoralists inside the reserve had been preserving. The borders of the game reserve are close to permanent water sources and so the *mlimbiko* located near to the reserve boundaries were therefore liable to damage and use by the illegal immigrants.

Resident pastoralists also caused problems. By early 1982 the dry-season *vitunga* had failed after resident pastoralists set up their *bomas* inside the reserved areas. In 1982 another meeting had to be called to re-establish the *vitunga* (Interviews EK 16/4/1996; ML 24/6/1996). Also, resident pastoralists tolerated the illegal immigrants around the edge of the reserve who were damaging their *mlimbiko*. They did this because of the insecurity of access that the resident pastoralists felt they had to the game reserve. They did not report illegal immigrants because they were afraid they themselves might be evicted from the reserve at any time. They did not want to endanger their position within pastoral society, should that occur, by informing on others who were not fortunate enough to have permits. Letters of complaint explicitly refuse to mention names (KWL 28/7/1977). Insecurity of tenure facilitated the breakdown of the management regime.

It has been suggested by some observers that the problems arose because of the disruptive interference of pastoral management by external forces. This is a simplification. Co-operation between pastoralists and external forces existed. The 1982 meeting over *mlimbiko* was attended by a large number of officials from the district and game reserve (Interview EK 16/4/1996). Moreover, there is evidence that reserve management and pastoralists co-operated in determining land use within the reserve. An order in 1983 (KWL 1/8/1983) instructs pastoralists who had built their *bomas* in a restricted area within the reserve not to return to live there in the next rains[21]. Thus, in Same District, the period of the 1970s and 1980s was not just one of conflict between pastoralists and external threats to their grazing management, but also one of internal threats to pastoralism and of various degrees of conflict, collusion and co-operation with external forces.

The removal of pastoralists and the internationalization of conflict
Much of this conflict over grazing management within MGR took place against a background of increasing attempts to remove pastoralists altogether. Ideological concerns had united in a new government resolve to remove them all from the area. In early 1977, at a district-level planning meeting, a firm decision to evict the pastoralists was reached, based principally on matters of policy and ideology rather than pragmatism (URT MKPR/G10/16/61): the decisions made earlier by Department of Wildlife officials which cancelled permission to live in the reserve; the villagization act which required Tanzanians to live together in villages; and, finally, the need to destock the cattle that exceeded the decreed stocking capacity.

These 'goods' were bound up in issues of security, of nation-building and development, but are not the same as the reactions to threats to resource def-inition and management that previous meetings had voiced. However, the resolve of 1977 was possibly short-lived and certainly ineffectual in the long term. Again, the state was not a united entity at this stage. Previously it had been represented by the Wildlife Department, now district and regional offi-cials were increasingly involved, and not all areas were willing to accept such a large, displaced population of pastoralists as would result from their evic-tion. The state was thus the site of conflict. Mangubulli (1992) notes that: 'Pastoralists gradually lobbied for sympathy and support from the local and national institutions. This made it extremely difficult for the Wildlife Division to sort out the conflict using police tactics.'

Records of the negotiations in this period are scattered, but it is apparent from one meeting in 1981 (KWL 13/6/1981) that pastoralists approached the Prime Minister's office in an attempt to stay on in the reserve. It is also clear that pastoralists' leaders were very much involved in choosing the new areas where they might stay.

Between 1981 and 1988 few records are available. It is not certain what happened that made it possible to overcome pastoralists' objections and the political influence that they wielded, but by the end of 1988 the process of

---

[21] This was shortly followed by a distressed cry for help from Yafuna Oseki, then the leader of the area, who was being threatened by local people who held him responsible for evic-tion and removal notices (KWL 18/12/1983). The tension demonstrates the practical diffi-culties of dual control and the fact that pastoral leaders were trying to put into practice reserve authorities' wishes.

eviction was firmly under way (URT G/C/MGR/77/91). Most had been removed by 1989. Further operations took place later to remove pastoralists who returned. Exclusion was enforced with severe fines which could frequently exceed TSh100 000 (Fosbrooke, 1992). Pastoralists allege that the evictions were on occasion violent, and that large numbers of stock were lost during the evictions and immediately after them. Currently, Maasai pastoralists are taking the government to court, seeking compensation and the right to use the game reserve.

After the evictions, the issues changed and sides divided. As discussed earlier, wider objectives are now being sought. For the conservationists the reserve is perceived to have been overgrazed by pastoralists and destroyed by poachers. No longer are rhino shot by the Wildlife Department for *shamba* raiding, but they and elephant have been devastated by large-scale poaching. The same Wakamba poachers mentioned in the first reports of the 1920s are still active, except that now they are supplied with weapons and ammunition by employers representing, or with access to, large international syndicates (Interview AM 26/2/1996). The area was also poached by Somalis.

The articles in the national and conservation press (Mduma, 1988; Sembony, 1988; Watson, 1991) voice the conservationists' concerns. Not only were pastoralists degrading a wildlife habitat, they were threatening a rare wilderness, and their supremacy in the area saw the last of the rhino and the virtual extinction of the elephant. These are conservation issues which transcend national boundaries. The eviction of pastoralists was seen as an important victory with transnational consequences.

With the growth of conflict and sites of conflict other players became involved. After the 1988 eviction, fines paid by the pastoralists were added to receipts from the Tanzanian Wildlife Protection Fund and the sums involved amounted to several million shillings (Mustafa, 1995). Internationally, the George Adamson Wildlife Preservation Trust became involved shortly after the evictions and began raising funds for the rehabilitation of the reserve and taking part in the actual rehabilitation work itself.

The international proponents of tightening up restrictions on human activity in the MGR have consistently identified human use and settlement, particularly by Maasai pastoralists, as the primary threat faced by the wildlife of the MGR. Mkomazi has been described as 'badly degraded' on account of 'deliberate burning by the Maasai people [and] the overgrazing situation', and this process of degradation has been linked to the 'unawareness, irresponsible attitudes, [and] lack of interest in the future world' of its former inhabitants (Simons and Nicolasen, 1994). In a speech, Tony Fitzjohn, the Field Officer of the George Adamson Wildlife Preservation Trust, described Mkomazi prior to 1988 as 'verging on a wasteland' due to 'those [the Maasai] who were seemingly incapable of getting their act together' (1994:12). Lest it be thought that these attitudes were only restricted to expatriate conservationists, in 1988 the then project manager of the MGR, Mr Materu, was quoted as saying that 'if pastoralists were allowed to have the reserve, their livestock would wipe out the vegetation and turn it into a desert in a very short time' (Sembony, 1988:18). A recent report blames the return of pastoralists to the MGR for the continuing problems faced by the

46

area's wildlife and environment ('Pastoralists re-endanger Mkomazi Game Reserve', *Business Times*, 12–18/4/1996).

The concerns of the pastoralists altered once they were evicted. Rather than claiming rights to the MGR *per se*, they now complain that to be evicted without compensation or preparation is a violation of their rights as citizens. Parakuyo and Maasai interests are promoted on the national and international stage under the umbrella of 'Maasai' interests and by 'Maasai' NGOs. Although they decried the loss of their grazing lands, they at first repeatedly stated that they do not want to fight the government and asked only that they be found other grazing grounds with access to MGR until these are found. Their principal concern was for the preservation of their livelihood and their pastoral way of life. The pursuit of these claims took them, without avail, to the Prime Minister's Office, the CCM party headquarters, the Minister of Internal Affairs and the Catholic Church (Mustafa, 1995). However, as all these attempts failed, international organizations became involved. With the sponsorship of the International Institute for the Environment and Development, the Legal Aid Committee of Dar es Salaam took up the case, which became altered slightly to one of human rights challenging, and still challenging, the legality of the government's action.

The issues involved in MGR have been altered by the changing context of African conservation and human rights debates. Conservation is now an issue of transnational importance, the local needs of a few pastoralists are held to matter little compared to the value of conserving endangered species, especially if the pastoralists themselves are guilty of environmental degradation. Similarly, the pastoralists, or sections of them, have joined the international discourse on human rights and the relatively recent concerns for the rights of indigenous peoples. Security concerns, for natural resources and people, derive their importance not just from what there is on the ground at MGR, but from what they signify internationally in the context of global needs and globally articulated rights and principles. MGR is, in a sense, being championed and has become the champion of several causes.

Searching for a solution

Mkomazi has reached an impasse. The deadlock between state authority and community rights drags on, both in the courts and in day-to-day interactions round the borders of the reserve. Currently conservation interests dominate, but only by virtue of a number of factors that are undergoing rapid change. These are firstly the temporary presence of conservationist scientists in the western end of the reserve; secondly the erratic conservation funding flowing to MGR; thirdly the current agreements between the Division of Wildlife (DoW) and conservation scientists in the reserve. While these factors continue, the conservation-dominated status quo may be just economically sustainable, though barely so, as is set out in more detail later. It is probably not politically sustainable, given the needs and aspirations of the communities adjacent to the reserve and their growing ability to command international advocacy and funding, and the tensions that inevitably ensue.

A number of powerful forces are coming to bear on the current impasse, and are increasingly likely to bring about change. As much as 25 per cent of

Tanzania's land has some level of conservation status, but it is a poor country and, with the pressures of cost-cutting and structural adjustment in state enterprises, there are barely the resources to manage its current conservation estate. Some conservation areas (Serengeti NP and Ngorongoro Conservation Area) generate substantial funds. Most other conservation areas do not break even. In Mkomazi, the only current source of revenue is derived from fines imposed on pastoralists caught grazing illegally. While representing a source of tension and hardship, these fines do not begin to cover the costs of running the reserve. At the time of writing, the manager of MGR is making key staff redundant. This makes it effectively impossible to enforce those policies of exclusion of grazing and other forms of currently illegal use in the face of the needs, aspirations and established resource-use activities of communities near the reserve (e.g. Kiwasila, 1995; Brockington, 1995, 1998).

In addition to this, there is a sea change in international and state attitudes to participation by nearby communities in natural resource management and in benefit sharing. Following the lead of community-based wildlife conservation and utilization initiatives such as CAMPFIRE and ADMADE (IIED, 1994), Tanzania is experimenting with a wide range of community-based conservation projects which seek to involve local communities in protecting the wildlife on their land, generally through some form of benefit-sharing from viewing or hunting game, but sometimes through low-impact community use of reserve resources. Ngorongoro Conservation Area has for decades made over a proportion of gate receipts to representatives of local government. Ruaha (Hartley, 1996) and Selous are recent attempts more closely modelled on the CAMPFIRE lines. Major donors strongly encourage such projects. At the other end of the scale there is a rapid growth of private luxury safari or hunting enterprises which negotiate directly with particular villages. Although the DoW has not yet approved the policy statement on community-based conservation formulated at the 1994 Arusha workshop (Hartley, forthcoming), the principle seems established.

There are particular complications in generating satisfactory community-based conservation projects along these lines around MGR. There is no buffer zone (a large population of some 30–50 000 abuts the MGR boundaries). Even the most optimistic projections show a very low capacity to attract and service tourists in MGR (20 beds over a maximum six-month season). Hunting is not currently felt to be sustainable or politically desirable. Most important, the population adjacent to the reserve is so large that any revenue sharing from tourism or hunting would work out as a trivial sum.

Although CAMPFIRE-style models are unlikely to work around MGR, there remains the possibility of low-impact use of reserve resources by communities with strong common property resource management systems in place. Ugalla Game Reserve, for example, has an established honey industry which does not conflict with the conservation values of the reserve. In Mkomazi, resource-use activities that mean a great deal in terms of local livelihoods, while having little impact on conservation values, could defuse the current impasse.

One of the factors underlying the swing to community-based wildlife management is the recognition of effective common property resource (CPR) management systems surviving and/or emerging in a wide range of situations

(Berkes, 1989; Bromley and Cernea, 1989; IIED, 1994). This chapter has detailed the evidence for well-established CPR systems of grazing management throughout the eastern part of the reserve up to the date of eviction, as well as the special reasons underlying the weakness of such systems in the western part of MGR once water sources were created and the area opened up to pastoralist grazing.

In addition to the potentially highly effective CPR management of grazing in and around parts of MGR, similarly long-established systems of CPR management of cultivable land, water allocation and beehive management operate on the borders of MGR (Kiwasila, 1995, 1996). There is clear evidence of well-established social infrastructures already in place in local communities to handle resource management issues around MGR.

Given this complex interplay of factors, what might Mkomazi be like 10 years from now? The scenario from the viewpoint of a conservation optimist might be that the international scientific presence will be maintained, that international conservation funds will continue to flow, that a much reduced game reserve staff will function effectively to limit illegal use of reserve resources, and that revenue from tourism and hunting, though inevitably low, will be put to such good use that the communities adjacent to the reserve will give the reserve their wholehearted support.

A more pessimistic view would see the scientific presence in MGR coming to an end and the decline and eventual cessation of international conservation funds. The reduced game reserve staff would be unable to exercise effective control. With rising pressure to trespass on reserve resources, increasingly punitive measures for those cases that are pursued would generate corruption and antagonism, while failing to stem resource degradation, possibly even eliciting vengeance targeting of conservation values (Lindsay, 1987; Western and Wright, 1994).

Somewhere between these extremes there may be a workable compromise. If it is to be achieved, it will be through a planning process that institutionalizes participation by all stakeholders, and uses a forum for negotiation, a process of consultation, and a level of transparency that allows the emergence of solutions that all can own. If this is not done, management policies will not work in practice. Even if the loser stakeholders do not have the power to get their own way, they have the power to undermine, block or destroy the aims of the 'winning' stakeholder (Lindsay, 1987; Western and Wright, 1994).

Given consultation, natural scientists could identify core zones of particular importance—for example, for biodiversity, rare species and migration corridors. Social scientists could help identify those resources that are of primary importance to communities nearby, as well as the possibilities, and problems, of common property resource systems on which to base their management. Communities adjacent to the reserve would benefit, not from negligible tourist or hunting revenue, but from the licensed and co-managed access to resources important to their livelihoods. MGR could be a model of the new Wildlife Management Areas envisaged in the current Tanzania draft wildlife conservation and utilization policy (Arusha, 1994).

Unpredictable 'wild cards' may drive the current impasse in unexpected and extreme directions. These include, for example, the controversial introduction of black rhino to a high-security enclosure in MGR (George Adamson

Wildlife Preservation Trust, 1994); the suggested shift to National Park status for MGR (perhaps as part of a cross-border Greater Tsavo conservation system [Ferguson, pers. comm.]); or the remote possibility of a legal victory by pastoralists in the current court case challenging their eviction. All of these are conceivable futures for MGR. Whatever that future, it is unlikely to be workable in the long run unless the principles of participatory consultation, transparency, and joint ownership of the outcome are maintained.

Acknowledgements and disclaimer

This work was funded by the UK's Overseas Development Administration (now known as the Department for International Development). The authors

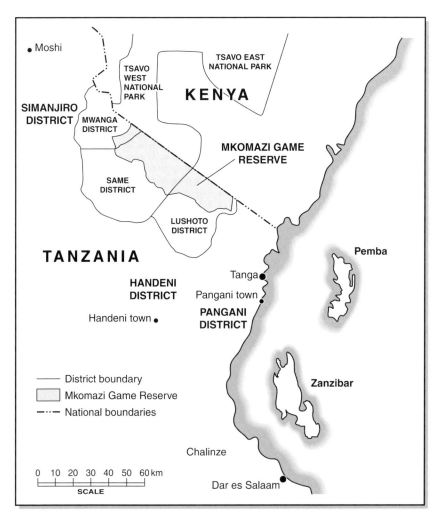

Figure 4. *Map showing the location of Mkomazi Game Reserve*

also wish to acknowledge the support of the Royal Anthropological Institute's Emslie Horniman Fund, the Parkes Foundation, the Kathleen and Margery Elliot Trust, the Central Research Fund of London University and the Graduate School of University College London and the United States Department of Education. The authors are grateful for the help and co-operation of the Institute of Resource Assessment, the University of Dar es Salaam, the Commission for Science and Technology of Tanzania and the Department of Wildlife. They are also indebted to the many members of local and district government and the countless other Tanzanians who live and work near to Mkomazi Game Reserve for their help, co-operation, welcome and warm hospitality.

The Department for International Development (formerly the Overseas Development Administration (ODA)) is the British Government Department which supports programmes and projects to promote overseas development. ODA funds supported this study and the preparation of the summary of findings. However, the views and opinions expressed in the document do not reflect ODA's official policies or practices, but are those of the authors alone.

Ethnic groups and the globalization process—Reflections on the Amazonian groups of Peru from a human ecological perspective

MAJ-LIS FOLLÉR

Introduction

The concepts 'ethnic groups' and 'ethnicity' are frequently used in the current social sciences, everyday political debate and in discussions on the causes of contemporary social, political and environmental problems. In this chapter these concepts are discussed from an interdisciplinary human ecological view on the relationship between human beings, environment and society. A human ecological study is distinguished from other social scientific studies of ethnic groups in that it considers the relation between human beings and both natural and social structures, and the link between individuals through their actions and reciprocity. Accordingly, in this essay ethnicity is analysed including all three corners of a 'human being–environment–society' triangle (Steiner and Nauser, 1993). Integrating these three dimensions and defining the relations between them is rather complicated, since we are dealing with an extremely complex web of causes, effects and interactions at different levels of aggregation. One appropriate method is therefore to combine empirical studies from various social, cultural and environmental settings.

A concept often used when analysing these relations is 'adaptation'. This concerns the interaction between man and the natural environment and can be seen from the point of view of the practices and activities of human beings that influence the survival of the population and involve cultural as well as biological factors. At the same time, nature has its own evolution. In this study, nature refers to the tropical rain forest, which is the subsistence base for the Amazonian population. The river changes its course, new plants and animal species evolve and still others disappear over time and space. A major theme is how human beings, as biological creatures, adapt to their physical environments through their culture, including their behaviour and lifestyle. Different aspects of this adaptation by human ecological and anthropological researchers have been widely discussed (Boyden, 1987, Hames and Vickers, 1983; Moran, 1979 and 1993; Sponsel, 1986) and I will elaborate the concept further on.

I wish to add one more theoretical concept, the 'theory of structuration' expounded by the sociologist Anthony Giddens and mainly limited to the social sciences. Nature is here seen as a product altered by humans through, for instance, agricultural practices, and not in the ecological sense as something existing outside and independently of human beings. The theory can be expanded to include ecological structures, meaning that ecosystems are composed of abiotic and biotic components which interact through the flow of energy, matter, and information, all of which vary in space and time (Steiner and Nauser, 1993). According to this definition, the ever-changing social and ecological structures constitute the framework within which the individuals or groups act, while it is this very action that creates or helps to re-establish those structures. This means that both the actions of people, here the ethnic groups, and the structure, such as the economic–political–cultural system, and the management of the resource base, must be taken into consideration in a reciprocal and dynamic way.

In this chapter the human ecological view on the process of globalization among ethnic groups is elucidated specifically in the context of the Americas through two historical perspectives: first, how ethnic groups have emerged over the years, and second, how they have assumed a certain identity through various social situations and encounters with people with a completely different world view. Against this historical background the accelerating processes of depletion of natural resources, population increase, urbanization, and the assimilation of 'traditional' cultures by the dominant society affecting Amazonian populations are analysed in the larger context of modernization, globalization and power.

Historical approch to ethnicity in Latin America

The present situation of ethnic groups in Latin America can be understood only from their historical development. Two distinct historical perspectives of interest for interpreting the encounter between Columbus and the people living in the Americas have been proposed by Crosby (1986) and Todorov (1982). Crosby sets up an ecological model of explanation to describe the encounter between the Spaniards and the indigenous people from the time of Columbus's voyages until the beginning of this century. He analyses the displacement and replacement of the native people and how these actions affected their survival. The 'Indians' are enclosed in the ecological context of their crops, wild and domesticated animals, weeds and disease agents. Crosby shows how the Europeans predominated in the encounter between the two 'biota', because of the attuned coexistence of the plants, animals, and microbes they brought with them. The diseases such as smallpox, whooping cough and measles, to which the natives had no prior immunity, killed up to 90 per cent of many native groups and in some cases eliminated them completely (Crosby, 1986).

This approach shows that no human actions are without their effects on the environment, and that the environment in turn is a continuous and active element affecting the survival of a group or an individual: human activity and social and environmental structures influence each other reciprocally. This refers to the duality mentioned above, that is, the human agents both act as members of their society within social as well as spatial–ecological structures, and, by this very action, also help to re-establish those structures (Steiner and Nauser, 1993:1).

Our understanding of the consequences of the European expansion for the people living in Latin America today has to start with this encounter. We are not concerned here with the first wave of immigrants, on foot, since its consequences and destiny belong to a long prehistory. The second wave— brought by the wind—was that of the Europeans. This marked the beginning of the 'construction of the other' in this region, and the 'creation' of the people whom we today call Indians or ethnic groups.

Todorov's approach is to understand the encounter between two very separate world views by interpreting how Columbus and Hernando Cortés, on the one hand, and the native Americans, on the other, were caught within their own social contexts, with neither of them being able to think beyond their own cultural limits (1982). This focus also includes the components of the 'human ecological triangle', but he treats them very differently from Crosby. Todorov defines Columbus's world view as consisting of three dimensions: natural (harmony between man and nature), human (culture and material wealth) and sacred. Columbus viewed the indigenous people as if they were a part of the landscape. 'His allusions to the inhabitants of the islands always occur amid his notations concerning nature, somewhere between birds and trees' (Todorov, 1982:34). The other reflection that Columbus made concerned their nakedness: '. . . the absence of clothes, which in their turn symbolize culture' (op.cit.). As a Christian, he also perceived them as pagans, without law or religion. He was only able to understand what he saw from his own cultural context in which clothes, wealth, and the expulsion of humans from Paradise stood for culture. He did not, in fact, have the capability, imagination or creativity to translate the people he met into the categories of another culture.

Columbus's initial image of the indigenous population obeys the same rules as his description of nature. He found them beautiful, good-hearted and peaceful, but from the beginning one can sense a feeling of superiority, which engendered protectionist behaviour. Columbus's attitude with regard to the people he met is based on his perception of them. Two components can be distinguished, which have survived in practice to our own days, in the relations between the colonist and the colonized. As a Christian, he conceived them as human beings with the same rights as himself; and this behaviour led to *assimilationism*, the projection of his own values onto others. The other component was the *difference* he saw, immediately translated into notions of superiority and inferiority. Both components of his perception of 'the other' are grounded in ethnocentrism, which is the identification of our own values with values in general, of our *I* with the universe, in the conviction that the world is one (Todorov, 1982: 42–43).

This historical background gives two different but converging explanations of the Western influences on today's Latin America and the indigenous groups. What we can see is that Columbus 'discovered' America, but not the Americans. Today, the rich part of the world has discovered the wealth of the tropical rain forest—Amazonas—but not the importance and value of the survival of either its inhabitants or various natural species. The continuum from Columbus to the modern Western view of the exploitable natural resources in the tropical rain forests is easy to trace in history.

The ecological perspective

From an ecological perspective, what we call 'traditional human societies' have, throughout history, been quite well adapted to their ecosystems. They have used natural resources from those systems at rates that did not disrupt natural flows and cycles, and in cases where their use of resources might have endangered the natural system, adaptation such as a nomadic lifestyle has often facilitated ecosystem recovery and maintenance. The populations have been small, at least in part due to the factors that naturally limit other animal species, including infectious and parasitic diseases and a high mortality rate among newborn and small children. This picture is undergoing a rapid change today as many indigenous groups in the Amazon lowland are confronted with the modernization process. Human activities are no longer only directed towards meeting the basic needs, but the previously rather isolated Amazonian groups are becoming integrated into the market economy through goods, products, tourism, and so on. From an ecological point of view, the ecosystems are threatened and sometimes destroyed, resulting in the disappearance of animal and plant species. The number of studies in the area has grown considerably during the '90s and there is today a variety of literature within the field of Amazon ecology and adaptation (e.g. Sponsel, 1986) and on changes in Amazonian indigenous anthropology (e.g. Viveiro de Castro, 1996).

For a more general discussion on adaptation, the process can be examined in four phases, which Boyden (1993) calls 'biohistory' in terms of the culture–nature interaction. The four phases, hunter-gatherer, early farming, early urban, and modern high-energy, differ from each other especially concerning resource management and energy consumption. Although there has been a shift towards the later phases, societies reflecting all four coexist today in, for example, the Amazonian region. When people from a range of biohistorical phases, with different consumption of non-renewable resources and varied world views, come together, change of some kind is inevitable. Biohistory is especially concerned with the impacts of societal activities on the biophysical variables of the biosphere, and on human beings. It pays attention to the processes of cultural adaptation that may be brought into action in response to socially and culturally induced threats to human survival and well-being (ibid.).

The process of adaptation may be regarded as changes and modifications of varying rapidity that enable a group to survive in a certain environment. The biological and cultural adaptations of human beings are essential for obtaining food, for protecting themselves against the stress of the climate through dwellings and clothing, for the socialization of children, as well as the care of the newborn, the sick and the aged within the group. Health and disease may be taken as positive and negative results of the capability with which human groups, combining biological and cultural resources, interact with their environment. Pathogens can breed only within certain demographic densities, which indicate basic shifts in the man–nature equation. The connection between mobility and the incidence of disease and epidemics has been noticed in the context of isolated groups (Crosby, 1986; McNeill, 1976).

From an ecological perspective, health problems can be seen as arising from the divergence between the environment to which human beings are genetically adapted and incidents in the disease pattern, when changes such as de-territorialization and urbanization occur. There is a constant adaptation to new conditions, but the biological nature of human beings is limited, and the discrepancies between the social and cultural changes and human biology create what he calls the 'principle of evodeviation', which is maladaptation (Boyden, 1987).

From a local or regional perspective, the environment imposes certain limitations on the survival of the group, such as the size of the group that has to find arable land for agriculture, other food products and water. Central to an individual's relation to the resource base is the local or traditional ecological knowledge which is the individual's or the ethnic group's collective memory. This knowledge embraces such survival strategies as familiarity with biodiversity, environmental assessment and information systems, which inevitably affect human well-being and survival (Follér, 1995 and 1997, Follér and Garrett, 1996). Ethnobotanical studies of the Amazon, with detailed categorizations of soil, plants and animals, help us understand the complexity of other knowledge systems besides the scientific ones. A comprehensive view of indigenous culture is essential to explaining how local people make use of certain plants for food, medicine or house construction, and avoid others. For example, Shipibo-Conibo, an ethno-linguistic group of approximately 30 000 persons living along the Ucayali River in the tropical rain forest of Peru and scattered in 100 to 120 villages over a large land area (Follér, 1990), name and classify aquatic and terrestrial animals into a complex consistent order (Tournon, 1994a and 1994b). Guillermo Arévalo, a Shipibo medicine man, has documented 400 medicinal plants used by the group, including the preparations for their therapeutic use (Arévalo, 1994).

The environment of the people living in the Amazon region is currently affected by the lifestyles of people living far away, with the result that their habitat and home are destroyed, entailing a threat to their survival as ethnic groups, since they are forced to expand beyond their natural physical limits and available resources. The people living in the Amazon are facing the problems of the scarcity of arable land for food production, the exploitation of non-renewable resources of minerals and energy within the region, as well as the exploitation of the forest for timber logging. Another threat is a rising population, coming from urban settlements, partly due to migration from the Peruvian Andes as a result of erosion on the mountain slopes and partly, in the case of Brazil, to an active government policy to give landless peasants plots within the Amazon (Moran, 1993:148ff). Increasing population causes pollution of water and air, with injurious health effects.

Species diversity has declined as a result of both floral and faunal species becoming extinct. The land and groundwater have been poisoned by pesticides and by mercury and other heavy metals (Boischio and Henshel, 1996; Gray, 1986). The rate of deforestation has been spectacular: during the 1980s and 1990s about 1.3 per cent of the forests has been destroyed annually, the highest rate of loss in the developing world (World Resources Institute, 1990). Furthermore, soil erosion caused by deforestation has been extensive and has led to river pollution, mudflows, and flooding.

The disruption that occurs between a local population and its environment may be perceived in a global context. Questions that might be raised are: 'What does the territory mean to the Amazonian groups and what happens when their land, the resource and subsistence base, is threatened?' One central concept is 'security': in this case, ecological or environmental security which concerns the maintenance of the local and the planetary biosphere as the essential support system on which all other human enterprises depend (Buzan, 1991:19). There is a wealth of current studies on the interrelationships between gender, identity, power, the nation-state, ecological security and the right to land for marginalized ethnic groups, as intertwined factors influencing the security of local societies (Buzan, 1991; Langlais, 1995; Stern-Pettersson, 1993). For the ethnic groups in the Peruvian part of Amazonia, state policy, transnational timber and oil companies, and significant guerilla movements such as *Sendero Luminoso* continue to be real threats.

Human actions always have unintended consequences; for the ethnic groups in the Amazon the consequences may be traced both to their own actions and to the actions of geographically distant structures. By thinking beyond the dualism between people and their habitat, structuration theory leads us to interpret and define components of a whole ecosystem in which people are but one constituent. Human attitudes, motives and values influence what people perceive and construe, how they use precise settings, and how they modify them over time. The interrelations between energy flows, material resources, human labour, and knowledge, communication and information should therefore be examined over an extended period of time in the context in which they occur (Lawrence, 1993).

Changes induced by modernization and globalization in the Amazon

The speed of change in a Western urban population might differ from that in an ethnic group living in the Amazon, but even within rather isolated indigenous societies such change is constant. The dynamic nature of culture can be seen in the way perceptions and strategies gradually evolve in indigenous societies as part of the process of adaptation to the resource-base. When social groups come into contact with other cultures, as they have throughout history, the changes become both more intense and more rapid.

One of the major current forces of change shaping human societies is modernization. It has its origins in Western Europe, but has spread to all parts of the world during the nineteenth and twentieth centuries, often in conjunction with economic development efforts, and has brought about worldwide cultural transformations. Some aspects of modernization are clearly beneficial to the survival of human beings, such as advances in health care, hygiene, new crops, technological and scientific knowledge, leading to, for example, a longer lifespan for humans in general. It is more difficult to measure changes in the quality of life due to modernization. Several consequences of modernization are both the solutions to many of today's problems and a part of the problem. Without modernization, the world population would not have risen to close on six billion, and many of today's epidemics, infectious and 'civilisation' diseases would not have existed without the present demographic structure. The current ecological problems, global and local, can also be seen as a continuation of the rationalization and modernization process.

To indigenous groups, modernization signifies that they are suddenly catapulted from their traditional ways of life into tension and conflict, both within their own group and in their interaction with other cultural groups.

Some caution is, however, advisable when using the notion 'traditional'. These societies may have experienced many changes due to interethnic contacts, natural disasters, and so on, even before the European contact. New tendencies seen today are possibly the erosion of the support system of the group and the breakdown of the extended family. De-territorialization and urbanization are just two more. However, these abrupt and rapid changes do not follow a uniform pattern and therefore need to be analysed, including the diverse components of the process.

Another major process of social change affecting the Amazonian population, and closely linked to modernization, is globalization. An important aspect of globalization is that it connects the local with the general and can be defined as: 'A social process in which the constraints of geography on social and cultural arrangements recede and in which people become increasingly aware that they are receding' (Waters, 1995: 3).

With globalization, the world is shrinking, and the dominant cultures of Europe and the United States are penetrating the local world of urban and rural areas in Africa, Asia and Latin America, reaching as far as the scattered and isolated Amazonian population. What we can see is that time–space distancing, disembedding and reflexivity mean that complex relationships develop between local activities and interaction across distances. In Amazonia, transnational timber logging and oil drilling by national and international companies, and the global network of narco-traffic are some examples of the shrinking distances and penetration of the local world.

Several scholars, among them the Norwegian anthropologist Thomas Hylland Eriksen, see globalization in a positive light. He emphasizes the vitality and originality occurring in the cultural encounter, which he calls 'creolization' (1994). The process implies a coming together of all humankind, a recognition of common values and goals, and an acceptance of cultural differences. This image of 'the world as one' is inherent in references to 'the global village'. International tourism, new broadcasting systems, computer networks and transnational industrial companies are just one side of it.

The serious inequality found in current societies is another side of globalization, which could also be largely attributed to the spread of capitalism and the market economy. Nevertheless, globalization is a part of the economic system of today, and what we see is mainly a one-way transmission of Western ideas, products and interests to other parts of the world. In this process, the knowledge and practices of local cultures are inevitably devalued.

The implications of globalization for the lives of the ethnic groups in Amazonia include the loss of local knowledge, de-territorialization, new diseases spreading through tourism, and modern high-mobility lifestyles. Andean flute music, handicrafts from indigenous groups, exotic food and native clothes are, of course, examples of transmission in the opposite direction. But what we see is a fragmented piece of what can be called 'folklorization' and 'exoticization' (Urban and Sherzer, 1991:11). We thus construct the role of 'the other' as a source of indigenous customs that can be relocated, and as an exotic image to attract the tourist industry.

Using Boyden's biohistorical perspective, we see a cultural encounter taking place between two different perceptions of the world. One of these cultures is able to dominate, thanks to its technological, military and economic power. This leads to a widening of the gap between rich and poor, reinforcing the marginalization and poverty of the indigenous populations. The marginalization is both physical—in that the ethnic groups are pushed into less desirable lands—and social and cultural—in that they exist on the edge of the prevailing economy, outside the power structure, in the periphery.

One question that has been raised is whether globalization implies homogenization or integration. Globalization merely implies greater connectedness and de-territorialization (Waters, 1995:136). How is it possible for ethnic identification to survive without a relation to a specific territory or a place? Among the Amazonian groups, place is often strongly connected with identity. Identity cannot be moved out of context. It is a complex phenomenon, a process of formation that continues and changes depending on external and internal factors. The various disciplines distinguish different aspects of identity formation. Political, ethnic, and gender identity are just some examples, and various identities may exist in one and the same person. The identity among the groups considered here, such as the Shipibo-Conibo, Ashaninka and Masigenka in the Peruvian lowlands and mountains, is strongly connected with language, cosmology, concepts of health and illness and territoriality, that is, the land and culture of their ancestors (Follér, 1990; Baer, 1992).

De-territorialization is often connected to the process of urbanization. The long-term trend of moving from small, scattered villages and towns to cities and megacities continues all over the world. Urbanization is a major force changing Latin America, and in Amazonia urban growth is about 6 per cent per year, according to the regional statistics (INEI, 1993). In a country like Peru, urbanization increases the marginalization of the ethnic groups. The transition from a rural, peasant, self-subsistent, and traditional way of life to one that is urban, and possibly supported by wage work, involves a significant breakdown of their social support system. They are facing new environmental problems and health hazards while dealing with the loss of the cultural identity and social network that they had in their villages. Distancing from the environment in which people have learned to make a living too often leads to poverty and a degraded life style.

The making of ethnicity in the Amazon

Two paradoxical facts characterizing the process of globalization and the ethnic situation in Latin America today are the difficulty of identifying the Indians in the Latin American melting pot of people of very different origins, and the overall reality of a multiethnic society. This can also be expressed as a dialectical trend towards homogenization, on the one hand, and pluralism, on the other. The idea of a modern, homogenized world culture, with shared values and attitudes, as a necessity for solving environmental problems and famines, population issues, energy consumption, and so on, is much advocated in current debate. But another trend can also be observed: ethnic groups around the world are resisting various aspects of modernization, for a diversity of reasons. The ethnic distinctiveness that will be discussed here concerns issues such as the role of the population in relation to territorial integrity, political autonomy and a certain control over the natural resources needed for survival.

In Latin America, few indigenous groups have any degree of guaranteed territorial integrity within the nation states that encompass them.

The representation of the indigenous peoples called native Americans, Amerindians or just Indians is undergoing an important transformation. An ethnic wave is passing through world society and is contributing to many international conflicts emerging in the South as well as in the North. Part of this wave is the appearance of new ethnic movements, some of them with an anti-colonial profile and a strong political aim of territorial control. As in many other parts of the world, ethnic groups in Latin America are increasingly aligning themselves with political movements for indigenous rights.

The globalization seen here as the deconstruction of the relationship between the local and the modern is not only a uni-directional trend of Western homogenization, but also the emergence of something new. These strategies of local persistence are expressed in the articulation of ethnic differentiation, which is shaping present-day world politics (Hettne, 1992).

In Peru, most Amerindians live in the Andean mountains, *la sierra*. About 65 ethno-linguistic groups coexist and inhabit the Amazonian region, *la selva*. They belong to 12 linguistic families, and they have their own languages, myths, religions and rationalities. This diversity is a value that has not been appreciated by the people governing the country.

Historically, these groups have been in contact with the Western world since the sixteenth century, through conquerors, missionaries, explorers and merchants. One of Columbus's men, Vicente Pinzon, discovered the Amazon estuary in 1500. But the interior of the Amazon region, later called the 'green hell', was not discovered until about 40 years later. The Spaniards arrived in the tropical lowland after first crossing the Andes. From then on the exploitation of natural resources, such as rubber, timber, gold, oil, and exotic animals, has intensified, and there is no sign of any decrease.

As mentioned above, Todorov explained how Columbus perceived the Amerindians as inferior as a result of his cultural restraints and religious narrowness. Other descriptions from the sixteenth century by proto-anthropologists and travellers such as Léry and Thevet indicate a similar perception of the inhabitants of Amazonia. They were still not seen as noble savages or cruel head-hunters, but even if their humanness was acknowledged, they were regarded as inferior, without knowledge of God, and primitive in their manners. Their technology, medical therapies and religions were also treated as inferior without any attempt at evaluation as to their appropriateness or function. These cultural traits were merely seen as different, and thus without sense, and condemned as worthless. The representatives of Western culture assumed an attitude of superiority in an ethnocentric way. This ethnocentrism has been presented as the only rational way of thinking.

The arrival of the Europeans led to many negative consequences for the native population, which was on many occasions vanquished, enslaved and killed. The technical superiority of the Europeans, with their guns and metal tools, and the power of the Roman Catholic church, which caused religious and psychological disruptions, were some important reasons for the defeat of the indigenous population.

The encounter frequently meant that the intruders imposed on the local inhabitants new values (religious, ethical and medical), and on their resource-base new crops and agricultural technologies. The indigenous groups were moved away, their villages or houses were destroyed, or the men were taken away to work with rubber or timber concerns and, more recently, with oil drilling or *coca* cultivation. Two processes can be defined: assimilation and resistance. The assimilation process means a loss of language, way of living, the medical universe; and integration into the more powerful culture. From historical and linguistic studies we know that many ethnic groups have disappeared, together with their language. Examples of resistance can be found in the first records from the central jungle, dating from 1557, when Juan Salinas de Loyola, a Spanish chronicler, described the people he encountered, enabling us to form a picture of their way of life. Other examples of resistance to the intruders can be traced from 1657 onwards (Heras, 1975; Regan, 1983).

De-localization was initiated some hundred years later by Franciscans and Jesuits who established mission stations in the region, *reducciones*, to pacify the indigenous population (Regan, 1983). The disastrous effect of the new infectious diseases that the intruders brought with them has been mentioned earlier. These decimated the indigenous peoples from the first moment of contact (Crosby, 1986). The depopulation of wide areas reflects both the ravages of the introduced infectious diseases and the dislocations associated with the incorporation of the indigenous people into the Western economic scheme (DeBoer, 1981).

During the post-colonial period, after Peru had become a sovereign state, Amazonia was increasingly penetrated by merchants and colonists from the rest of the country and abroad. Amazonia was regarded as an immense common property filled with natural resources. Combined with the ethnocentrism of the immigrants, this encouraged conflicts over land. In 1849 a law was established which made it easier for foreign colonists to acquire land and settle down in the region (Chirif and Mora, 1976). This can be seen as the beginning of the marginalization of the indigenous inhabitants of Amazonia and the destruction of the fragile tropical ecosystem, of which the colonists had no understanding and no relevant ecological knowledge.

The rubber boom in the late nineteenth and early twentieth centuries intensified the destruction of the environment and signified further resettlement of the ethnic groups. The indigenous population was again captured, enslaved, relocated and, this time, put to work tapping and collecting latex until the rubber market collapsed around 1910.

The increased settlement in the Peruvian jungle following the rubber boom made it necessary for the government to regulate and define rights to land and exploitation of resources. A law in 1909 did not even mention the indigenous groups in the area (Rosengren, 1987:46). Not until 1957 was landowning by the lowland ethnic groups taken into consideration in Peruvian law. *Comunidades nativas* is the most common settlement pattern today, and a law from 1968 acknowledged the legal right of native groups to exploit more extensive land areas, including the right to use and sell natural resouces such as wood and game, and the right to collect other resources. The authorities gave the community a legal deed, *título comunal*, to the land.

This administrative and legal organization still exists, but has been more and more undermined by various changes in the constitution. The latest threat to the survival of the ethnic groups and their right to land in the Peruvian

Amazon comes from the present leader of the country, President Alberto Fujimori. The congress has approved a new law, and the future of the *comunidades nativas* is once more seriously menaced (Aroca and Maury, 1993). One risk with the new constitution is that it gives opportunities to sell the collectively owned land to colonists, who may commercialize and exploit it for timber felling.

The globalization of the Amazonian region and its incorporation into the market economy have had devasting effects on the ethnic groups since they are socially and culturally exhausting processes leading to overexploitation of the ecosystem. In this process the indigenous groups have had to struggle for territories and resources, for their language, world views, religious rituals and medical practices.

The ethnic groups encountering the nation state

If we see the Amazonian population in earlier times as composed of relatively isolated and autonomous groups, their situation is now totally changed. Ribeiro (1971) viewed the assimilation process as consisting of five stages: isolation, intermittent contact, permanent contact, integration and extinction. Probably there still exist groups at all the stages, especially in Brazil with its enormous area. In the Peruvian part of the tropical rain forest, the riverbeds and fertile flood plains are densely populated, and there have been armed conflicts, cultural revitalization, religious movements, repossession of resources and other manifestations to guarantee their right to land. The ethnic groups have been incorporated to a greater extent into the nation state, and this has had certain implications.

For the people living in the Amazon and their encounter with the nation state, three characteristics of the state are especially important (Urban and Sherzer, 1991:8). These are its claim to have a monopoly over the legitimate use of force within its territorial boundaries, its assertion of autonomy related to other states, and its gradual development of citizenship as the form of membership in the collectivity.

Today a trend can be seen questioning the more established conceptualization of indigenous people. New studies focus more on the processual nature of indigenous identities, instead of transforming collective self-representation of particular social groups as indigenous (Field, 1994).

A brief summary of the changed view of ethnic groups within social science can be obtained from two sources. The first is a rather traditional or static anthropological approach influenced by Boas, which bound language, material culture, and cultural identities together. The second is British structural functionalism, which envisages social relations as a homeostatic organism in which individual and collective behaviours are defined by cultural norms and values in order to maintain social equilibrium.

Another approach to the study of ethnic groups emerged with Barth's *Ethnic groups and boundaries* in 1969. His central tenet is that ethnicity is a form of social organization. This implies that 'the critical focus for investigation becomes the ethnic boundary that defines the group rather than the cultural stuff that it encloses' (1969:15). The critical feature of ethnic groups is, according to Barth, the characteristic of self-ascription and ascription by others.

62

What is new in Barth's work is the shift from a static to an interactional approach to ethnicity and the differentiation between ethnicity and culture. Barth presents ethnicity or ethnic identity as an aspect of social organization, not of culture. He also includes environment and ecology in the main framework to understand how cultural differentiation and ethnicity are linked to the concept of 'niche' (Barth, 1994).

This approach is still highly valid in the discussion on boundaries between groups, between 'us' and 'them', and in order to see the processual and relational views in the definition. Ethnic groups are seen as interest groups operating within larger societies, among whom markers of ethnicity are produced through interactions with other social sectors. Notions such as markers or negotiating ethnicity also give rise to the dynamic view of 'who are the Indians?' There are historical examples of how indigenous groups invented and reinvented traditions as a part of the reproduction of their identities (Elsass, 1992). According to this approach, the survival of an ethnic group, the gap between extinction and assimilation or acculturation, can be derived from its cultural potential, such as cosmovision, language, a logical structure in the way of thinking, local knowledge (including ethnomedicine and shamanism), perception of nature, and so on. Nevertheless, the term 'ethnic group' is ambiguous and vague, and the relationship between ethnicity and other types of identity, social classification and political organization, such as class and gender, is changing constantly (Hylland Eriksen, 1993).

Today the ethnic groups of Latin America are fighting for survival through their own organizations for self-determination. They are working together through various local and national federations. A basic political aim of these federations is territorial control and access to natural resources; this is the central focus of indigenous rights throughout the world. Every indigenous community must be able to conserve, use and organize its resources freely to ensure its survival through coming generations. Secure land is of fundamental importance to indigenous people who wish to continue their own way of life. Their sense of identity is strongly coupled to the perception of their existence within the forest. This collective identity is in turn essential for their survival as an ethnic group.

Guaranteed territory is a key to the long-term protection of the South American rain forest. Natural resource management strategies that are culturally appropriate and economically sustainable are being sought for the area. Global changes and the impact of these changes on human society have become important items both in research and on political agendas.

Just as 'Indians' did not live in the Americas until Europeans invented the term and its social positioning, the multitude of distinctive indigenous societies of these continents became 'ethnic groups' only as their territories were incorporated into the colonial, and later republican, national regimes. Ethnicity and ethnic groups should be understood as processual terms that signify changing identities in relation to colonialism throughout history, rather than as a set of more or less fixed categories.

Since the first encounter with the Europeans, an interface has been created. The nature of this interface depends on the nature of the encounter. Highland groups such as the Aymara and Quechua comprise numerically large populations that in their own way have internalized European social and cultural forms since the contact, while lowland people, living in small, dispersed groups, have remained more isolated and closer to precontact conditions for a long time (Urban and Sherzer, 1991).

Conclusions

The process initiated by colonial intervention in the Amazon, leading to a destruction of livelihoods, is almost akin to an unavoidable human and natural calamity. The encounter signified a biological disaster for human beings concerning the disease agents brought from Europe against which the people had no immunity and which nearly led to their extermination. From Todorov's perspective, the cultural encounter signified that the superiority in the context of the European value system and during the long colonial history led to the marginalization, de-territorialization and cultural impoverishment of the ethnic groups and destruction of the tropical rain forest, their home. The action of the Europeans and what they brought with them in the way of biological agents, plants, crops, animals, microbes, on the one hand, and economic, political, religious agents, on the other, and the interaction at this special historical event, form the background for explaining and understanding the present situation.

The two perspectives reinforce the calamity for the ethnic groups in the Amazon. I would like to describe it as an incorporation of European (Western) biological and cultural elements into their own framework of social life. In this process a geographically unbounded 'global' setting emerged. The cholera epidemic in 1991 was just one more dagger thrust from the biological (lack of immunity to the new bacteria) and social (poverty) results of globalization (Follér and Garrett, 1996). These factors interact and minimize the possibilities of survival for the ethnic groups in Amazonia in the way they have chosen to live. Through transsocietal processes, globalization is involving the exchange and flow of goods, people, information, knowledge, microbes and biota.

Global de-territorialization means that people are displaced or migrate in search of survival for ecological or political reasons. One effect that cannot be denied is that young people who move to the cities forget the language, last name and cultural manifestations binding them to the environment of their ancestors.

Changed patterns of land use and the systematic harnessing of all natural resources for the continual enhancement of global industrial production and trade have had devastating implications for the livelihood and survival of ethnic groups. Ethnic survival in the modern world would be possible and meaningful if its own intrinsic dignity were recognized, and not only seen in the context of progress and growth. If the nation state has homogenization as a primary goal, difference will appear as resistance—and that is what we see in Latin America today.

The international United Nations summits—in Stockholm about the environment, in Rio about environment and development, in Cairo about population, in Copenhagen about social development, in Beijing about women— have been the most obvious symbols of the massive amount of analysis, discussion, and action being directed toward the future of the planet Earth.

Ethnic groups all around the world have also at last entered into this mutual dialogue concerning their future. The value of their way of life, their way of thinking and their traditional ecological knowledge has slowly begun to be recognized. Western civilization has begun to realize that it probably has much to learn from the indigenous groups in order to ensure a sustainable development.

In the future we will observe ethnic groups and individuals choosing from a variety of paths. Whether they choose to articulate their ethnic differentiation or to become integrated in the process of the big global 'melting pot' or creolization will depend on the interplay of internal and external factors. What we can see today is the creation of new institutions to organize the interests of ethnic groups. The double character, or duality, of this action is apparent: where the free action creates the prerequisites for its own limitations.

Increasing competition, expanding strategies—Wage work and resource utilization among the Paliyans of South India

CHRISTER NORSTRÖM

Introduction

THIS CHAPTER CONCERNS the Paliyans of the Palni Hills[1], southern India, a people categorized as hunters and gatherers in the ethnographic literature.[2] I will give some tentative ideas concerning their resource strategies and the way they elaborate these in order to secure subsistence assets. My data are based on 24 months of fieldwork, mainly between 1993 and 1995.[3]

The significance of cultural values, norms and meanings for how people utilize available resources is generally recognized within the social sciences. However, within studies of 'hunters and gatherers' this understanding has played a minor role. The reasons for this we can find in two general paradigms: human evolution theory and world system theory, which have dominated hunter-gatherer studies over the years (Barnard, 1983; Bender and Morris, 1988).

The 'evolutionists', in search of 'pristine' hunters and gatherers, view contemporary hunters and gatherers and the way their societies work as mainly determined by their natural environment. The most extreme kind of these theories is 'the optimal foraging theory', where resource strategies are supposed to be correlated to ways of procuring optimal calories within the shortest time (Winterhalder and Smith, 1981). The advocates of the second paradigm view contemporary hunters and gatherers as a category constructed by Western scientists. They claim that these groups of people do not, in any significant way, differ from their neighbours. According to this view contemporary hunters and gatherers have, for a long time, become poor among other poor due to the expanding and all-encompassing capitalist economy (Wilmsen and Denbow, 1990:489). In both these views, cultural values, norms and meanings are played down: in the first case because technical and environmental factors are considered to determine behaviour; and in the second because these peoples are viewed as politically and economically so weak, compared to the surrounding society, that whatever culture we grant them will not, to any significant extent, influence their place in contemporary society.

---

[1] The Paliyans live on the eastern slopes of the Western Ghats, along the border between Kerala and Tamil Nadu (Gardner, 1972). This chapter only deals with the Paliyan of the Palni Hills. I use pseudonyms for personal names and places in the Palni Hills to protect the integrity of the local people.

[2] Dahmen, 1908; Gardner, 1965, 1966, 1969, 1972, 1985, 1988, 1991a, 1991b, 1993; Manndorff, 1960; Sherring, 1975; Thurston, 1909.

[3] My fieldwork was sponsored by a two-year grant from the Swedish Agency for Research Cooperation with Developing Countries (SAREC).

The uneasiness among some scientists over these paradigm controversies within hunter-gatherer studies (culminating in the famous 1990s 'Kalahari debate'[4]) and the focus on generalized structure-oriented theories have created a shift towards theories of social change and real world problems of applied research (Burch, 1994:446).

This general shift in research emphasis, and the ethnographic studies it has generated, has given more attention to the interplay between actors and the forces they represent at the local level. However, in many of these studies there is still a strong tendency to consider change as something mainly coming from outside, losing sight of the potential of contemporary hunters and gatherers to '. . . incorporate "other people" as economic as well as social resources. . .' (Bird-David, 1988:30), useful for maintaining their own social systems and values. The assumption seems to be that influences from neighbours among hunters and gatherers in terms of food and dress habits, or settlement patterns, or generally intimate social and economic relations with others, are incompatible with the social systems and basic values of hunters and gatherers. It is as if contemporary hunters and gatherers could not have motivations and ambitions which include resources outside their traditional hunting and gathering mode of life without undermining that very same life.

It is recognized that in South India hunters and gatherers (Hill Pandaram, Nayaka (Naikens) and Paliyans, among others) have been engaged in economic pursuits within a modern cash economy in combination with hunting and gathering for a long time. At the same time they have been able to uphold a certain degree of autonomy (Morris, 1982(a):64; Bird, 1983a, 1983b; Gardner, 1985). Morris and Gardner, when considering the 'contact' situation, mainly focus on how the character of the modern cash economy determines the social systems and habits of south Indian hunters and gatherers, without clearly accounting for their point of view as to why they became part of trade and plantation work. In contrast, Bird-David[5] puts forward the thesis that these economic pursuits become parts of the hunters and gatherers' traditional 'pre-existing pattern' (1983b:81). Even though the Nayaka partly changed their 'production (wage labour), consumption (rice) and distribution (money)' (ibid.), Bird-David suggests that these activities should be seen as new opportunities for upholding the Nayaka socio-economic structure, rather than undermining it. In a later article she introduces the category 'modern' hunters and gatherers (1992), which refers to those hunting and gathering societies that combine: '. . . hunting and gathering and various other strategies, including engaging in wage work, trade, occasional cultivation and stock-keeping, and even (in Australia and North America) government and office work, as well as drawing welfare benefits' (op.cit.:22).

It could be argued that Bird-David's 'modern' hunters and gatherers, and the possibility of upholding their socio-economic structure, are a special case only applicable under very particular circumstances. Her fieldwork is based on one local group of Nayaka, 70 people, who have been involved in local

---

[4] Barnard, 1992; Lee, 1992; Lee and Guenther, 1991; Solway and Lee, 1990; Wilmsen and Denbow, 1990.
[5] Earlier known as Bird.

trade of non-timber forest produce, combined with wage work in a rubber plantation established in their vicinity, and later some occasional cultivation, all taking place within a limited area (Bird, 1983a). However, my own field data from the Palni Hills, which include studies of about 3000 Paliyans pursuing a wide range of economic activities, support her main argument.

Tamils in the Palni Hills express their views of the Paliyans with statements like 'they never stay in one place'[6] and 'they come for a while, then shift back to the forest, it's their habit'. Although the Paliyans are more settled and less forest-oriented today than earlier, these characteristics are probably still what makes the Paliyans significantly different in the eyes of other groups in the area. When Paliyan individuals, families, and sometimes groups of families, shift from one place to another, this often implies that they change from one kind of subsistence resource to another, or from one combination of resources to another. This correlation could suggest that the resources themselves are the main reason for these shifts. Such material determinism would not take us very far in explaining the Paliyans' resource strategies, however, especially if we look at these shifts in the light of their own explanations.

When asked about different resources, the Paliyans easily explain what, from their perspective, are the virtues and drawbacks of different economic activities. From that to comparing different resources and putting them into a specific preference list is something that, so far, no one has carried out. The Paliyans' answers reveal the fact that they do not have any clear preferences among the options. This does not mean that they do not avoid certain kinds of economic activities. It means that the resource and its procurement as such does not always seem to be the main reason for their choice. This becomes clearer when they explain why they shift subsistence resources within the same area, or why they turn up in a different area. The reasons for choosing one place are often connected with the reason for leaving another.

Although available resources determine their range of choices, the Paliyans' own discussions and actions indicate that other considerations than pure subsistence needs, involving cultural values and norms, become part of the way they structure and develop strategies for securing subsistence assets. However, as has been pointed out in recent discussions within cognitive anthropology (D'Andrade and Strauss, 1992), human action is not directly derived from cultural constructs. Strauss emphasizes this point by taking a new look at the nature and sources of human motivation. According to this view:

> ... on the one hand, motivation depends on cultural messages and is realized in social interaction, but on the other hand, that motivation is not automatically acquired when cultural messages have been imparted. Knowing the dominant ideologies, discourses, and symbols of a society is only the beginning: there remains the hard work of understanding why some ideologies, discourses, and symbols become compelling to social actors, while others are only the hollow shell of morality that may be repeated in official pronouncements but is ignored in private lives (1992:1).

---

[6] All Tamil expressions have, for simplicity, been translated into English.

The question of how cultural messages are internalized is not something I will dwell on in detail here. Strauss's combination of cognitive anthropology and sociocultural models, however, suggests that we keep as our research focus the actors' actions and their comments on why they undertake these actions.[7] In a similar vein, Gudeman and Rivera see economic and cultural models as: '. . . products of long conversations, fashioned by communities of discussants' (1990:14). Further, 'models and their lexicons emerge through the agreement, argument, and reflection of humans engaged in practices and conversations, both verbal and textual' (ibid.).

A focus on people's actions and voices is also in line with Long's important remark in his studies on actors, structures and interfaces in rural settings. He stresses that we have to recognize that: '. . . social action undeniably entails the notion of choice, however limited, between different courses of action, as well as some way of judging the appropriateness or otherwise of these' (1989:224). This notion of choice and a certain degree of autonomy among the Paliyans, otherwise living in a world dominated by Tamil caste groups, will be elaborated on in this chapter. My concern will be on Paliyan resource strategies, but not only because this level of Paliyan life has changed significantly during the last decades. Paliyan subsistence activities are also their main link to outsiders, and therefore become for them the most important realm for creating a wider social space in a shrinking physical world.

People and resource utilization in the Palni Hills

The Palni Hills are an eastern offshoot of the Western Ghats, the major mountain chain of southern India. Situated in Tamil Nadu at the border of Kerala, with an area of 2400 km^2, it drains two of the more important river systems in Tamil Nadu: on its northern side the Cauvery and on its southern side the Vaigai. With its steep hills, reaching 2500m above sea level, and narrow valleys, the climate is tropical, turning to subtropical at higher elevations. The hills are covered with a mixture of tree savannah, riparian and dense evergreen forests. At higher altitudes there is a mixture of grasslands and evergreen mountain forests.

Among the people now inhabiting the hills, approximately 300 000, there are only two groups who claim descent from the area, the Paliyans and the Puliyans. The Puliyans were subsistence cultivators when their land was taken over by plain Tamils migrating up the hills between the sixteenth and seventeenth centuries (Nelson, 1989). These caste groups (Mannadiyar, Asariar, etc.), together with later arrivals of Telugu-speaking Chettiar, still dominate, to a large extent, the rural areas of the hills. The Paliyans were not that much affected by these transitions. They inhabited the more inaccessible areas within the valleys and forests along the slopes. When the Paliyans refer to this period, they claim: 'We lived on yams, honey, and monitor lizards. If we met strangers we ran away out of fear.'

In the nineteenth century, the British started plantation cultivations and commercial forestry in the mountainous areas of southern India. By the

---

[7] Strauss expands on sociocultural models advocated by Bourdieu (1977), Geertz (1973) and Ricoeur (1979).

69

beginning of the twentieth century these had firmly established themselves. In the Palni Hills, and especially along the southern side, coffee and cardamom were the most suitable crops. Large parts, mainly in the upper areas, were cultivated with exotic tree species like eucalyptus (*Eucalyptus globulus*) and wattle (different species of *Acacia*). Although there was a trade of crops, timber, and other forest products to markets and places outside the area even before the advent of the British, such trade now steadily expanded into a modern market economy (Larsson and Norström, 1993). Today we find a situation where cash crops and commercial forestry totally dominate the economic picture in the Palni Hills. Land suitable for cultivation is in short supply, resulting in high land prices. During the last few decades (if not earlier), economically successful groups from the plains have competed with the hill people over the land. However, large parts of the Palni Hills are still well forested, in spite of increasing population, expanding and intensifying agriculture, commercial forestry, and overgrazing and fuelwood collecting, the latter especially in the foothills. In parts of the hills the flora and fauna are in such good condition, although under severe threat, that the Tamil Nadu Government, in co-operation with a local environmental organization, have proposed a national park or sanctuary in the area.[8]

Another important fact for the development of the Palni Hills was the creation of the hill station Kodaikanal by American and British missionaries during the second half of the nineteenth century. Kodaikanal is today the administrative centre and the only town and urbanized area of the hills. With its history of international representation, the influential 'leadership' of the town (today a combination of Westerners and Indians) has played, and still plays, a significant role in the development of the hills. With the help of their widespread networks, local organizations have been able to attract significant amounts of international funds for 'development' work in the area. Several of these organizations, with programmes oriented towards the poor, have become important actors in the rural areas, especially since the 1980s. Some of the same forces have been active in creating the Palni Hills Conservation Council, one of the best-known local environmental NGOs in India.

The Paliyan economy

The Paliyans talk of an earlier period when they based their economy on the gathering of plants and hunting of animals, typically giving a condensed answer to complex issues and questions: 'We lived on yams, honey, and monitor lizards'. I found that this statement encompasses a way of subsistence involving more than 200 different plants and animals (cf. Gardner, 1993). They also use this statement as a contrast to their economic strategies of today, when most of them, from time to time, are involved in wage work for others. Wild yams (different species of *Dioscorea*) have been their staple food. When they started to work for others, rice, as part of payment, became increasingly important. At what period wage work started, differs from one local group to another. The most common answer is that the eldest generation of today as children followed their parents to work, while their parents were

---

[8] Palni Hills Conservation Council, 1986 and Tamil Nadu Forest Department, 1994.

brought up only on forest resources. This would mean that many of them became involved in work relations with outsiders about 40–50 years ago. Some Paliyans may have done this even earlier and there are reasons to believe that they have never been totally isolated from others. However, the intensity and content of these external relations seems to have varied over time.

Today we can find Paliyans as daily labourers within plantations, grazing livestock for others, or their own goats and cattle, collecting non-timber forest produce (including fuelwood), cultivating cash crops, paddy (rice) and millet on their own land, clearing roads and paths, or doing occasional work for the forest department and environmental organizations (for example, collecting seeds from the forests). No other group in the hills is involved in such diverse economic pursuits. To this we should add that a majority of the Paliyans still hunt and gather forest resources. To be able to see how their economy works, three of the more important areas of resources used by the Paliyans today are examined: plantation work, trade and cultivation.

Plantation work
The local people in the Pandju valley, on the southern slopes of the Palni Hills, told me that in the Sangutumalai area, a valley further to the west, cardamom estates already existed at the end of the last century. The first estate established close to the Pandju valley was Suraj estate. The land was opened up in the 1920s by a retired Indian major from the British Indian Army. Today it is owned by a wealthy family of Nadar caste from the nearby plains town Bodinayakkanur. The head of the family, Kalliyanagam, runs the family business together with his four sons. In Pandju valley and its surroundings there were at one time eight cardamom estates running simultaneously. Three estates are still running and some cardamom is also cultivated by local hill Tamils.

When Kalliyanagam took over Suraj estate in the 1960s, he hired some Paliyans in the neighbourhood to work as watchmen. Some of them may have worked for the former owner. Kalliyanagam's accountant at that time re-established the contacts. Later on, other Paliyans joined the estate and together they formed three sibling groups.[9] One of these sibling groups was Karuppan's group,[10] who stem from the area. Two other sibling groups, those of Ganeshan and Murugan, came from Sangutumalai at the time when Murugan married one of Karuppan's sisters.

The Suraj estate consists of 143 acres of forest land and is leased from the government through the forest department for 19 years at a time. The cardamom plants (small cardamom, *Ellettaria cardamomum*) are planted within the forests at an elevation of 1000–1500m above sea level. These uninhabited

---

[9] The usual settlement group among the Paliyans was a sibling group, their marriage partners, children, and their parents, if alive. With the shift to bigger settlements and villages, especially since the 1980s, the normal Paliyan settlement today includes several sibling groups, although they may still occupy a separate area of the settlement.

[10] For simplicity I am using 'Karuppan's group', etc., to designate a Paliyan sibling group. The personal name stands for the eldest living male. This is sometimes practised by the Paliyan themselves, especially in a village setting where more than one sibling group lives together.

and forested areas are also, unfortunately for the growers, the habitat of several species of wild animal. Bison (gaur), deer, wild boar, birds, and especially monkeys are significant competitors for the cardamom plants and harvest, easily devastating the crop if the land is not protected. This was one of the major problems for the early growers and became even worse when cardamom became good business and the cultivations expanded in size. One solution was to find people to watch over the land; however, it was not easy to find people in the plains who would stand the harsh climate for extended periods of the year and who could swiftly move around in the dense and steep terrain. Because of this, many owners of cardamom estates along the southern slopes of the Palni Hills hired local Paliyans.

The Paliyans consider watchwork on forest estates and plantations convenient, because it is easily combined with food collecting and hunting, the plantations being within their traditional forest grounds. If any small game turned up during their beat they hunted it. If there was little or no food in their settlement, they would dig wild yams and collect fruits, either during the day or on the way back to the settlement. There was no effective way for the owner to check their work duties, since the Paliyans were very much on their own. However, if the owner found that wild animals had destroyed the cardamom plants or fruits, the Paliyans were blamed.

Payment was in kind, usually low-grade rice brought up from the plains. Each person was paid per day and each working day was noted in the account-book kept by the accountant. On Suraj estate it was the normal procedure to clear the account once a month. The rice was carefully measured by the accountant at the main house, according to the number of working days for each individual. Once a year, during festival time, they were also given some simple clothes as payment or 'bonus', as Kalliyanagam would put it: a shirt, a *lungi* (waist cloth worn by men), or short trousers for males and a *sari* for the females.

The work arrangement between the owner and the Paliyans was loosely formulated. The owner made, through his accountant, a verbal agreement with each family or someone within the local group whom they, the owner and accountant, considered as representing the group. This would, in most cases, mean either the male of a nuclear family or the eldest male within a sibling group. The deal implied that the Paliyans agreed to come to work during the season, but did not state exactly how many working days or how many workers. They should watch the estate from morning to evening. As watchwork on cardamom estates is difficult to quantify, especially to estimate the positive effect of protection related to numbers of watchers, having a demand for a specific number of Paliyans or working days was not really necessary. The owner was mainly satisfied to have a group of Paliyans coming most of the days.

This loosely regulated system gave individuals within the local Paliyan group plenty of room to stay away if they chose to, as long as the group sent enough workers to the estate over time. According to the Paliyans, this meant that 'they could come and go as they wanted'. The Paliyans did not want to regulate the work too much and were satisfied to get part of their food from the estate owner. As each individual and family would regulate this according to their own choices, the number of working days varied a lot between them and from one month to the next. This need for a certain degree of autonomy from the estate owner was clearly expressed through the general Paliyan refusal to settle down within the estate. Kalliyanagam could not understand why they preferred to stay in those 'simple huts out there' or, as in the case of Ganeshan's family, 'even live in a cave!', when they could come and stay on the estate.

The main controlling instrument for the estate owner was to give the salary in advance. When the Paliyans accepted the advance, they agreed to do the work according to the amount of rice given. This gave the owner an idea of how much work he could expect in the near future. Because of this debt the owner could also, to some extent, prevent the Paliyans from changing their minds and going to work on other estates, or staying away too long for other reasons.

This debt system could in some cases be developed into debt bondage. This occurs when workers become deeply indebted to the estate owner, who is then able to force people to pay off the debt by work. The permanency of debts forces the labourer to work for the owner continuously, in some cases for several years. However, the Paliyans working on Suraj estate claim that they never accumulated any debts during this period.

The ordinary situation on Suraj estate was that the Palisyans either got an advance for a period not longer than a month, or lived on wild yams until the next payment time. Arrangements changed from one month to the next, and also varied from one family or individual to another. If nothing exceptional happened, life would go on like this during the season. Next season the owner would expect them to be around again and the Paliyans would expect the accountant to come and look for them. This work arrangement continued on Suraj estate between the Paliyans and the owner from the 1960s until the middle of the 1980s.

This economic system was, however, not always untroubled. A Tamil plantation owner could not easily absorb forest people into the system just by mere economic force and political power. The relations between the Paliyans and the estate owners were full of tensions. To uphold the system needed a lot of negotiation and bargaining between the parties involved.

The estate owners had, through debts and co-operation built up between each other, a certain degree of control over the Paliyans, but without the Paliyans' full consent the arrangement was in most cases difficult to uphold. That was something Kalliyanagam had to learn at the end of the 1970s, when a major conflict developed. One of Kalliyanagam's foremen was caught stealing cardamom. During this conflict the owner accused some of the Paliyans of being involved in the theft, and he and his staff threatened, and even beat, some of them. He said that if they did not confess he would take them to the police and they would be put in jail. The Paliyans denied the accusations and decided that they did not need to accept such treatment. Murugan's and Ganeshan's families left the area, returning to their close relatives in Sangutumalai, their original home. Karuppan's family, however, did not feel involved in the conflict, and continued its relation with the owner.

Murugan's and Ganeshan's families stayed in the Sangutumalai area for more than a year, at which point Kalliyanagam sent one of his accountants to the area to ask the Paliyans to come back. According to Kali, Murugan's younger brother, the accountant came and spoke 'soft words'. The accountant informed them that the owner did not mean what he had said and would be happy to have them back. With these smooth words, both Murugan's and Ganeshan's families decided to go back to the area, taking up the work and the relations with the Suraj estate again.

This was the only major conflict to which my informants referred. However, over the seasons minor conflicts arose regularly. Some of these conflicts occurred when the foremen blamed individual Paliyans for insufficient watchwork when there was a loss of harvest or damaged plants, for not regulating their debts in time, or for minor thefts of different kinds.

If individual Paliyans felt that they were mistreated too much in these conflicts, they chose to stay away from the estate. This could be for a couple of days or for more than a year. If the owner wanted them back he sent the foreman to ask them to forget the conflict and come back again. These conflicts were considered by both parties as conflicts between the owner and the individual Paliyans, or, from the Paliyan point of view, as a family matter. This meant that if an individual Paliyan stayed away because of conflict, other Paliyans did not feel obliged to do the same. Most of the members within the nuclear family would stay away, but that was not the rule.

An additional problem, in the relation between the owner and the Paliyans, was the conflicts within the local Paliyan group. A common way of solving a conflict between two parties among the Paliyans, either within a family or between families, was one party deciding to leave the settlement. Often this included leaving the area and whatever work arrangements they had with landowners as well. During these conflicts, the landowner, in his own interest, sometimes tried to mediate.

To summarize, what is found here is an economic arrangement between the Paliyans and the owner of a cardamom estate in which both parties try to benefit according to their own economic strategies. The owner aims at maximizing the output of his crops to increase his profit. Although he had to expect a certain degree of loss of harvest each year, he could reduce the loss significantly by using the Paliyans as watchers of the land (it may be important to remember that this period was a boom in Indian cardamom business, and that losses of harvest were normally economically counterbalanced by the cardamom position on the international market) (Pruthi, 1992:63).

The Paliyans used the payment from the owner primarily as an additional food resource, and secondarily as a source of clothes and other goods. This arrangement decreased some of the pressures on their ordinary hunting and gathering economy, a pressure which seemed to be at its height in the cardamom harvest period (August–December), when their main staple food, wild yams, is less abundant or almost absent in many areas of the hills. However, it is also important to recognize that rice became a very much appreciated food item among the Paliyans.

Work on cardamom estates was the most common wage work for Paliyans along the south-western slopes of the Palni Hills until the 1980s. When India lost its monopoly on the international market at the end of the 1970s, several estates were closed down and others were not kept in good shape. Since then, many Paliyans have shifted their interest towards daily labour on silk cotton (*Bombax ceiba*) and lime (*Citrus aurantifolia*) plantations, some of them only returning to the cardamom estates during the harvest season (then doing weeding and harvest work). Others never went back.

In the silk cotton and lime plantations they do weeding, harvesting, and, in some cases, transport the harvest down to the markets. In the Pandju valley there is no regular pattern to this work. Each family shifts their interest between different landowners depending on their or the landowners' needs, and on the extent to which they can keep up friendly relations. In some cases Paliyan families have worked for the same landowner for several years, in other cases the Paliyan families shift regularly.

A landowner who wishes to hire Paliyans as daily labourers enters a Paliyan settlement and asks them to come for work. Usually the landowner chooses a man whom he considers to have some influence over his fellow people, one who may know the work situation as well as how keen the others in the settlement are to take up work. Some of the other Paliyans may also turn up. Together they decide the payment and work period. This agreement is not binding, especially not if no one has debts to this landowner. Most of those who agreed will turn up for work, but the frequency over the period will vary a lot from one individual to the other. Payment is usually offered in either cash or rice. A few big landowners practise a system of advances which circumscribes the independence of their workers. Usually they give up to Rs1000 (about two months' pay) in advance, and only allow repayment through work. A few Paliyan families started to work under these conditions in 1995 and still have debts. However, most Paliyans in the area have been able, sooner or later, to end these kinds of debt relations.

Despite the income from wage work, most families still collect wild yams and other forest plants, together with some small game hunting. Some Paliyans also have small kitchen gardens, a few goats and poultry.

Trade in non-timber forest produce

The collection of non-timber forest produce (hereafter NTFP) from the forests of southern India has a very long history and forest people have, from early times, been involved in this trade. The degree of Paliyan involvement in NTFP collecting varies a lot from valley to valley. Most local groups do at least some collecting. In the Pandju valley they have not, in their lifetime, been involved in any regular sense; however, the Paliyans in Nelli valley, on the northern side of the hills, have turned into 'professional' traders of NTFP in recent decades. In 1994, 26 families, out of a total of 31 families living in the valley, were involved in collecting NTFP (if we include fuelwood collecting). Most of these families get their major income from this work.

According to them, it all started about 20 years ago. At that time some of them stayed far up in the valley, inside the forests, living on food-collecting and small-game hunting. During this period, plains people used to bring up cattle for grazing during the dry summer months. Some of the Paliyans came into contact with a Kavundar caste man who had been asked by forest contractors in his home village to arrange for the Paliyans to start collecting NTFP for them. From this point, NTFP collecting increased and, because of the continuing demand, it has also attracted Paliyans from neighbouring areas to settle in the valley.

The right to collect NTFP is sold by contract by the government through the forest department by a system of auction and lease. The contractor, who takes the area on lease, either by himself or through agents, approaches local people to collect for him.

In the Nelli valley the contractors have remained the same for many years. One person has the contract for lemon grass oil and another one for most of the other produce. Both of them have their business centre in the nearby town of Palni. The produce is collected mostly by the Paliyans, who are approached at their settlements at the start of the season for each product. Palanichamy, the local forest ranger, told me that in 1994 there was a total of 41 different NTFPs leased out in this area. The most important ones for the Paliyans are lemon grass (*Citrus flexuosus*), gooseberry (*Emblica officinalis*), galnut (*Terminalia chebulla*), and a palm leaf (*eenji, Phoenix silvestris*) used for making broomsticks. Apart from the above, two other kinds of forest produce have importance for the Paliyans in the Nelli valley: fuelwood and one kind of bamboo. The last items are not within the authorized list of NTFP in the valley and are therefore considered by the authorities as illegal to collect. This leads to special considerations when collecting and selling them.

The organization of NTFP collecting of galnut, gooseberry, *eenji*, etc., is very similar. The contractor shows up in the settlement at the start of the season. As prices are not fixed from one year to the next he makes a deal with the villagers that he will pay a certain amount per quantity and that, within a certain time, he will come back and pay for what they have collected. There is no fixed quantity that they should collect. The contractor signs a paper given to the collectors for each product, certifying that the Paliyans are collecting for him during a specific period. The paper serves as a proof of legality in case the Paliyans are checked by someone from the forest department.

How often and how much each individual or family collects is up to them. The contractor has no direct way of influencing their decisions, but the price he is ready to pay influences the Paliyans' motivation. If they consider it too low, they do not go. Occasionally the contractor and Paliyan individuals negotiate a number of days and how much pay, but this usually results in quarrels. Normally, though, they will reach an agreement. The contractor can give some small, short-term credits, but, according to my information, no long-term debts are accumulated.

For collecting these NTFPs the Paliyans either go singly or in small groups. Co-operation is not necessary for completing the tasks. Each individual, man, woman, or youngster, collects according to their capacity and gets paid for their own harvest, although young people normally give part of their pay to their parents. Collecting teams are not regulated in any sense and often change from one day to the next. Their own way of putting it is that 'they go as they like'.

Normally they will leave in the morning after breakfast, returning in the late afternoon. If the collecting area is far away, they can stay one or two days in the forest. When going in a group, they go together to the area of collection. There they split up and each person selects a tree. If the yield is not enough for everybody they go to the next area, leaving behind what they have collected so far. In the new area the procedure is repeated. When everybody has collected enough, they pick up all the yield for the day and return to the settlement at the damsite. There each individual stores the harvest in his or her family hut until the contractor comes to close the deal.

Lemon grass oil extraction is a more complex operation and needs cooperation between several individuals. The Paliyans do this in families and about 10–13 families are engaged each year. Simple sheet metal stills are provided by the contractor (six units in 1994) and are kept by the families in the settlement. The extracted oil is kept in plastic cans containing 22 litres. To extract that amount will take one team about 17 days, during which time each team has to stay at the extraction site. To reach the sites takes a 3–5 hour walk from their settlement. The extraction sites are selected for two main reasons: availability of lemon grass and water. Sometimes four or five groups could be out at the same time, and each family makes between three and five trips per season, depending on the seasonal availability of lemon grass.

There are two other, less common, ways of organizing lemon grass oil extraction. In one Paliyan settlement on the north-western side they combine the extraction of lemon grass oil with food-collecting and hunting of small game. This local Paliyan group still regularly uses wild yams as its staple food, collecting wild yams every other day, the whole year round. Whatever extras they need, they buy out of the income they get from selling lemon grass oil. They themselves own the stills and, instead of selling via a contractor, they sell the oil directly to a market one day's walk away. Another difference is that they supplement the wild-growing lemon grass with their own cultivated lemon grass.

Still another way is found in a valley on the northern side, where some Paliyan families extract lemon grass oil for landowners from the plains. They use both wild and cultivated lemon grass. The Paliyans are paid daily wages and this system resembles other kinds of daily labour for landowners.

Fuelwood and bamboo collecting are, as has already been mentioned, considered illegal by the authorities. The reason is that these activities are looked upon by the government as important causes of the degradation of the forest cover. Compared with NTFP collecting, fuelwood and bamboo collecting in the valley brings in many more people, also involving caste people. The demand for fuelwood comes from the nearby plains villages with a total population of more than 10 000. Bamboo is a common material used in villages and towns for different kinds of constructions.

Because of the heavy demand for fuelwood all year round in the area, the Paliyans often turn to it when they need an income. Usually local hotel owners and wholesalers in the nearby villages go to the Paliyans for fuelwood. The Paliyans will bring fuelwood down to the Paliyan settlement and keep it there. Before dark, or early in the morning, the buyers turn up and the deal is settled.

Cultivation of the land

Some Paliyan families seem to have done occasional cultivation on their own for a long period of time. In the Pandju valley in the 1960s they used to clear small areas in the forest and cultivate ragi (*Eleusine coracano*) or millet (*Setaria talica*) for their own consumption. In several other areas they have also tried to cultivate ragi or millet, later adding cash crops like banana (*Musa paradisica*) and castor oil (*Ricinus communis*). After some years they usually have to abandon the land because of objections from the forest department or Tamil landowners in the neighbourhood. Today some Paliyans are able to cultivate small plots of land, usually with cash crops like silk cotton, lime, castor oil, or bananas, some of these within Reserved Forest Land.[11] As this is still considered illegal by the authorities, the cultivators need to give certain amounts as bribes to the forest department guards to be able to continue.

A few isolated cases of land distribution to the Paliyans from the government have taken place. However, only a few Paliyan families, mainly on the south-western side of the hills, have been able to secure this land. The main crops they cultivate are silk cotton and lime.

In Kombaikadu, a valley on the eastern tip of the hills, land was distributed by the government in the 1960s to landless families, including both Puliyans (see above) and Paliyans. This was done on the initiative of some local Tamil politicians (and coffee growers) close to the Kamaraj Government, the Tamil Nadu government at that time. The Puliyan were able to keep this land. The Paliyans lost their land within a couple of years to influential landowners in the neighbourhood. Today the Paliyans in Kombaikadu work as daily labourers on the Tamil landowners' estates in the valley, combining such work with some food-collecting and small-game hunting in the surrounding forest and occasional collecting of NTFP.

In the Pandju valley the government allotted 120 acres of land for cultivation to 40 Paliyan families in 1991. The Paliyans still control this land, but have had a lot of trouble with encroaching neighbours. However, the conditions of their land vary a lot. They have cultivated some lime and silk cotton, but only a few families have been able to make the input necessary to get the first harvest (it takes four to five years for lime and silk cotton to reach maturity). Several individuals and families have left the valley for extended periods to work in neighbouring valleys, either because of subsistence needs, or conflicts with fellow Paliyans (both within or between families) or with Tamil landowners in the valley. Some, from the beginning, never bothered about the land, mainly because they felt they would never be able to accumulate the input necessary for cultivating it. The ongoing conflicts with the neighbouring landowners have also discouraged many from cultivating their own plots.

The few families who achieved their first small harvest in 1995 were those who had hung onto their land, and through hard work on others' land were able to invest some of their earnings in their own fields. However, the best cultivated are the plots belonging to two Paliyan families who used the income from some holdings further up the valley which they had gained 10 years previously.

A third case of land distribution took place in the Sangutumalai valley to the west of the Pandju valley. Here 40 Paliyan families were given land with the help of the local village council in the valley. Most of these plots are still in the hands of the Paliyans and are today well established with lime and silk cotton. To be able to run these plots on a family basis most of them

---

[11] An administrative unit, referring to the state-owned forest in India.

78

lease out the silk cotton. This is also common in the few other places were Paliyans have been able to establish silk cotton cultivations. The silk cotton harvest needs more labour input than a family can provide. Paliyans usually lease it to neighbouring Tamils for a relatively small sum of money, when compared to the average rate of leasing silk cotton in the area.

Many Paliyans in the Palni Hills have eagerly tried to cultivate land. Because of competition from neighbours and the government, and their own methods (including insufficient input) many have failed, but still hope to be able to do it in the future.

Some concluding remarks on the Paliyan economy

I have chosen to describe in some detail three important resources used by the Paliyans in the Palni Hills. To give a more complete picture of the Paliyan economy, let me make some comments on plantation work in the coffee estates within the 'coffee belt' in the lower parts of the eastern Palni Hills. In this area most land is cultivated and less forest remains. This limits the alternatives for the Paliyans, compared to other areas of the hills. Most of the Paliyans living here work regularly on the estates, although some hunting and gathering is possible, as well as NTFP-collecting. Some Paliyans cultivate in the forest, but it is an unpredictable pursuit because of forest department control. In this area we find the only Paliyan group who claim that they no longer use any forest food resources at all. The reason is that they stick to a part of a valley where there is no forest. Here in the coffee belt, where competition over land is very high, some Paliyans have joined a local political organization demanding land for the landless people in the area.

There are also three groups of Paliyans who are more forest-oriented than average. One group, mentioned above, are engaged in lemon oil extraction. A second group of about 15 families mainly stay in the forest deep down in a valley on the northern side, living on wild yams and other forest resources, occasionally extracting lemon grass oil and collecting fuelwood for outsiders. Another group of 15 families only trade honey to one contractor, otherwise staying in the forest. They live in Sirumalai, a smaller hill area a short distance to the south-east of the Palni Hills.

In most areas there is a great demand for Paliyan labour. They are considered to be skilful workers, more used than others to the conditions prevailing in the mountains and forests. They work for lower wages and make fewer additional demands than caste people, who are usually well organized. Although the Paliyans are considered rather unpredictable, as regards coming to work regularly, the landowners feel that they are easier to handle than caste people, especially if it comes to open conflicts.

The Paliyans can still use forest resources if they so choose, although forest food for most of them has become secondary to their diet today. With this in mind we can conclude that Paliyan resource use varies a lot, depending on opportunities as well as Paliyan interests.

Paliyan norms and values

Social life among south Indian hunters and gatherers has been described as putting '. . . a normative stress on the self-sufficiency of the individual, and on symmetrical relations' (Morris, 1982a:109). This includes the fact that there are no corporate groups above the level of the family and 'pervasive emphasis on sexual egalitarianism' (Morris, 1982b:180). Gardner proposes that these societies have 'an individual-autonomy syndrome' including the following traits:

> . . . pressure on children for self-reliance, independence, and individual achievement; individual decision making in matters having to do with family, power, property, ritual, etc.; extreme egalitarianism; techniques for prestige avoidance and social levelling; absence of leaders, what Meillassoux and Woodburn call instantaneous or immediate economic transactions; individual mobility and a corresponding openness and turnover in band membership; resolution of conflict through fission and mobility rather than by violence or appeal to authorities; bilateral social structure; a general tendency toward informal arrangements and individually generated, ad hoc structures; and relatively high levels of interpersonal variability in concepts, beliefs, and manner of expression (1991a: 548–9).

Although Gardner's use of 'individualism' and 'egalitarianism' has been criticized for not incorporating different notions of these concepts and that they are taken out of context (Fawcett, 1991; Grinker, 1991; and Guenther, 1991), the above list serves the purpose of highlighting a sharp contrast between the Paliyan and the Tamil society. Where individual Paliyans strive for being able to decide on their own what to do and with whom, the Tamils are oriented towards intercaste relations, the subcaste (intracaste), and especially the joint family (Östör et al., 1992; Uberoi, 1993). In situations of co-operation between Tamils and Paliyans, the Tamil notion of group co-operation often clashes with Paliyan ideas of individual autonomy and the down-playing of authorities.

When outside organizations co-operate with the Paliyans, the representatives of the organizations expect at least a minimum of co-operation between the Paliyans within the settlement. If that fails, the organizations, which usually build their work on groups and especially those living in a settlement rather than families or individuals, get confused. In the Pandju valley an environmental organization has been, for more than a year, trying to support the Paliyans in their effort to cultivate plots. During that period more than a third, and sometimes more than half, of the Paliyans have been in other valleys, only occasionally visiting the Pandju valley. When a field assistant from the organization asked one of the older Paliyan women in May 1996 why all the people migrate to other places, she answered: 'Earlier they used to stay in different places. If you want them to stay in one place it may take five to ten years. In this village some persons do not like unnecessary talk. If someone talks about their personal life they will move to another place.'

The value of self-reliance, individual decision-making, and social levelling, makes Paliyan conflict-solving tend towards group fission (cf. Baxter, 1972). In earlier times the major conflicts arose out of competition over partners, either through rivalry or disagreements over suggested marriage unions between families. Today economic transactions and increasing economic and social diversity within the local group are new reasons for internal conflicts.

The case of land distribution in the Sangutumalai valley, mentioned above, shows that internal conflicts have a strong impact on the Paliyan settlement pattern and co-operation. About 15 years ago 40 Paliyan families were allotted pieces of land for cultivation. A village with stone houses was built for them. Because of several conflicts only 11 families still remain there, and they are divided into two factions.

The strong emphasis on egalitarian relations between men and women among the Paliyans is questioned by the Tamil gender view. For example, in the economic relations between Paliyans and Tamils, the Tamils always strive to make the arrangements between men, with a tendency to exclude women from decision-making. However, individual decision-making among the Paliyans makes it difficult for men to make decisions for the women. Even if women are sometimes excluded in discussions about work arrangements, they will be included at the family level. If no consensus is reached within the family, the man can only speak to outsiders on his own account.

The Tamil feeling that the Paliyans are different and not fully included within the Tamil life and culture is deep rooted. It is clearly expressed by the story around the notion of *sambal kundi*. Translated, *sambal kundi* means 'holy ash on the arse' and is used as a derogatory name for Paliyans by local Tamils. I heard this expression for the first time when a young coffee grower named Pandian recalled that a landowner colleague of his used the expression when he was admonishing one of his Paliyan workers for not being careful enough towards his young wife. She was pregnant for the fifth time, and the girl was not yet twenty years old.

Pandian, who is the fourth generation of a Nadar coffee-growing family in the area, told me that his family had hired Paliyans on their estates for decades. To illustrate the Paliyans' independent character, he gave me the story behind the expression *sambal kundi*:

> Once upon a time Lord Shiva came down to earth. When he was walking in the forest he suddenly came up to a man lying on his knees on the ground carefully watching something. Lord Shiva, who was used to being worshipped by all people, was surprised by this man who seemed to ignore him, so he called for the man's attention. When he did so the man said, remaining bent over and without losing his concentration on the ground, 'I am totally busy trying to catch the rat in this burrow, but you can throw some holy ash on my arse', pointing with his arm towards his own posterior.

'This fellow was a Paliyan', Pandian concluded.[12]

If the above points to significant differences between the Paliyans and the Tamils, we should not underestimate cultural similarities, a partly shared culture that must have been developed over a much longer period than the 'contact' period referred to in this chapter. The Paliyans speak Tamil and there is no trace of them having had their own Paliyan language, which indicates long and close relations with Tamils in the past.

---

[12] Stories like this are also used by 'upper' castes to explain why some groups should be, because of misbehaviour in earlier times, considered as 'low'.

Apart from this fact the religious realm is maybe the area where the similarities become most prominent. Paliyan worship shares the elements and structure of Tamil worship (Milner, 1994:172–80), and especially what Fuller (1992) calls 'popular Hinduism', the everyday devotion to gods and goddesses at the village level. This realm of shared culture is clearly expressed in the use of Paliyan spirit mediums (*samiyadi*) as healers by Tamil families and individuals. Several Paliyan *samiyadis* in the Palni Hills have regular Tamil 'patients' coming from nearby villages as well as from bigger towns like Madurai and Coimbatore. To make possible these sessions, and the communication involved, the Tamils and the Paliyans need to share the same basic ideas about certain types of illnesses and the relations between gods, spirits, and people's behaviour (Bharati, 1993; Dumont, 1986; Gardner, 1991b; Harper, 1957; Moffat, 1979).

Paliyans are also very well aware of the basic codes of conduct between themselves and other caste groups. Although they place a strong emphasis on individual autonomy and know that they can manage in the forest on their own, if they have to, this fact never leads them to express superiority towards Tamils. Their place as a group considered 'low' in the eyes of Tamil society is generally accepted, and anything in their behaviour that would challenge that pattern is carefully avoided. My impression is that to be able to uphold these relations in everyday life it would need knowledge and a shared culture with the surrounding society far greater than they could have achieved during a couple of decades.

My point of view is that the Tamil society is not another 'world' for the Paliyans, and may never have been. The Tamil society is, rather, another part of their world which they have been able to share, more or less, over time. Earlier they would share this world as little as possible, their reluctance expressed by the statement: 'we ran away out of fear'. Today the possibilities open to them of sharing the Tamil world are significantly different, and how they go about doing this, with the differences and similarities between them and the Tamils, will be dealt with in the next section.

Securing subsistence assets and widening the social space

Bird-David introduced the term 'wage gathering' to encapsulate the Nayaka's ability 'to interpret their new experiences in traditional terms', where 'wage' stands for the new items introduced from the outside through wage work, and where 'gathering' stands for the traditional system's interpretation of these external relations (Bird 1983b:82). From this she develops what she calls a prototypical model of modern hunters' and gatherers' mode of subsistence, building on four interrelated features: the autonomous pursuit of resource-getting activities, diachronic variation of resource use, synchronic diversity within groups, kin, and household, and the continuous presence of hunting and gathering.

Gardner suggests that the Paliyans have developed an 'oscillating biculturalism', where decisions to avoid relations with outsiders are 'a function of external socio-political harassment', and where most decisions to take up work for others are 'attributable to the pull of techno-economic opportunities' (Gardner, 1985:425).

In spite of the advantages of these models in emphasizing the autonomous character of south Indian hunters and gatherers, I have difficulties in sharing their notion of culture and regret the absence of references to the construction of cultural models on an individual level. To look at culture as units, basically determined by different economies where the only contact between cultural units takes place out of the necessity to uphold the units, plays down the degree of shared culture between Paliyans and Tamils, and leaves out the dynamics of cultural flows, changing motivations and individual diversity at the local level.

Paliyans today are oriented towards both their own traditions and towards Tamil society. If there was once a time when they could remain on their own, that time is now long gone. However, the Paliyans do not seem to regret this. If their physical space has decreased, they feel that their social space has increased. Therefore they are more concerned with the outcome of their relations with modern Tamil society than with the preservation of a tradition in 'isolation' from Tamil society. To understand this concern and the Paliyan behaviour, here focusing especially on their economic behaviour, we need to combine several levels of Paliyan cultural constructs.

First, there are the basic needs that must be fulfilled and that also contribute to feelings of status. Today all Paliyans need some cash for clothes, and a minimum amount of commodities. If they do not have this they feel that they will be looked down upon by others. Therefore all Paliyans have some economic relations with outsiders. Some families are more eager to gain resources above a minimum level, to give their children a Tamil education, establish stone-house villages, spend more on weddings and other ceremonies, etc. If they are able to achieve some of this, they feel more on equal terms with their Tamil neighbours, but this requires a high degree of mixing with outsiders.

Second, their values and norms decide the outcome of social relations, both internal and external, once they have been established. These values and norms, some of them referred to above, were basically established in the traditional Paliyan setting. If conflicts arise, and independence is sought to reduce social pressure, forest resources become important. At the individual level a combination of these factors would determine, in relation to possible opportunities, the outcome of their behaviour.

What I am suggesting here would need a more careful elaboration. However, this way of combining different motivating levels of cultural constructs resembles what D'Andrade calls 'cultural schemas' (1992:28). A schema is '. . . a sort of program; a procedure by which objects and events can be identified on the basis of simplified pattern recognition' (ibid.). These schemas have three important aspects: they make possible the identification of objects and events, they have the potential of instigating action (they can function as goals), and they are hierarchically organized (op.cit.:28–30).

For the Paliyans this would mean that they seek outside resources because they need them, enjoy them, and they increase their social space, including respect from the outside. However, if internal or outside relations come into conflict with their self-esteem, they are still, in most cases, prepared to break off these relations.

The important task for the anthropologist would be to identify these schemas and put them in a social and cultural context, interpreting people's statements as well as their actions. To end this account, let me, in a simplified form, give some examples in Boxes 1, 2, and 3.

Even though the availability of different economic opportunities is not normally determined by local people themselves, as long as there are alternatives, people can to a certain degree make their own choices. In that sense they also become, more or less, parts of shaping future possibilities. The examples below indicate that even if Paliyan choices are limited, they still

---

Box 1. Andi and Kuppi

Andi and Kuppi are the elder brothers of five siblings. Their parents joined the cardamom estates in the Pandju valley in their young days. Apart from getting additional subsistence assets, they claim, as do many old Paliyans, that they enjoyed becoming friends with Tamil people. Earlier they had been too afraid to approach Tamils, something they felt they did not need to be anymore.

In the 1980s, when the cardamom business declined, Andi and the others decided to try out some cultivation on their own, in combination with work on the estate. The estate owner did not approve, and when Andi insisted, he was thrown off the estate. Kuppi, his brother, and their father decided to stay on the estate. Andi and the others continued cultivating for the next five years. During this period they were mainly dependent on wild yams.

At the end of the 1980s new opportunities arose. With the support of an outside organization Andi took the main initiative to establish a Paliyan village further down the valley, with land for cultivation granted by the government. Kuppi was invited to join, as were all other Paliyan families in the valley. Kuppi never did. His main reason was that work was more secure and easier on the estate. He also had another reason which he was not too outspoken about: at this time he had two wives, a practice common among Paliyans. However, polygamy is illegal in Tamil Nadu and to move down to the village site would expose his family situation more explicitly to outsiders.

Kuppi's decision to stay on the estate was commented upon by Andi: 'He prefers to be a slave'. Andi was very clear and outspoken about his own motives. He felt that his children should live differently from previous generations, and he was prepared to work hard to achieve this. His land is in good condition today. He and his family have also adopted Tamil customs more eagerly than most of the other Paliyans in the valley. Among other things, he once went to the famous Tamil pilgrims' temple in Palni Town. He also put one of his sons in a Jesuit boarding school in the hill town of Kodaikanal. For him this is a matter of prestige among the Tamils. He often tells them that 'we are no beggars, we can provide for ourselves'. In some of the other Paliyans' eyes this has gone so far that they jokingly call him Thevar Andi (Thevar is a title used by some of the local Kallar landowners to designate their caste group).

Box 2. Mani

Mani was born in 1970. Until the end of the 1980s he lived with his mother and siblings in a forested area close to the Pandju valley. Here they usually stayed in caves and lived on wild yams and other forest resources. At this time they were asked to join a nearby cardamom estate. When Andi's plans for getting land from the government were realized (Box 1), Mani and his family decided to join them. Mani said that they did so because Andi promised them land, a stone house, a bank loan, and a school for the children. Mani stayed in the village and got married there. They tried to cope by working for landowners, collecting wild yams, etc., and also cultivating some of their land. In 1994, however, he decided to leave for a cardamom estate further to the east and never returned. His mother had by that time already joined this estate because of conflicts with her husband. What made Mani make this decision was, by his own account, a combination of two events: he lost his wife to another man in the village and he was accused of theft. To avoid these conflicts he abandoned his land and moved.

Box 3. Sethu and Muthumani

The married couple Sethu and Muthumani also live in the Pandju valley. Muthumani was once married to another Paliyan and lived in the south-westernmost portion of the hills. Here they worked for others, but also had some land of their own. They were quite well-off by Paliyan standards. However, Muthumani was very jealous of her husband. She suspected him of having relations with other women. Finally they separated. Through a landowner in the area she came to the cardamom estate just to the east of the Pandju valley about 15 years ago. Here she met Sethu. When Andi (Box 1) started the settlement in Pandju valley, they decided to join it in 1991 for the same reasons as Mani (Box 2). Muthumani's jealous and quarrelsome manner had not disappeared, however, and she often accused Sethu of being unfaithful to her. Until the end of 1994 Sethu preferred to work on the cardamom estate because of these continuing quarrels, only coming back to Muthumani to rest for a couple of days now and then. If he and Muthumani were to cultivate their land at the village site, she had to do it.

At the end of 1994 everything changed. One day Sethu was climbing for jack fruits (*Artocarpus heterophyllus*) owned by the estate owner, when he fell and severely injured his arm and chest. He was hospitalized for a week, and was unable to work for many more weeks. Sethu had expected some support from the estate owner in this situation, but the landowner did not bother. However, Muthumani supported him throughout and Sethu decided never to go back to that landowner. Although Muthumani is still quarrelling with Sethu, they now stay in the Pandju valley, working for other landowners and trying to keep up their land.

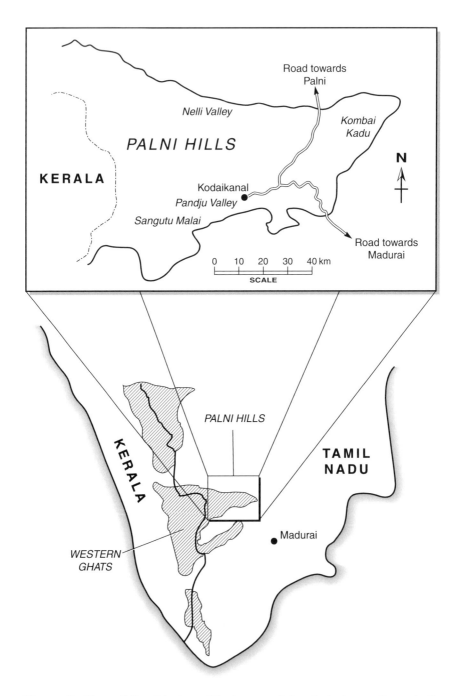

Figure 5. *Map of the Western Ghats mountain chain in southern India and the Palni Hills area*

86

have choices enough to allow them to act according to individual principles embedded in their own values and ambitions. In the case of Andi (Box 1) he and his family could, by 'going back' to wild yams, decrease their dependency on the estate owner. That new situation paved the way for establishing their own village some years later, according to Andi's and others' new ambitions. However, half of the Paliyans in Pandju valley never joined the village. The choices they made were nothing that Andi and the proponents for the village could do anything about. Even though Andi wanted everybody to join, and did not like their decisions, he had to respect their right to make their own choices, even his brother Kuppi's refusal to join, all according to Paliyan rights of individual decision-making.

It would be difficult to account for such different individual actions as the above examples present by only referring to structural forces. By moving closer to the individual, without losing sight of existing structures, taking into account different levels of cultural schemas, such as Paliyan ambitions embedded within their own value system, and the way they are combined by individuals, gives a more reasonable account of what actually happens in Paliyan life.

Conclusions

The Paliyans in the Palni Hills use several subsistence resources, and in many cases change them regularly. Sometimes they live almost solely on forest resources and sometimes become fully engaged in the modern cash economy. This makes them involved in intimate relations with both the forest and mountain areas, as well as with their Tamil neighbours. Whatever the reasons for their earlier 'isolation' in the forests, the Paliyans today seem to recognize that their life is part of Tamil society. That does not mean that they feel totally powerless in this situation, although competition over resources and social space is intense. The enormous variation of Paliyan resource utilization is ample proof of this. To understand this complex situation I have suggested that we need a more actor-oriented approach to the study of hunters and gatherers, including the study of individuals' ambitions and motivations, to be able to represent the dynamics of real life. This would need a more detailed analysis than the one I have presented above and should also include a closer look at other actors in the areas, embedded in regional cultures and power relations.

Agroforestry intensification in the Amazon estuary

EDUARDO S. BRONDÍZIO

Introduction

AGRICULTURAL INTENSIFICATION lies at the heart of today's sustainable development agenda, and has been treated as the major focus of technology transfer to rural populations. Although it is common practice in the literature to criticize the way the term 'agricultural intensification' has been defined and applied, there have been few attempts to translate that into rural development policies and agricultural practices on the ground. The use of the term 'intensification' is frequently applied to factors of production, such as energy and capital input, rather than to land-use in general. Hence, classical accounts of intensification have the tendency to quantify it as proportional to increases in energy, technology, and capital input to a given area. Another dominant definition is that based on Boserup's model that refers to intensification as the process of increase of the frequency of use (or cycles of use) of a given piece of land. These focuses tend to overlook the maintenance of output yield over time and its relationship with other land-use and socio-economic facets of agriculture. This approach leads to emphasis on the substitution of local land-use strategies by external technology based on energy and capital intensive systems primarily focused on export-oriented agriculture. While concentrating on that, the tendency is to neglect investment to improve the existing socio-economic and physical infrastructure that would enhance local production systems, without threatening the local resource basis and economic and food security.

This chapter discusses the application of intensification parameters to a food production system, the *açaí* agroforestry (*Euterpe oleracea*) of the Amazon estuarine flood plains. *Açaí* fruit is a top-ranked regional staple food, grown on the flood plain, and its management and production have become the main economic activity for a large number of estuarine towns. *Açaí* agroforestry is based on locally developed technology that maintains intensive, long-term staple food production in forested areas with simple technologies.

Amazonian *caboclos* (native Amazonian rural populations) living in the flood plain have historically been the major contributors to regional agriculture and the forest economy. As the population grows in urban centres, their role and the use of the fertile flood plain tend to increase. Even more than mechanized agriculture and ranching which was the cause of upland deforestation, flood plain agroforestry has reached the crossroads of intensification and has become a major regional food production system.

Despite its major importance, the *açaí* production system is generally regarded as mere extractivism, and has been treated as such in national socio-economic surveys, by local populations, and by scholars (see examples of different considerations in Anderson, 1990, 1992; Calzavara, 1972; Chibnik,

1991; FIBGE,[1] 1988; Homma, 1993; Lima, 1956; Ross, 1978). This is not only a result of the region's socio-economic history based on export-oriented extractivism and the outside control of resources, but also a consequence of the way agricultural intensification has been defined. The rigid boundary drawn between different food production systems has labelled forested areas, such as those used for *açaí* agroforestry, as 'unproductive,' or at best 'extractivist'. Agricultural intensification, conventionally defined, is a synonym for deforestation, also implying an ability to keep a place deforested over time.

This chapter is organized into four main parts. First, agricultural intensification is discussed in the context of land-use. Second, an interdisciplinary and multilevel approach to understand agricultural and land-use intensification is proposed. The third part focuses on the case study of the production system of *açaí* agroforestry, while discussing its management and production. The fourth part develops an analysis of the suitability of using conventional intensification parameters to agroforestry production systems, such as the case study presented. The chapter ends with considerations about the implication of agricultural intensification for rural development in the Amazon estuary.[2]

Agricultural intensification, sustainable development and global change agendas

The last few years of agricultural intensification research[3] may be divided into two main trends, both related to a broader discussion of the so-called sustainable development and global change agendas: first, the review of intensification analysis based on small-farm agriculture and resource management, and second, the focus is on land-use analysis that places agriculture within a broader spatial and temporal landscape context, proposing nested scales of analysis at local, regional, and global levels.

The best example of the first trend is the outstanding work of Netting in *Smallholders, Householders* (1993), evaluating and highlighting the importance and significance of small-farm intensive agriculture in the world. Netting's book redefined intensification not only in the light of sustainability and productivity, but revised the myth of the unproductive and backward small farmer characteristics historically associated with peasant agriculture. According to him:

Defining intensive agriculture in terms of yields per unit of land over time emphasizes output as the dependent variable, and it does not prejudge the effect of economic inputs of labour, capital, or technological change. Increases in these independent variables, singly or in combination, on a

---

[1] FIBGE's definition of vegetal extractivism: 'the process of exploiting natural vegetation resources that includes gathering or harvesting products such as wood, latex, seeds, fibres, fruits, and roots, among others, by rational means, allowing sustainable production over time, or, in primitive and itinerant form, allowing, usually, a single harvest' (author's translation from FIBGE, Fundação Instituto Brasileiro de Geografia e Estatística. 1988).

[2] For additional details on *açai* agroforestry intensification, see Brondizio and Siqueira, 1997, where some sections of this chapter have been previously presented.

[3] For a review of agricultural intensification studies see Brondízio and Siqueira, 1997.

constant land area, may intensify its use (cf. Burton and White, 1984; Bradley et al., 1990), but this must be demonstrated by the analysis rather than assumed (ibid. p. 262).

The disruption of small-farm agriculture in favour of modern energy-intensive technology has lessened to a degree and has promoted more extensive forms of land-use.

The second important trend of agricultural studies emerging in the 1990s, is a result of the association between interdisciplinary research in ecological anthropology and landscape—land-use ecology. Two main factors have contributed to this. On the one hand, ecologically oriented anthropologists have scaled up their local unit of analysis due to the need to understand agriculture and economics on a broader regional scale (Brondízio et al., 1994a; Conant, 1990; Moran et al., 1994; NASA, 1990; Wilkie, 1990). On the other hand, ecological and physical sciences working on a global scale have perceived the need to scale down in order to understand the impact of local land-use strategies on global processes (Dale et al., 1993; NRC, 1992; Shukla et al., 1990; Skole and Tucker, 1993).

Various convergent themes have contributed to this process of integration. The increased demand for food in less developed countries, the global effects of deforestation upon biogeochemical and hydrological cycles, and the loss of biological and crop diversity are closely related to a model of agricultural expansion based on energy-intensive, export-oriented production systems. By demonstrating the contrast between the complexity and efficiency of local land-use strategies and the impact of conventional agriculture and cattle ranching, social and ecological scientists have been the main critics of such development approaches. In this process, the tools of analysis have also changed. Site-specific measures of agricultural activity have been used in conjunction with remotely sensed data and Geographical Information Systems, making possible the extrapolation of spatial and temporal scales. In this research agenda, the dimensions of agricultural change tend to become more complex. Rates of fallow regrowth and frequency of crops, such as those proposed by Boserup (1965), may be tested, as well as the environmental impact and sustainability of production systems. As Behrens et al. state, 'by mapping processes of human disturbance onto a landscape, translating them into the spatial domain, it becomes possible to derive quantitative measures of intensity and diversity' (1994:280). However, the ability to shift the level of analysis depends on the ability to translate information across scales with a minimum loss of detail, a condition that can only be achieved through interdisciplinary research and methods.

Agricultural intensification in the context of land-use

It is clear that intensification models and the comparative analysis of food production systems, such as *açaí* agroforestry, need to integrate a larger array of variables. Intensification does not proceed linearly, dependent on one factor (e.g. population growth or market demand), nor is it ahistorical; instead, it occurs as a combination of these factors with other variables such as internal population dynamics and opportunities offered by external sources (e.g. incentives from development projects). Thus, it responds to multilineal

90

processes combining variables operating on multiple scales that interconnect regional, local, household, and individual levels.

Land-use history becomes an important component of agricultural analysis, since it reflects the correlation between the present condition of plant and soil interaction and past socio-economic events and management practices motivating land-use change. Thus, it provides a better understanding of the land-use impact of a particular technique. The focus on *processes* of land-use intensification (i.e. coexistence of land-use strategies) is more relevant than characterization of *stages* of intensification (i.e. frequency of a crop in a given area). A land-use based approach makes it possible to grasp the process of coexistence between intensification and deintensification as related to temporal variation of land-use strategies. For instance, increased intensification in one production zone coexists with transient deintensification in another. This is the case regarding many estuarine populations in the Amazon that have virtually abandoned swidden agriculture in the upland forest in favour of *açaí* floodplain agroforestry production and trading. However, the thriving regrowth of fallows subjected to swidden agriculture allows manioc agriculture to be reconsidered at any time if the need arises. Another common case in the estuary is that of areas that have borne the repeated heavy impact of agricultural machinery (in general presented as 'intensive') which, besides creating dependency on tractors and fertilizer, has limited the regrowth capacity of vegetation, thus constraining future uses of the area. Within this framework, patterns of intensification may be defined in terms of the capacity of the ecosystem to sustain future uses. Hence, variability in land-use intensification can be reinterpreted in terms of flexibility of economic and ecological strategies, rather than in terms of input/output ratios at one point in time only.

Another important aspect to be considered in a multilevel analysis of intensification is related to the unit and scale of analysis of land-use systems. By putting site-specific measures in a regional perspective, one needs to scale up from a garden plot, to a farm, to a community of people, to a landscape and finally, to a regional level of intensification. For instance, the impact of agriculture on the vegetation and soil complex imposes an ecosystemic function on the landscape, which is thus seen within a spatio-temporal setting. One may ask how much one practice affects the regrowth capacity of vegetation at the site and how it changes landscape heterogeneity over time. In other words, a highly intensive system in the short-term (e.g. artificially fertilized agriculture) that limits the use capacity of the land in the long-term can be seen as extensive rather than intensive, and temporally unsustainable. The ability to maintain continuous use and a larger economic portfolio (i.e. the opportunity to shift to other activities) defines intensification as a dependent variable of sustainability, that is, accounts for the ability to maintain production over time, without constraining change in the production system in the future.

A conceptual structure for an interdisciplinary analysis of intensification

Interdisciplinarity is the most important paradigm faced by scholars working with socio-economic and environmental issues today. The complexity of rural development problems, for instance, requires an approach frequently beyond our disciplinary boundaries and scales of analysis. Isolated disciplines are limited in their understanding of, and solutions to, complex problems such as tropical deforestation. The present work is based on the assumption that an interdisciplinary study can only be achieved on the basis of three main structures. First, there should be an understanding of the historical evolution of the disciplines or fields involved; second, there should be unifying themes allowing integration of, and communication between, the areas involved; third, there should be a middle ground and integration between deductive and inductive approaches.

Historical evolution of the disciplines

Although widely discussed, the interdisciplinary approach is frequently confused with the 'sum of disciplines' instead of the 'integration' of disciplines. Among other reasons, the constant appropriation of another discipline's methods without a clear understanding of its theoretical context causes this problem. The greatest barrier to interdisciplinarity is the lack of consideration of the historical processes that have united or split particular disciplines. It is not only the acceptance of differences and similarities that makes the interdisciplinary approach possible but furthermore, it is the understanding of the historical context in which such processes occurred.

This study is not only grounded in the historical development of different disciplines but also in the convergence of paradigms among these different areas. Of special significance to the theoretical and methodological approach developed in this work are the fields of ecological and economic anthropology, vegetation ecology, ecosystem ecology, ethnoecology, landscape ecology, and remote sensing and geographic information systems (GIS).

Today we live at a moment in history that allows a level of disciplinary integration never before thought possible. On the one hand, vegetation ecology has been widely revised and broadened with the emergence of landscape ecology, whereas ecological anthropology and human ecology have engaged more directly in a large-scale perspective that allows the study of human problems at different levels. In parallel, the revision of the ecosystem concept in favour of both anthropology and ecology, and the emergence of a global change agenda have permitted a stronger unifying structure, absent during the 1960s and 1970s. However, in order to make integration possible, co-operation between disciplines needs to go beyond methodological sharing to more serious theoretical synthesis. It is important to make clear, however, that the speciality within each discipline must be maintained while each cultivates unifying themes as a bridge to integration. When tied to a wider context, disciplinary specialization is the most important contribution of science.

Unifying themes

Unifying themes or questions are proposed here as the main strategy of interdisciplinary work, since they encourage the development of analytical structures in which different paradigms can be related. Questions that have meaning for the social, biological and physical sciences can be developed, based on the use of key variables. The present study is based on three main unifying themes.

The first unifying theme is the intensification of food production systems. This reflects the driving forces behind changes in land-use. At the same time, it reflects the contrasts and dilemmas of different production systems, and the search for new parameters of sustainability and development paradigms. The second unifying theme is land-use. Land-use reflects the socio-economic dynamics of the landscape, while combining the actions and decision-making of individuals, communities, and institutions. It is a theme of great relevance frequently used in the physical, biological, and social sciences, and allowing integration of these areas. Finally, the third unifying theme is global change. Global change reflects the relationship between land-use and intensification of production systems with multi-scale ecological processes, such as biogeochemical cycles. At the same time, it challenges the integration of levels of analysis of different disciplines, in order to explain how local processes influence regional processes, and regional processes influence global processes. It has the potential of linking the analysis of human behaviour operating at each of these levels.

The method of multilevel analysis of land-use/cover change

The idea of constructing a multilevel method of land-use/cover analysis follows the current trend, especially in human ecology, of designing research methods from the perspective of the 'minimal data set'. The integration in the research design of socio-economic, cultural data with physical data builds a common ground for analysis fundamental to interdisciplinary attempts, and makes possible comparative analysis and data sharing among different disciplines. The concept of minimal data set design was developed by Moran (1995). It includes data on demographics, economics, social organization, production systems, health and nutrition, market, agriculture, vegetation cover, soil, climate, and ethno-ecological dimensions of resources. Although broad and inclusive, the method proposed here resembles the Land-Use/Cover Change Science Plan's suggestion of an analysis that should grasp simple, but strong relationships between driven forces and land-use/cover change (LUCC Science Plan, 1996). A land-use/cover analysis provides us with tools that connect human behaviour in relation to economic forces and management strategies, with ecological aspects of land cover.

The method, as proposed in Figure 6, is aimed to be developed integratively, using inductive and deductive approaches on different scales, by combining field research with laboratory/library work. Fieldwork is designed to inform laboratory work with satellite images and maps. In addition, laboratory work can precede fieldwork and inform it through preliminary analysis of land-use patterns and settlement distributions. It is important to note that in both approaches, research starts without any fixed scale of analysis, but nevertheless follows the idea that data collected at one specific level must be able to inform other levels. Hence, the samples at one level may need to be aggregated at a higher level or be used separately when necessary. This is a characteristic advanced from the hierarchical progressive contextualization approaches (Slobodkin et al., 1980; Vayda, 1983; O'Neill et al., 1986) in which problem-oriented questions are put into a larger and lower relationship structure uncovering new important variables at each level. Such research design avoids a definition of boundaries prior to ecological, socio-economic, and historical contextualization of the problem in focus.

The method of multilevel analysis of land-use/cover change (Figure 6) is built upon a structure of four integrated levels of research: the landscape/regional level; the vegetation class level; the farm/household level; and the soil level. The model relies upon a nested sampling procedure that produces data that can be scaled upwards and downwards independently or in an integrated fashion. The integration of multi-temporal, high-resolution satellite data with local data on economics, management, land-use history, and site-specific vegetation and soil inventories aims at understanding eco-logical and social dimensions of land-use on a local scale and linking them to regional and global scales of land-use dynamics. The assessment of land-use and land-cover change as a function of socio-economic and ecological factors is a fundamental step in understanding the sustainability of current forms of land-use and the consequences of these actions on the region's land cover.

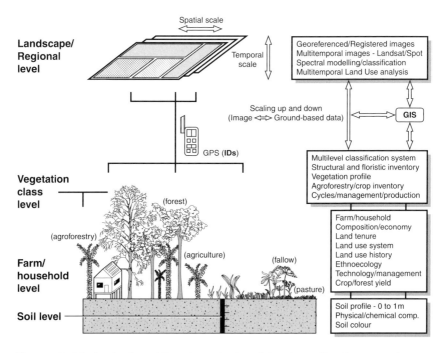

Figure 6 *Method of multilevel analysis of land use/land cover change* (from Brondízio, 1996).

Case study: the intensification of *açaí* agroforestry

Açaí agroforestry systems—management, planting, and production
Açaí agroforestry management has been the focus of a considerable number of studies in the Amazon estuary, especially after the 1980s when a marked increase in fruit production was observed (Calzavara, 1972; Lopes et al., 1982; Anderson et al., 1985; Jardim and Anderson, 1987; Anderson, 1988; Murrieta et al., 1989; Anderson, 1990; Jardim, 1991; Anderson, 1991;

Anderson, 1992; Anderson and Iorys, 1992; Peters, 1992; Neves, 1992; Jardim and Kageyama, 1994; Hiraoka, 1994; Brondízio et al., 1993a; Brondízio et al., 1994a and b; Moran et al., 1994; Brondízio and Siqueira, 1997; Brondízio et al., 1996). Based on FIBGE production data for 1991 (around 110 000 tons of *açaí* fruit is produced in the region), we estimate that the commercialization of *açaí* fruit generates US$15 m for producers, US$1.5 m for transportation, US$3.75 m for market brokers, while the processing and commercialization of *açaí* juice accounts for US$55 m. We can estimate that *açaí* fruit supports an economy of at least US$75.25 m in the estuary as a whole (see Brondízio, 1996 for more details). However, this does not take into account the *açaí* consumed directly by riverine households.

Despite such attention, many aspects of *açaí* agroforestry systems are still unknown, such as a better understanding of levels of management intensity, spatial distribution of managed areas, and associated planting techniques. Management requires understanding at two levels: site-specific and land-use. Whereas site-specific knowledge can reveal the level of management applied to changes in structural and functional characteristics of the vegetation stand, it is limited in showing the spatial extension of these areas. Spatial analysis of management is important in revealing interactions between areas managed at different intensity levels and their interrelationship with other land-use classes.

Surprisingly, few studies have dealt with the production output of *açaí* agroforestry (for an in-depth analysis of *açaí* agroforestry production, including a comparison with all accounts presented in the literature, see Brondízio, 1996). Management of *açaí* agroforestry has as its primary goal raising the level of production of *açaí* fruit. Questions emerge, however, as to what level, at what pace, and to what degree continuous site maintenance yields increments in production. Furthermore, it is relevant for the producer to know how management influences the distribution of production during the season, and whether it increases the flexibility of producers to decide upon the harvesting period according to market fluctuations. Can the producer control these variables through management practices?

Study area and data
The study area is located in the estuarine region of the Amazon, on Marajo Island, in the county of Ponta de Pedras, state of Para (see Figure 7). It is a transitional region between two macro-environments—natural grassland and forest—and most of the region is flooded forest (Pires, 1973; Prance, 1980). The human population of the region can be found in small urban centres, or scattered along the river banks in a typical pattern going back at least to the rubber boom of 1880 to 1920 (Wagley, 1953; Moran, 1993, 1974; Parker, 1985).

The data presented in this essay refer to two years of research which focused on understanding the production system of *açaí* agroforestry and its relationship to land-use change. However, research in the area started prior to this, in 1989. Special attention has been given to three populations representing different economic and land-use patterns. This includes a population reliant upon swidden agriculture and flood plain agroforestry, a second population with a land-use system in which swidden agriculture has been virtually

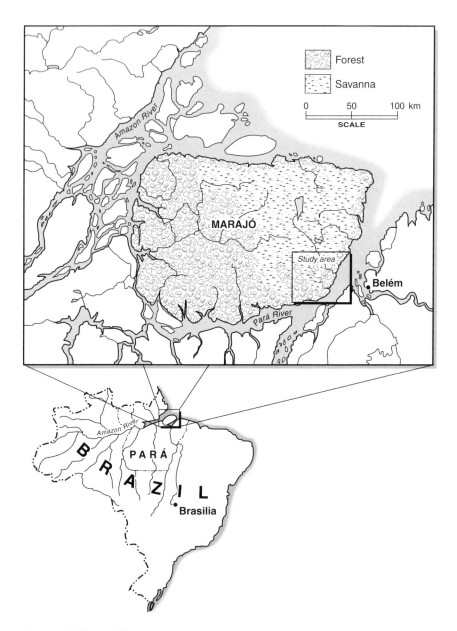

Figure 7 *Map of the Amazon estuary*

abandoned in favour of flood plain agroforestry, and a third population with a land-use system based on the coexistence of mechanized agriculture and pasture and, to a lesser extent, flood plain agroforestry. Ethnographic, socio-economic, and ecological accounts concerning these populations can be found in Murrieta et al. (1989); Murrieta et al. (1992); Siqueira et al. (in

96

press); Neves (1992); Brondízio and Neves (1992); Brondízio et al. (1994a); and Murrieta (1994).

This chapter takes advantage of a series of previous published and unpublished works focused on land-use change and landscape analysis of the study area. Methodology and results concerning the use of satellite images to classify 15 land-use/cover classes, including unmanaged flood plain forest, *açaí* agroforestry, and three stages of forest succession can be reviewed in Brondízio et al. (1993a and b, 1994a, 1994b, 1996); Brondízio (1996); Moran et al. (1994); and Mausel et al. (1993). Special attention has been given to the integration of levels of analysis, i.e. scaling up and down data from household and site-specific vegetation inventory to the local and regional scale as comprised by satellite images of the Landsat TM series.

Methods

Agroforestry inventory. Stand inventories were developed for 10 fields characterizing different levels of management of *açaí* agroforestry (for extensive data see Brondízio, 1996). Although the selection of areas with differential agroforestry management was based on interviews with local *açaí* producers, a concern with the spatial distribution of the sites on the TM satellite image was also taken into account. During the inventory, four adjacent plots (25 × 25m) and four nested sub-plots (2 × 5m) were randomly distributed in the managed area. In each plot all the trees (Diameter at Breast Height, DBH >10cm) were identified, DBH measured, as well as stem and total height. In each plot all *açaí* (*Euterpe oleracea*) with DBH > 5cm were counted, taking into account the number of stems per clump. In the sub-plots all the individuals were identified and counted, and saplings (DBH > 2cm) were measured for DBH and total height. In the unmanaged flood plain forest site, the number of plots and sub-plots was doubled (i.e. eight plots of 25 × 25m). These data were incorporated into a database and related to image characteristics through the co-ordinates obtained by the use of GPS (Geographical Positioning System). Establishing the relationships between the database and the image was accomplished using ARC/INFO 3.4 software.

Agroforestry fruit production experiment. Four different producers and eight different sites were selected to measure *açaí* fruit production during the whole harvesting season of 1994. Experimental plots were located, based both on the producer indication of the site (with respective history) and on preliminary analysis of area boundaries and characteristics. In each site a 25 × 25m plot was marked. For delimitation a cord was used to fence the plot off and restrict the use of the area for the purpose of the experiment only. A sub-plot of 10 × 10m, was set up inside the plot, and marked in the same way. Sub-plot location was based on a stratified random selection.

In the large plots (25 × 25m) a complete inventory of all tree individuals (DBH >= 10cm) and all *açaí* individuals were measured for species identification, DBH, total height, and number of *açaí* stems per clump. In this area, all *açaí* bunches were weighed. In the small plots (10 × 10m) all *açaí* clumps and respective stems were labelled in order to account for production at the individual level, the number of bunches per stem counted, and the location of each clump mapped. Each producer was trained and oriented to proceed with the experiment, and a notebook prepared to be kept with the producer during the harvesting season. However, the research team was present for most of the time to monitor the harvesting in all the sites. Figure 8 presents a summary of the results of the production experiments' for the eight sites of *açaí* agroforestry and unmanaged flood plain forest.

RESULTS

Population and management terms. *Açaí* palms occur in abundance in estuarine flood plain forest, varying in density and distribution depending on environmental and anthropogenic factors. Different management and planting strategies transform these areas into *açaí* agroforestry, or, as termed locally, *açaizais*. The term encompasses different intensities of management, population densities, and structure, as well as a diverse range of species composition. The term 'agroforestry' is used here to designate the temporal and/or spatial association between wood species (e.g., *açaí*, rubber, coconut, hardwood) and non-wood species (e.g., banana, medicinal plants), and husbandry (e.g., swine and ducks) in a given area under human management. This description follows the international definition of agroforestry systems accepted by the International Center for Agroforestry Research (ICRAF).

The three main means of *açaí* agroforestry development are: (1) management of native stands; (2) planting of *açaí* stands following annual or biannual crops, that is, *roçado de varzea*; and (3) combined management and planting in native stands. The management of native stands can be understood at two different levels: forest stand and plant levels. At the forest stand level, thinning and weeding techniques are used. At the plant level, management focuses on pruning techniques. Planting, however, involves both the forest and plant levels. Nevertheless, one needs to account for the use of these techniques in a similar fashion in planted *açaí* agroforestry. During the development of the *açaí* stands, weeding and pruning are used to encourage the development of seedlings and to control the density of stems per clump. These techniques are maintained continuously over the years during the formation of a mature *açaí* stand, which over time is also subjected to thinning of wood species, as in other managed sites. These techniques will be described in more detail here.

Defining levels of management intensity The intensification of production systems on the Amazonian flood plain has been frequently associated with deforestation, and an increase in energy input and labour to a given area. This approach has frequently contributed to a biased analysis of locally developed agroforestry systems. Agroforestry systems that mimic native forest are 'invisible' to the analysis of most researchers searching for conventional measures of intensification. This leads to its characterization as extensive, partially extractivist, and not dependent on labour and energy input other than for gathering.

Defining intensification parameters for locally developed agroforestry systems is a challenge that requires analysis at different levels. While site-specific data on vegetation structure, composition, and development can

Stand inventory data[1]

Site	Tree Species	Total individ.[2]	No. of clumps	Clumps/m³	Stems/Clump	% açaí B.A.[4]	Avg. height (m)	Bunches harvested	Avg. bunch weight (kg)	Tot. fruit prod. (kg/ha)	Tot. baskets (baskets/ha)[5]
								Production data			
1	31	141	16	0.025	6.1	18.99756	10.1	31	3.5	1392	116
2	6	196	41	0.065	4.6	49.54148	8.3	55	4.5	3568	297
3	5	196	76	0.12	2.4	65	8	177	5.5	12240	1020
4	6	156	56	0.089	2.6	52.62673	7.1	130	5.2	8904	742
5	14	147	46	0.07	3.02	29.05014	8.09	56	3.9	2612	217
6	8	191	75	0.12	2.7	50.16234	7.1	125	4	6476	540
7	7	168	41	0.065	3.8	52.84785	9.4	57	4.1	2984	249
8	7	169	38	0.06	4.4	49.31838	9.2	71	3.9	3788	315

[1] The sampled area in all the sites was 625m²
[2] Considering each stem (DBH = 5cm) as an individual
[3] Absolute densty of Clumps (clumps/m²)
[4] Basal area (m²/ha)
[5] Considering average basket weight = 12kg

Figure 8. *Table showing inventory and production data for sample plots of açaí fruit production experiments*

reveal the degree to which intensification is taking place, it frequently fails to show the spatial particularities associated with it. By nature, the flood plain is not an indivisible tract of land where expansion occurs in a homogeneous fashion. Rather, it resembles a network of sites where different levels of intensification are present, composing a mosaic of more intensively managed sites interconnected by less intensive areas.

Data show a consistent similarity of structural and floristic parameters that characterize *açaí* agroforestry and its management in relation to intensification. Furthermore, these data reinforce the notion of *açaí* agroforestry as a complex management of the structural and floristic composition of the flood plain environment, as well as a significant and consistent control of this production system. In summary, one can propose the use of two main sets of intensification parameters in *açaí* agroforestry. The first is composed of measures of clump and stem density, that is, the density of the production unit per square metre or hectare. The second is a function of management practices on the production units, such as average height, number of stems per clump, and the contribution of *açaí* stems to overall site structure and floristic composition. Therefore, management should be seen as a combination of these parameters. This is important because production does not respond only to density of production units but also to the level of maintenance of each unit. For instance, a site of high *açaí* density but characterized by excessively tall or old stems and an unbalanced number of stems per clump may have the same production output as a lower-density site with well-managed production units. In other words, one parameter can offset the other, and so they need to be integrated.

Density of stems and clumps. The density of stems and clumps is the main indicator of management level, since it reflects the dominance of the production unit at a site. At the study sites in Ponta de Pedras, the number of clumps and stems per hectare can be aggregated into three main groups: low density, medium density and high density. Low density is generally found in flood plain forests, whereas medium and high densities are present in intermediate and intensively managed areas. In low density conditions, there is an average of 150 clumps (450 stems) per hectare, while this number can be up to five times greater in managed areas and nine times greater in some cases. Most of the study sites lie in the medium density class, that is, an average of 500 clumps and 2000 stems per hectare. However, more intensively managed sites present more than 800 clumps and 3000 stems per hectare.

The density of stems, however, is not a single measure of intensity, since production output does not respond to these factors alone. Large numbers of stems may include young and unproductive stems, as well as older and taller stems that are also relatively unproductive. There seems to be a general pattern of medium density in most of the managed areas in Ponta de Pedras, as well as in the literature. This may be the optimum density of productive units for a number of reasons. At the study sites, one can see that this density can be achieved after five years of management and maintained over the years. It is likely that the maintenance of productive clumps at such a density requires less labour input while achieving substantial production. Whereas a high-density area may provide a larger production output, one may ask whether the additional labour input to maintain these areas is rewarded by greater output. It is interesting to note, however, that after the medium-density level there is no perceivable change in stand structure. There is a clear increase in *açaí* I.V.[4] during the first phase of management (around three years) from around 20 to 40 per cent. The next phase gives evidence of another jump in *açaí* I.V. (from 40 to 65 per cent), representing the clear dominance and increased density of *açaí* at the site. However, despite the increase in density, I.V. remains the same level as at medium-density sites. It shows that other forest species still play a structural role within a high-density *açaí* agroforestry stand, just as they do in areas of medium density. In summary, despite the fact that density of productive units (stems and clumps) is the most practical indicator of management level, high density areas often have the same structure and composition as areas of medium density. This fact reinforces the idea of analysing intensification by looking not only at site-specific factors but also at the spatial level, that is, the distribution of managed areas in relation to unmanaged sites.

Species composition. The number of species drops abruptly during the first phase of management (from one to two years), but it stabilizes gradually over the following years, despite the large increase of *açaí* clump density in intensively managed sites. Similar species diversity can be found in areas that present twice as much clump density and twice as many years of management. In other words, *açaí* agroforestry maintains a minimum number of species despite the intensity of management. There is no indication of single dominance of *açaí*, which makes *açaí* agroforestry always appear similar to flood plain forest, despite its nearly monocultural status, that is, dominance of production units over other species. This is remarkable, since most of the tree species can be characterized as productive. This reinforces the argument that *açaí* agroforestry are sites of intensive production, despite their structural appearance. The unveiling of the structural changes resulting from management can support this argument.

Stand structure. In flood plain forests, *açaí* stems contribute less than 15 per cent (less than 10 per cent in one case) to total stand basal area, and represent less than 20 per cent of total individuals. As management proceeds, this contribution tends to increase to a level of 50 per cent of total biomass, and up to 90 per cent of total number of individuals. Few changes in basal area occur in the first three years of management, but *açaí* tends to reach 50 per cent of total basal area in five years and corresponds to more than 80 per cent of individuals. It is interesting to note the similarity of basal area measurements in both flood plain forests and *açaí* agroforestry. Management does not radically change stand biomass, but instead influences which species contribute to it. Basal area ranges from 29 to $31 m^2$/ha in flood plain forest.

The maintenance of basal area in managed areas is an indicator that it is possible to achieve intensification of management and production without

---

[4] Importance Value (I.V.) is a percentage index that combines relative density, frequency and dominance aspects of a species; it is a practical way to provide a logical arrangement of 'dominant' species in a given stand.

disrupting structural-functional characteristics of the forest. Changes in the relationship in average stand height and contribution of *açaí* stems to total basal area are subtle in structural terms, but may result in dramatic increases in production output. A comparison of flood plain forests and *açaí* agroforestry shows a decrease in average canopy height from 19m to 16.5m and a change in first stem height from 12.4 to 10m. This change is proportional to the increase in the basal area of *açaí*. However, in intensively managed sites, *açaí* density and basal area increases but average stand height is maintained, indicating that despite the level of intensification, stand structure tends to have similar characteristics. This is one of the reasons behind the classification of *açaí* agroforestry as areas of extensive extractivism: they look just the same as flood plain forest.

Planted açaí *agroforestry: the* roçado de varzea

Roçado de varzea is an intensive intercropping system that combines annual, biannual and perennial crops in a spatio/temporal sequence resembling stages of secondary succession. This agroforestry system is developed in areas of high flood plain (*varzea alta*) that are only occasionally reached and fertilized by tides. This system has been described in Siqueira et al. (in press), Brondízio (1996), Brondízio and Siqueira (1995); Moran et al. (1994), and Hiraoka (1994).

A *roçado* is prepared by slashing and burning. During slashing, species considered important, such as rubber trees, remain untouched. Once the area is burned, careful cleaning removes unburned branches and prepares the area for intercropping. A description of a sequence of *roçado de varzea* is presented in Brondízio (1996). As noted by Hiraoka (1994), *roçados* are unique in the sense of plant combination. Each producer can make different spatial and temporal arrangements of plants. However, the techniques used to plant a *roçado* are similar among producers, as is the end result characterized by *açaí*-dominated agroforestry.

Planting usually starts with a mixture of annual, short-cycle crops and biannual species. In this fashion, banana and pineapple are planted right before annual crops are sown. Another commonly used biannual species is sugarcane, alternated with banana. Short-cycle species such as pumpkin, watermelon, and cucumber are dispersed around the site, while other annual crops, such as maize, rice, okra, sesame, and sweet manioc are planted in alternating rows or clustered in particular arrangements. In addition to annual and biannual species, perennial fruit trees, spices, and medicinal species are planted, such as coconut, papaya, peach palm, orange, lime, *cupuaçu*, breadfruit, and cacao, among others. By the end of the first year, a rich diversity of economic species is in place.

The first products of a *roçado* are the annual species that begin ripening after the second month, such as pumpkin and cucumber. Three to four months later, annual crops such as maize and sesame are ready for harvest. In both cases, the produce is consumed by households and the surplus taken to the market. Six months after planting, banana and sugarcane begin to dominate ground cover, although some other species are still cropping. By the end of the first year, banana, sugarcane, and pineapple begin cropping. The overall structure of the *roçado* is characterized by the dominance of these species followed by perennial trees. Following the first year, *açaí* seedlings begin to appear in the understorey of the banana stand, which shows the first signs of the next stage of agroforestry, characterized by trees. Producers usually encourage *açaí* seedlings during this period by weeding around them. *Açaí* seeds are both randomly sown and planted in specific spots. *Açaí* seedlings are also planted to speed up the process of *açaízal* formation.

Açaí colonization is strengthened by the dispersion of seeds from neighbouring *açaízais*, mainly during high floods that occasionally reach the *roçado*. Between the first and second years, the producer harvests a wealth of bananas, sugarcane and pineapples. Although these crops will continue producing over the next three years, productivity will fall drastically after the *açaí* take over the canopy and overshadow other species. As the end of the second year approaches, the *açaí* start to outdo the banana in height and to dominate the area. Producers report that in some *roçados* the vigour of secondary succession species, including *açaí*, is remarkable, requiring intensive labour input for weeding. In some cases, if the producer cannot control the vigour of regrowth, the *roçado* is left for regeneration until a stand dominated by *açaí* is established. Only then will weeding, thinning, and pruning proceed. However, in most cases the producer maintains a clear understorey that facilitates the development of *açaí* and other fruits. It is locally known that a well-shaded *roçado* (with banana for instance) is the best strategy for weed control. For this reason, some producers prefer to work harder during the preparation and planting of *roçados* in order to prevent weeds taking over in the future.

After the third year, the *açaí* start to dominate and overshadow banana and sugarcane. *Açaí* production begins within three and a half to five years of the establishment of the *roçado*, when other fruit species such as coconut, cacao, and *cupuaçu* begin producing as well. At the end of five years, the *roçado* already has the structure and composition of agroforestry. Pruning is carefully carried out during this period to balance *açaí* clumps, usually characterized by a wealth of offshoots. When the *roçado* is completely developed and carefully maintained and managed, it has a high density of *açaí* clumps and a relatively clear understorey where fruit trees can be seen. Unmaintained areas resemble a thinned flood plain forest that, despite being dominated by *açaí*, is characterized by a large number of flood plain trees on the way to overtaking the canopy. As noted by Hiraoka (1994), if left unmaintained, a *roçado* will return to a forest-like structure and composition after some years.

The development of a *roçado* therefore imitates stages of secondary regrowth, while creating an economically productive agroforestry that can be maintained for decades. Two of the sites described in this chapter, for instance, are *roçados* over 20 years old that have been maintained, giving a high level of productivity over these two decades. Whereas nowadays these areas resemble a managed flood plain forest, the *açaí* agroforestry areas are ones in which regrowth has been managed to increase the efficiency of cultivation. Hardwood species for household use that represent market value, such as *Virola surinamensis*, are generally maintained during weeding and thinning, thus increasing the value of the area. The technique of managing *roçados* represents one of the most important strategies of flood plain agricultural intensification for the region, with the potential of providing for household consumption and representing income and increased property and resource value, while providing output for market. This agricultural system is hardly comparable to other systems in terms of production output.

Açaí *agroforestry production: measuring different units of production*
Bunch production. A large, heavy *açaí* bunch at harvest is what producers aim for. Good management has a significant impact on fruit production at this level; it increases both the average bunch productivity and the frequency of more productive bunches in intermediate and intensively managed areas.

Stem production. Access to information about fruit production at the stem level is of major importance to understanding the effects of management on site productivity. Generally, the data indicate that stem production tends to be higher in managed areas when compared to unmanaged sites. There is a close relationship between stem height and fruit production. The higher productivity of stems in a specific height class (e.g., 10 to 12m) is a clear parameter to guide management. Stems growing in unmanaged areas, that is, with more canopy closure, tend to grow taller, thus putting more energy into development than into bearing fruit. There is a general trend indicating that large DBH correlates to higher fruit production. Producers recognize that in intensively managed areas, an *açaí* stand is usually composed of individuals with larger DBH and shorter heights.

Clump production. Clump production is a function of quantity and quality of stems, that is, the stem's productivity and number, respectively. Unmanaged and initially managed sites had the lowest production, while the highest yield was shown at intensively managed sites.

Site production. The association between management pattern and site productivity shows a positive correlation between clump density and production output.

The production pattern resulting from the experimental sites closely corresponds to the level of management at the sites. The three basic groups of *açaí* agroforestry with regard to clump density can thus be related to output production. Group 1, occurring in unmanaged sites, has an average of 256 clumps/ha. In this group, the production output average is around 1392kg/ha/year, that is, an average of 115 *açaí* baskets/ha. Group 2, occurring in newly and intermediately managed sites, has an average of 672 clumps/ha. In this group, output production varies from 2600 to 3800kg/ha/year, i.e., an average of 266 *açaí* baskets/ha. Finally group 3, characterized by more intensively managed sites, has between 900 and 1200 clumps/ha. In this group, production varies more widely from 6400 to 12 000kg/ha/year, an average of 760 *açaí* baskets/ha.

Açaí *production compared with other crops*
Figure 9 provides a comparison between *açaí* and other crops and concludes this analysis of *açaí* production. Crop return is presented in energy terms (calories per gram) and in terms of economic return. It is important to mention that it does not include the cost of production, which is expected to be

Crop	Location	Reference	Productivity (kg/ha)	Consumption (kg/ha)[1]	Calorie yield	Economic return[2] (US$/ha/year)
Rice	Flood plain	Lima (1956)	4500	4500	15 556 500	900
Maize	Flood plain	Lima (1956)	600	600	2 179 800	180
Beans	Flood plain	Lima (1956)	550	550	1 870 000	319
Rice	Upland	POEMA (1994)	1500	1500	5 185 500	300
Maize	Upland	POEMA (1994)	600	600	2 179 800	180
Beans	Upland	POEMA (1994)	802	802	2 726 800	465.16
Manioc	Upland	Brondízio (1996)	12000	3002	10 266 840	960
Açaí (unmanaged)	Flood plain	Brondízio (1996)	1390	695	1 267 680	152.9
Açaí (intermed.)	Flood plain	Brondízio (1996)	2612	1600	2 918 400	287.32
Açaí (intensive)	Flood plain	Brondízio (1996)	6476	4600	8 390 400	712.36

Assumptions:

[1] Total amount available as food for consumption
Manioc is based on the average productivity of manioc flour
Açaí is based on the yield of juice (considering 6 litres of juice/açaí basket)
[2] Average price December, 1994 (field data)

Figure 9 Table showing productivity and economic return of major crops

105

much higher for grain crops such as rice, maize, and beans, since they require higher labour allocation and the acquisition of seeds.

In the flood plain, intensively managed *açaí* ranks as the crop with the second highest output, after rice. The average economic return of rice is US$900/ha/year, while intensively managed *açaí* provides US$712/ha/year. However, as discussed in the previous section, *açaí* producers can distribute their harvesting over the season, depending on price fluctuations. This is the case of the producer on experimental site 3, who received US$2272/ha/during the year of this experiment. This is not true for rice or other grains, which are generally sold at once, with the result that producers cannot take advantage of higher prices. Rice cultivation also has higher costs (of site preparation, labour allocation and seeds). Other products extracted from *açaí* agroforestry are not included, such as heart of palm, wood, and other fruits. This indicates that the combination of rice and *açaí* in the *rocados de varzea* provides the best economic return in the flood plain environment, in the short-term (rice) and long-term (*açaí*). This is also significant in terms of the calorie yields of these crops: rice and *açaí* provide the highest return in calories.

Most interesting, however, is the economic potential manioc represents in the upland area. It provides conditions for achieving the highest economic return of all crops, including intensively managed *açaí*. The high productivity of manioc, added to its very low production costs, makes it the most interesting crop in the upland area. However, its production declines after the second year of cropping, while *açaí* yields continuous long-term production. Thus, the economic return of manioc cannot be compared to that of *açaí*, due to its extensive nature. *Açaí* agroforestry is a continuous production method, and its economic returns must be calculated taking into account the maintenance of production over time. The combination of manioc and *açaí* with rice agroforestry is the most promising agricultural strategy in the area, since it combines both high economic return/ha and the highest production of calories/ha, with a lower environmental impact when compared to mechanized agriculture and pasture.

Manioc is even more significant when compared to other upland crops such as beans and maize. It provides three times the economic return of rice, five times that of maize and twice that of beans (see Figure 9). This is also true in terms of calories, thus helping to explain the overwhelming historical preference of local populations for manioc as the most important staple food in the region in caloric terms.

The production cost of beans in mechanized crops in Praia Grande was estimated to be around US$350/ha. This includes labour, machinery, fertilizers, pest control, harvesting and processing, which can also be applied to rice and maize since they are similar crops. This indicates that only beans have a positive economic return, although low (US$165/ha) when compared to manioc and *açaí* (even in unmanaged areas). In summary, the combination of *açaí* in the flood plain associated with manioc in the upland area provides the best combination in terms of economic return and household food supply. Although rice provides the highest return, this figure does not consider production costs, which are higher. The association of rice in *rocado de varzea* followed by banana and other fruits, and by *açaí*, is the best economic strategy on the flood plain. In the uplands, manioc is still the best option available.

From site-specific to micro-regional level

Based on the area of *açaí* agroforestry and flood plain forest classified using Landsat TM images (see Brondízio et al., 1996), we can estimate that the study area as a whole (4764ha of flood plain forest) presents an economic return of US$869 523/year. This figure is based on commercialized production only and does not include household consumption. The study area represents only 16 per cent of the municipality of Ponta de Pedras, but it shows the importance of *açaí* agroforestry in the local economy. This is the equivalent of 25 per cent of the total *açaí* production estimated by FIBGE for the municipality. Thus, the total *açaí* economy in the area may yield approximately US$5 million/year, assuming an average seasonal price. When compared to all other agricultural products together (manioc, beans, rice, coconut, and fibre), *açaí* contributes five times more money to the local economy, and 11 times more when compared with forest products (lumber, charcoal, rubber latex, and heart of palm [FIBGE 1990, 1991]).

In summary, *açaí* agroforestry represents the best economic alternative for the region, while at the same time causing minimal impact on the land cover. The association of *açaí* and rice in the flood plain with manioc in the upland areas seems to provide the best agricultural strategy for local producers. Rice production is compatible with *açaí* agroforestry when part of *rocado de varzea*. Incentives for intensifying this production system may result in the agricultural development of the region in the near future.

Implications of intensification models for understanding agroforestry systems

The application of conventional measures of intensification to Amazonian agriculture is challenged by numerous constraints. Nevertheless, as previously discussed, these limitations are not unique to the region, but rather to most small-scale agriculture in the tropics. A primary problem is the focus on a single agricultural activity instead of land-use systems into which an agricultural field fits as part of a larger economic and subsistence strategy. This assertion reiterates two concepts discussed above: first, the importance of seeing agriculture within a spatial context, and second, the coexistence of intensification and de-intensification of agriculture as part of a larger land-use strategy (Guillet, 1987; Netting, 1993). To these remarks one can add a large body of literature on Amazonian flood plain populations showing more intensive use of the flood plain, associated with extensive swidden in the uplands, correlated to other economic activities, such as fishing, extractivism, hunting, and cattle ranching (Brondízio et al., 1994a; Denevan, 1984; Hiraoka, 1985; Meggers, 1971; Moran, 1989; Padoch, 1989; Roosevelt, 1989).

The most problematic application of intensification models is related to agroforestry activities, especially in cases such as *açaí* agroforestry, where the distinction between agroforestry and native forest is not clear. Concerning the case of *açaí* agroforestry, the flaws of current methods of measuring intensification in the evaluation of the production system can be explained by five main reasons: forestry structure, technology, spatial dimensions, the 'hidden harvest', and flood plain cycles.

107

Forest structure

The most serious constraint on the understanding of *açaí* agroforestry, using conventional measures of intensification, is related to forest structure and the frequency of production. This is because this system does not fit into the usual intensification measures, such as Boserup's 'frequency model', which labels clearing as the beginning of the productive process. Actually, *açaí* agroforestry may be assigned to both extremes of Boserup's model. First, management of the flood plain forest does not substitute forest for bare soil. In other words, it does not follow the conventional agricultural path of deforestation–crop–fallow commonly used to assign intensification to a production system. Rather, management transforms forest into forest, changing not its structure and function but the dominance and diversity of trees by economically desirable species. As a result, an *açaí* stand resembles (to an outsider) a regular forest and not an agricultural site. There is no category such as food-productive forest in conventional intensification models, and for this reason, managed *açaí* agroforestry may be characterized as 'unproductive land', or as it has been so far, as mere forest extractivism.

A planted *açaí* agroforestry (i.e. derived from a flood plain garden), as described earlier, may be characterized as one of the most intensive extremes of Boserup's frequency model. A flood plain garden starts by producing short-cycle crops (e.g. pumpkin, rice, and maize) during the first months, continues with annual and biannual crops (e.g. banana and pineapple), and then produces a smaller quantity of fruit trees (e.g. pupunha and coconut) and larger quantities of *açaí* fruit. Production in this area may be continual and uninterrupted in the long-term as long as management is maintained. In other words, it fits neatly into the more intensive, multicropping category of Boserup's model. However, in mature *açaí* stands, one cannot discern whether they result from forest management or whether they are an advanced stage of a flood plain garden. Hence, the application of Boserup's model to define intensification is highly paradoxical, placing *açaí* agroforestry at both extremes of intensification, that is, continual cropping versus non-cropping, and failing to incorporate its long-term efficiency and productive capacity which are independent of high technological, labour, and capital input.

Technology

It is common sense to say that *caboclos* have inherited the agricultural knowledge of pre-Colombian populations relating to flood plain agriculture. However, as discussed in the past section of this study, the application of this knowledge has been shaped by both historical factors (e.g. extractivism) and by available market opportunities. *Açaí* agroforestry is part of this process. As a result of increased rural migration to urban centres, the demand for *açaí* fruit has increased exponentially in the last 20 years, creating a prosperous market for the fruit. The large natural occurrence of *açaí* palm in the flood plain, associated with its ecological productivity, makes it highly responsive to management. Management occurs at the species level, gradually affecting the vegetation as a whole, making these areas hardly distinguishable from flood plain forest to an outsider. *Açaí* producers have managed both natural populations in flood plain forest, and intensively planted *açaí* palm in flood plain gardens, that is, *roçado de varzea*, associated with annual and perennial crops. The relatively low labour requirement with virtually no specialized tools, characterizes the system as technologically very simple compared to mechanized agricultural production, for instance. In general, the agroforestry garden follows the same path of secondary regrowth by starting with annual crops interplanted with a few of the slower-growing species of fruit and native trees associated with *açaí*, the density of which is gradually increased until high biomass agroforestry is in place.

At this point, the vegetation combines the functional and structural characteristics of the forest with the economic returns of agroforestry. During the first three years, the garden produces grains, tubers, and fruits uninterruptedly until it is replaced by a mature *açaí* stand that shades out other species. Once an *açaí* agroforestry is in place, its production will be continual as long as appropriate management is maintained. Production is not only in terms of *açaí* fruit, but includes heart of palm as well. However, only axes and machetes are used to prepare and maintain these areas. Although technologically simple, this process involves specialized knowledge about the species and plant-soil interactions. Therefore, any account of technological input in this system cannot rely simply on a comparison of the energy-intensive agricultural technology involved, but should include considerations of accumulated management knowledge, specialized labour, efficiency of production, and sustainability.

Spatial dimensions

The spatial distribution of *açaí* agroforestry is composed of a complex patchwork of production sites interconnected by both managed and unmanaged forest. Intensively managed or planted *açaí* agroforestry may be recognized by the dominance of the *açaí* palm. However, areas in the process of management and transitory flood plain gardens (from annual to perennial crops), although still in production, tend to be confused with unmanaged forest or secondary growth. Therefore, understanding the management intensity of *açaí* agroforestry cannot be based only on a site-specific inventory but must incorporate analysis of the spatial dimensions and interrelationships between areas under different levels of management.

Three levels of management may be described in relation to both site-specific structure and spatial arrangement: unmanaged, intermediately managed, and intensively managed (including planting of flood plain gardens). Unmanaged areas are continuous stretches of flood plain forest that structurally and functionally are not regulated by *açaí* palm but where *açaí* may be a dominant species. In contrast, intensive areas are clearly dominated by *açaí* palm. However, defining an intermediate level of management requires both an understanding of the site-specific dominance of *açaí* palm, and the spatial connections between intensively managed and unmanaged areas. In other words, intermediately managed areas are composed of sites of intensively managed areas interconnected by unmanaged forest. Thus, intermediately managed areas indicate a progressive expansion of intensively managed areas that become interconnected as management proceeds, a process that can be called 'progressive spatial intensification'. Although site-specific assessment can convey the level of management applied to change structural characteristics of the vegetation, it is limited to conveying how intensification of management proceeds in spatial terms. Shifting scales of analysis are thus required to explain the intensification of *açaí* agroforestry since it is a function of its spatial dimensions, as previously discussed. In this case, there is no clear boundary between extensive and intensive *açaí* agroforestry, since one is the product of the other.

In summary, such a pattern of progressive expansion of intensive sites poses a challenge to straightforward measures of intensification based on input (energy, labour, capital) per unit of area, and to measures of crop frequency based on the contrast between productive and unproductive areas.

The 'hidden harvest'

The subsistence economy of tropical agriculturists involves more than edible products (Ellen, 1982). The literature on non-timber products of tropical forests has flourished in the last few years, as well as the search for alternatives to deforestation and better knowledge of local economic strategies (Hecht et al., 1988; Nepstad and Schwartzman, 1992; Plotkin and Famolare, 1992). Although at times considered almost impossible to measure, taking into account non-edible and/or non-marketable products in agroforestry systems is fundamental in understanding the relevance of these areas in terms of supplying the household with food, raw materials, medicine, and providing market opportunities sometimes even more profitable than crops. A good example is Hiraoka's work in the Amazon estuary (Abaetetuba, Pará state) demonstrating the importance of miriti (*Mauritia flexuosa*) to household income. The market of miriti fruit represents 13 to 15 per cent of total household income (1994).

Secondary output of *açaí* agroforestry involves both household and marketable products with varying values. Raw materials such as fibres and stems used to build homes and fish traps contrast with highly valuable hardwood extracted during management. Although the market value of hardwood may be easily assessed, it is much harder to do so for non-timber products. However, studies have shown that forest products account for a considerable part of the local economy, and in some cases may exceed other activities, such as agriculture and ranching (Hecht, 1992; Peters et al., 1989). In summary, access to a large portfolio of timber and non-timber products in agroforestry areas guarantees market independence in terms of raw materials, and is an important part of both the household and market economy that should be considered when accounting for agroforestry productivity.

Flooding cycles

Another contradiction in the application of Boserup's model to define intensification of flood plain agriculture is noted in Chibnik's book *Risky Rivers* (1994), based on his work in the Peruvian Amazon. Chibnik cites Park (1992) to claim that the frequency model does not fit into the flood plain cycles, since agriculture is regulated by the seasonal rise and fall of rivers. Besides that, production in this area varies yearly, largely due to environmental conditions rather than to variation in technological and labour input. This is less of a problem in the estuary, where flooding is regulated by the daily tides, but it is true for most of the Amazonian flood plain that is seasonally flooded. In

110

summary, comparison of frequencies is not adequate in this circumstance, and even production output needs to be considered as a variable less dependent on technology and labour input per se, but strongly dependent on environmental variables such as annual rain or flood patterns.

Agricultural intensification and its implications for rural development in the Amazon estuary

This study has identified a series of constraints on the application of intensification parameters based on conventional agriculture to production systems such as agroforestry. Agricultural intensification, conventionally defined, is a synonym for deforestation and also implies the ability to maintain a place deforested over time. Forested areas, such as those used for *açaí* agroforestry, have been labelled 'unproductive' or at best 'extractivist'. The use of the term 'intensification' has been associated with factors of production such as energy and capital input, rather than with land-use in general. This focus tends to overlook the maintenance of output yield over time and its relationship with other land-use and socio-economic facets of agriculture. As previously discussed, considerations of intensification of flood plain agroforestry systems should take into account factors such as differential technology, forestry structure, hidden harvesting, flooding cycles, and the spatial dimensions of these areas, instead of focusing on input components. An interpretation of intensification in the context of land-use may help to avoid the assumption that externally induced changes increase the income and well-being of local populations. Besides that, it avoids conventional development strategies that tend to introduce export-oriented production without considering their impact on the local economy and food security.

Additional implications for development strategies may be foreseen. First, emphasis should be placed on diversification and the coexistence of land-use strategies, both intensive and extensive, concerned with long-term production capacity and increased property value that guarantees conditions for household reproduction. Finally, efforts should be concentrated on agroforestry strategies that allow uninterrupted multicropping, while increasing the value of land and providing diversified yields over time. The technique of *roçado de varzea* represents one of the most important strategies of flood plain agricultural intensification for the region, with the potential of providing reliable household income and increasing property and resource value, while providing output for market and household consumption. The association of grain and fruit production in the short-term with *açaí* in the medium and long term produces a level of economic return for *roçado de varzea* greater than most other crops.

Moreover, it is important to emphasize the significance of manioc as an upland crop. Manioc may provide a reliable economic return and it supplies, in addition to *açaí*, the most important caloric source in the region, while at the same time being a low-cost crop adapted to soils of limited fertility. However, due to its extensive nature, manioc production cannot be compared in the medium and long term to the economic return of flood plain agroforestry. Thus, the development of a more intensive and sustainable system of manioc cultivation, allied to intensive flood plain agroforestry, needs to be

111

considered as a priority in agricultural research. To date, flood plain agroforestry represents the best strategy of agricultural intensification and income generation in the region without the displacement of local populations, without deforestation, without reducing the diversity of land-use, and without destroying the resource basis, while also providing the most important source of income for local populations.

In the context of creating a new economic development concept based on social justice and environmental grounds, it is important to modify our conception of *caboclos* as a social category. In this sense, the contribution of Netting (1993), which can also be applied to *caboclo* populations, is enormous. Although avoiding the use of the term 'peasant', probably because of the meanings attached to the word, Netting has contributed to the redefinition of the peasant categorization in a more dynamic and dialectical way in addition to adding a more positive view of the role peasant farming plays and has to play in the world of agriculture.

Improvements in *caboclos* agricultural systems should come with socioeconomic infrastructure and extension services, rather than focusing on technological changes to production systems. The lack of infrastructure in terms of energy, transportation, extension services, and co-operative organization has led rural producers to political isolation and economic dependency on middlemen and patrons. Access to basic services, such as health care, education, transportation, as well as an infrastructure to commercialize forest products, should be priorities in order to guarantee the social and economic development of the region.

Incentives for the development of intensive and sustainable agroforestry systems can turn the region into a large food producer aimed both at local and export marketing. In parallel fashion, small-scale transformation industries should be promoted as ways of aggregating value to local products, increasing employment, and improving the circulation of money within the region. The development of estuarine agriculture associated with the management of timber, fishery, livestock, forest products, and transformation industries can turn around the extractivist stigma that burdens the region's population and economy into a promising land. This study has tried to point out the contradictions associated with agricultural intensification, as well as with *caboclo* production systems, as a way of contributing to future development strategies in the region. Recognizing the role this system plays in regional food production may contribute to a shift that sees the production system no longer as extractivist, but as no less than forest farming.

Acknowledgements

This study was made possible by a grant from NASA—Global Change Fellowship Program to E. Brondizio (3708–GC94–0096) and a graduate student equipment grant from the Midwestern Center of the National Institute for Global Environmental Change (NIGEC). Earlier field studies in the area and researching this study were supported by the National Science Foundation (grant 91–00526) from the Geography and Regional Science and the Program on the Human Dimensions of Global Environmental Change (P.I. Emilio Moran), the Wenner-Gren Foundation for Anthropological Research

(P.I.E. Moran), and grants from the Brazilian National Research Council and the Museu Goeldi in Brazil (P.I. Walter Neves, CNPq 403534/90–9; 150043/90–2). The author is equally thankful to ACT/Indiana University for its financial and infrastructural support during the development of this research and the support of EHBRAPA/CPATU in Belém.

The author has 'no words' to thank Professor Emilio Moran for his advisory skills during the development of this research and the collaboration of Dr Walter A. Neves and Rui S.S. Murrieta. I specially acknowledge the assistance and friendship of the *açaí* producers who collaborated with the production experiments and have taught us extensively about flood plain agriculture and management. The author acknowledges the assistance of Lucival Rodrigues Marinho (in memory) and Jair da Costa Freitas for their work with plant taxonomy and field research. I am indebted to the continual support locally of our friends Valois Delcastagne and Socorro V. Ribeiro, and the people of Praia Grande, Marajo-acu, Paricatuba, and Ponta de Pedras as a whole. The author is thankful for the collaboration of Vonnie Peischl (Administrative Co-ordinator of ACT) for her constant help during this research. Finally, *obrigado* to Andréa D. Siqueira and Maíra S. Brondízio. The views expressed in this essay are the sole responsibility of the author and do not reflect the views of the funding sources or collaborators.

Rules, norms, organizations and actual practices—Land and water management in the Ruaha River basin, Tanzania

JANNIK BOESEN, FAUSTIN MAGANGA and RIE ODGAARD

Introduction

THE SUSTAINABLE MANAGEMENT of natural resources through local institutions is one of the research themes of a major research initiative carried out by Tanzanian and Danish anthropologists, political scientists, sociologists, geographers and agronomists in the Ruaha River basin of Tanzania (see Figure 10). Under the umbrella of 'Sustainable agriculture in semi-arid Africa', the research is conducted on this and two additional themes: (1) changing resource utilization and livelihood strategies, and (2) water balance and nutrient cycling in semi-arid agro-ecosystems. The aim of the research is to:

○ improve understanding of the state and dynamics of environmental degradation in semi-arid parts of southern Tanzania;
○ improve and integrate natural and social science methods applied to study and to explain environmental degradation;
○ explore how local perceptions and knowledge can contribute to the development of more sustainable methods of farming; and
○ develop strategies for sustainable agricultural production, aiming to increase production stability and productivity without irreversible land or environmental degradation.

This chapter presents some of the analytical and conceptual understandings of institutional aspects of local resource management, which we are working towards as guidance for the work on the research theme given here.

As the research theme currently has to be integrated with results from the two other themes, it will focus particularly on the management of land and water resources for agricultural and pastoral uses, and will focus on the dynamics of changing resource management mechanisms.

The field of natural resource management is one of the areas where political scientists, economists, anthropologists, geographers and other scientists have traditionally converged with their different, sometimes opposing, approaches. In such a multi-disciplinary field, and particularly for inter-disciplinary research, one of the important prerequisites is that communication is not impeded by different interpretations of similar words, terms and concepts, but instead leads to a common understanding of their theoretical implications, etc. Among the concepts which have been used differently by the above-mentioned social scientists is 'institution' (in this chapter there will be no time for 'sustainability'!). Although since the 1970s writers like Ciriacy-Wantrup and Bishop (1975) have emphasized the importance of considering institutional aspects in resource management, scholars are not in agreement about the exact definition of the concept, resulting in ambiguity and confusion.

To provide an appropriate context for our discussion on land and water management in Tanzania, we start out by highlighting the different ways of conceptualizing 'institution', concluding that the important aspects of resource management for analysis include such diverse elements as knowledge systems, rules and norms, organizations, and conflict resolution mechanisms (whether we agree to call them all institutions or not). Resource management is dynamic, shaped by and shaping people's changing patterns of interaction, and by the different purposes people attach to natural resource management.

Conceptualizing 'institutions' and their role in natural resource management

Relating institutions to organizations

One of the issues which calls for clarity and consistency, when analysing institutional aspects of natural resource management, is whether to make a distinction between 'institution' and 'organization' or to view them as overlapping, and hence use the terms interchangeably. For example, Uphoff (1986) has noted:

> The terms *institution* and *organization* are commonly used interchangeably and this contributes to ambiguity and confusion. Three categories are commonly recognized: (a) organizations that are not institutions, (b) institutions that are not organizations, and (c) organizations that are institutions (or vice versa, institutions that are organizations) (Uphoff, 1986:8).

A quick review of the literature on institutions supports the above observation by Uphoff (1986). There are writers who use the concepts institution and organization interchangeably, and those who make a clear distinction between the two concepts. According to writers like Uphoff (1986, 1992) and Maganga (1995), an institution may or may not be an organization. Others, like North (1990) and Ostrom (1992), make a clear distinction between the two terms.

In his thesis, Maganga adopted the definition put forward by Uphoff (1986) in which '. . . institutions, whether organizations or not, are complexes of norms and behaviours that persist over time by serving collectively valued purposes' (quoted from Maganga, 1995:33).

Using the two terms interchangeably, and categorizing institutions in a continuum ranging from the public, participatory and private sectors, Uphoff (1992) lists some of the areas where institutions might play a role in natural resource management:

○ mobilizing resources and regulating their use;
○ generating and interpreting location-specific knowledge;
○ facilitating quicker and less costly monitoring of changes in the status of resources;
○ conflict resolution;
○ conditioning people's behaviour (through community norms and consensus); and
○ encouraging people to take a longer-term view by creating expectations and a basis for co-operation that goes beyond individual interests.

In contrast to Uphoff (1986, 1992) and others who write like him, North (1990) makes a clear distinction between institutions, which he views as 'rules of the game', and organizations, which he views as 'a set of players, a team, working within the framework of the rules towards specific objectives'. North (1990:3–4) defines institutions as follows:

> Institutions are the rules of the game in a society or, more formally, are the humanly devised constraints that shape human interaction. In consequence they structure incentives in human exchange, whether political, social, or economic. . . Institutions reduce uncertainty by providing a structure to everyday life. They are a guide to human interaction. . . Institutions include any form of constraint that human beings devise to shape human interaction.

According to North, institutions can be both formal (constitutions, laws, property rights) or informal (sanctions, taboos, traditions and codes of conduct) and they may be created (e.g., a constitution) or they may simply evolve over time, as does common law.

North thinks it is very important to distinguish between institutions and organizations. Although, according to him, organizations, like institutions, provide a structure to human interaction, this structure consists of human beings, while the other is composed of rules, laws, etc. Hence, to him, organizations include political bodies (political parties, the senate, a city council, a regulatory agency), economic bodies (firms, trade unions, family farms, co-operatives), social bodies (churches, clubs, athletic associations) educational bodies (schools, universities, vocational training centres), and so on.

Elinor Ostrom (1992:19) defines institutions in the following way:

> . . . an institution is simply the set of rules actually used (the working rules or 'rules-in-use') by a set of individuals to organize repetitive activities that produce outcomes affecting those individuals and potentially affecting others. Hence an irrigation institution is the set of rules for supplying and using water in a particular location.

Ostrom distinguishes between institutions and organizations by emphasizing the visibility of organizations: '. . . organizations are visible and measurable (consist of human beings), while the rules in use by the organization consist of common knowledge (which people have in their heads) or [those that] are written down on paper.'

She elaborates further:

> All rules contain prescriptions that forbid, permit, or require some action or outcome. Working rules are those actually used, monitored, and enforced when individuals make choices about actions they will take in operational settings or when they make collective choices. . . Enforcement may be undertaken by those directly involved, by the agents they hire, by external enforcers, or by a combination of these. Rules are useless unless the people they affect know of their existence, expect others to monitor behaviour with respect to these rules, and anticipate sanctions for nonconformance (ibid.).

Institutional change

As North (1990) states: 'Institutions are creations of human beings. They evolve and are altered by human beings. . .' His new institutional economics explanation for institutional change, which rests on assumptions about rational profit-maximizing individuals, has been criticized, however, for a failure to account for changes in preferences (ideology), which have nothing to do with economic considerations (Gunnarsson, 1991; Knudsen, 1995).

Knudsen (ibid.:78) distinguishes two ways of viewing institutions: either as a micro-level phenomenon which is created by actors for specific ends, or as a macro entity which structures human action:

> There are, broadly speaking, two ways of viewing institutions among social scientists. The first is the 'bottom up view' which sees institutions first of all as the outcome, the aggregate of individual action. . . Here institutional change results from actors' changing preferences or changing opportunities (opportunity set), what we could term a 'voluntaristic' view of institutional change. . . The other approach takes a normative perspective, arguing that institutions shape people's action and preferences. In this view, changing preferences come about as a result of institutional change, what we could term the 'deterministic' position.

The latter quotation points to the importance, in order to understand the dynamic aspects of institutions and institutional change, of taking as the point of departure people and their struggle to bring about changes, rather than the institutions which they have created, but which they are constantly challenging and changing through their daily practices and actions.

Following Long's actor-oriented approach, which implies that concepts '. . . are grounded in the everyday life experiences and understandings of men and women, be they poor peasants, entrepreneurs, government bureaucrats or researchers' (Long, 1992:5), Nuijten in a study from Mexico conceives '. . . of organization as a set of practices'. This, according to her:

> . . . implies that organizing is not limited to formal institutions but can take the many forms in which peasant smallholders and other people are organized in their everyday life. It is further argued that, instead of seeing organizations as bounded social systems, as the objects of analysis, we should analyse organizing as a process (1992:204).

To support this view she refers to Wolf (1990), who argues:

> . . . that we should get away from viewing organization as a product or outcome, and move to an understanding of organization as a process. He suggests that we should make a start by looking at 'the flow of action', and by asking what is going on, why it is going on, who engages in it, with whom, when, and how often. By approaching organization as a process, the focus is shifted from looking at the functioning of an entity with its own 'rules', 'principles' or 'culture', to the creation and reshaping of different organizational forms (quoted from Nuijten, 1992:204).

Natural resource management mechanisms, their purposes and change

This discussion on institutions, organizations and change, while general and therefore abstract in character, provides insights which are useful for the study of natural resource management. Our study of natural resource management takes as its point of departure people's interaction with other people (and with the environment) concerning natural resources, especially land and water. It looks at both the norms and rules in use, as well as the organizations that help structure people's actions in relation to natural resources, as outlined by most of the authors mentioned earlier. The present authors all agree that norms and rules on the one hand and organizations on the other hand, must be distinguished as different categories, though rather similarly defined by the authors quoted. However, some of the authors adhere to the semantic position that these are all institutions, while others reserve that concept for norms and rules. Consequently, we tentatively suggest using the more neutral term 'resource management mechanisms' to include them all.

Departing from the abstract discussion of institutions, it is furthermore our contention that rules and norms and organizations do not exhaust the types of mechanisms involved in natural resource management, i.e., in structuring people's actions when dealing with natural resources. We are tentatively working with two more categories of resource management mechanisms:

○ Knowledge systems, experiences, habits, which are also 'a guide to human interaction' and 'structure incentives in human exchange', and are to a great extent shared socially, but which are not backed by social sanctions for non-conformity like rules and norms.
○ Conflict articulation and resolution mechanisms, possibly the dynamic element, including bargaining, manipulation, etc., in the arenas created by the other three types of mechanisms.

The literature presented also reminds us, however, that while such resource management mechanisms structure people's interaction, they are themselves human constructions, which are constantly changed by people's actions, be they organized and deliberately directed towards changing the way resources are managed, or simply actions that contravene a rule to make it obsolete or alter it. The study of resource management, therefore, must be concerned with how it affects people's use and handling of natural resources; but perhaps even more with how, when and why people change their resource management mechanisms, and how that affects people's use and handling of natural resources.

Very often, for example, change will come about through conflicts when pressures on resources grow and power relations between stakeholders change. Conflicts unfold in the form of conflicting interests and subsequent actions in relation to natural resources, but also through competing perceptions of the resources and their maintenance, and differentiated access to manipulation of the resource management mechanisms. But their emergence, forms, and outcomes are influenced by changes in pressure and demand on resources and in power relations, which are themselves consequences of changes in population, production and economic and political structures.

In the next section we elaborate on the four categories of resource management mechanisms and give some preliminary examples of their dynamic character from the Ruaha River basin.

One reason why the conceptual discussion of institutions and organizations may sometimes appear overly abstract may be a certain tendency to discuss institutional change in general, irrespective of the particular purpose for which institutions are created and maintained. However, if rules, norms, organizations, etc., are human constructs, they are constructed with a purpose and maintained with a purpose—which may be more or less specific, differently interpreted and reinterpreted by different stakeholders, and which may, of course, undergo change.

In the case of resource management mechanisms their general purpose is, of course, resource management, i.e., they are created or emerge because there is a social demand for certain management functions to be performed. This is not to deny all the conflicting interests and powerplays surrounding the creation, functioning, and change of resource management mechanisms, only to reiterate that these are to a large extent focused precisely on the management functions performed by the rules and norms, organizations, etc. Change, therefore, must be studied in relation to changing interests in, and demands for, the performance of different resource management functions. Some considerations concerning management functions and change are presented below, based on studies of water resources management in the Ruaha River basin undertaken by the authors (MWEM 1995).

Changing natural resource management in the Ruaha River basin, Tanzania

Knowledge systems, habits and experiences

One of the categories of resource management mechanisms which we have identified refers to people's behaviour and behavioural patterns as they are guided by knowledge systems, habits and experiences but not backed by social sanctions, yet which to a large extent are socially shared. This is contrary to what is the case with rules and norms, to be dealt with later.

There is an increasing body of literature on indigenous technical knowledge and its importance for local people's use and management of natural resources. However, we believe it is important to see even knowledge systems as integrated parts of management systems as such, in the sense that knowledge systems help structure people's behaviour. Shared knowledge and experiences are, at the same time, no doubt some of the more fluid management mechanisms. These are constantly being reinterpreted and changed, as well as deviated from, because every individual develops her or his own ways of doing things. Alternatively, they invent a new technology or improve the one they already have.

Examples of people inventing their own specific small pushcarts or trolleys, developing special ways of lining irrigation furrows, or experimenting with ways of improving the fertility of their soil are numerous in the Ruaha River basin. They often build on time-honoured experiences—and successful innovations may spread like bushfire (while others mysteriously do not!). In contrast, local knowledge has also often been used in passive resistance to enforced management imposed by both colonial and post-colonial authorities.

We have not yet worked with this issue in detail, but it seems that despite the growing literature on indigenous technical knowledge, the study of it still has a long way to go. We do not, as yet, know of much work being done on the specific aspect of knowledge as a resource management mechanism in its own right, which was only briefly touched upon by Maganga (1995). Also, changes in knowledge systems have to be discussed in this connection: is it actually better to conceive of people having a catalogue (Richards, 1985) of knowledge or practices from which combinations can be freely chosen, or of a range of co-existing knowledge systems rather than the scientific/indigenous knowledge dichotomy (Agrawal, 1995).

Rules and norms and actual practices in land and water management

As argued earlier, rules and norms have to be understood as a product of human interaction: that is, people make rules and norms, they follow or violate them and they change them. We shall now deal with the rules-in-use and the rules and norm-generating organizations and groups of people.

To understand the dynamics of the rules and norms in use related to land and water management, it is essential to consider the nature of the legal system in which major parts of them are embodied. In relation to this, it is important to draw attention to the fact that Tanzania is a country with legal pluralism, that is, the legal system is composed of statutory as well as customary laws. One important difference between statutory law and customary law is: that while the first mentioned is unified and formally written and changed in court judgements and legislation, customary law is unwritten and is continuously subject to reinterpretation, change, and diversification.

That customary laws form part of the legal structure in Tanzania is an oft-forgotten fact. Thus many problems have arisen in the country as a result of outsiders (private enterprises and donor agencies among others) uncritically accepting official rhetoric; such as that all land and water belongs to the nation, and therefore such resources can be utilized for whatever purposes and by whatever persons the government allows. (Some examples of this are analysed in Lane, 1990; Kiwasila and Odgaard, 1992; Mustafa, 1993; Mwaikusa, 1994, among others).

For the majority of people in the Ruaha River basin, access to and use of land and water are regulated according to customary rules and norms. However, although our main focus here will be on customary arrangements, these arrangements will be dealt with within the framework of the dual law system. Formal legislation is becoming increasingly important, not only in the form of state regulations impacting on the functioning and change of customary management systems, but also due to the fact that enterprises, groups of people and private individuals are increasingly trying to get formal titles to land (this is especially true in areas with land pressure), and trying to ensure formal water rights, especially in areas with large as well as small-scale irrigation activities (see, for example, MWEM 1995).

The unwritten and flexible nature of customary law implies that we are dealing with a very complex phenomenon. Conceptually, therefore, it is important to be aware that customary law may refer to four different things (summarized from Armstrong, 1992:31–2; for further elaboration in a Tanzanian context, see also Odgaard and Maganga, 1995):

○ the customary laws of specific ethnic groups;
○ customary law which is applied in courts;
○ customary law which is applied by so-called traditional authorities (chiefs, headmen, and family councils outside the state law system); and
○ living customary law, that is customs and practices of the people today and the principles underlying these practices.

At the same time as these four dimensions of customary law indicate a history of dynamic changes, they are, as we shall see, also all reflected in the various land and water management systems found today in the Ruaha River basin.

The dynamic aspect of the historical development of customary law is, as stated previously, very important to keep in mind. As mentioned by Sara Berry (1993), there is a bulk of recent literature (see, for example, Moore, 1986 and 1989; Chanock, 1982; Shivji, 1994; and URT, 1994) which has shown that customary laws are not 'static perpetuations of pre-colonial norms, but new systems of law and adjudication based on colonial administrators' interpretation of African tradition' (Berry, 1993:24). Customary law has, however, also been reinterpreted and affected by post-colonial state intervention and post-colonial policies. One of the major policies having interfered with customary arrangements in Tanzania is the *Ujamaa* policy, the implementation of which meant that millions of people were to be moved and resettled away from their home areas. During the villagization period, these movements implied the extinction of customary rights both for the people who were moved and for those who inhabited the area in which they were settled. Customary arrangements in relation to land-use and the division of labour have also been violated by state intervention directly into production and reproduction systems.

Since the mid-1980s, when people were officially allowed to move back to their areas of origin, the number of cases of people reclaiming their customary rights to land has exploded in Tanzania. At the same time, the people who have in the interim been moved to, or have immigrated to, the areas to which the indigenous inhabitants are returning, are faced with severe problems of maintaining rights to land.

However, customary rules were not static before the colonial intervention either. There is historical evidence that norms, rules and customs were ever changing before the colonial era, as a result of peaceful interaction between various ethnic groups, or due to conflicts, warfare and conquest occurring between neighbouring groups, impact of long-distance trade, population movements, and so on.

Changes from within the customary rule systems themselves also occurred, due to gained experiences showing that one rule may be better than another, or to increased pressure on resources, and internal competition (see, for example, Gulliver, 1957 and 1961; Moore, 1989; Odgaard, 1997; Koponen, 1995).

To illustrate further these processes of change, we shall now look at the rules-in-use in the Ruaha River basin in relation to land and water resources.

The population of the Ruaha River basin is today ethnically very mixed, but previously the dominating ethnic groups were the Hehe, Sangu and Bena. The cultural and resource management systems of these groups have been described as being quite similar (see, for example, Mumford, 1934). A brief general summary of Hehe, Sangu and Bena indigenous customary laws (number 1 above) states that:

> ... villagers do not possess any absolute ownership of land and their ownership really amounts to a form of right of occupancy, the effectiveness of which depends upon residence in a certain village combined with the actual use of this land at some particular time. It is regarded as private in that only one man may use it, the right to use it can be inherited and it may be alienated by way of a gift. Its possession, however, is not absolute in that it cannot be sold and when once a man leaves a village or abandons his land, then in the absence of any claimant the land once more becomes a portion of the communal lands of the village. (Mbeya District Handbook, quoted from Odgaard and Maganga, 1995:21.)

A few details should be added to this brief summary. One is that according to custom a man must provide his wife or wives with a *shamba*, whereas no provisions are made for the children. When a child becomes old enough he acquires land in the same way as any other adult. Moreover, a landowner may rent out his land to another person against payment, but never for more than a year. Large parts of the Ruaha River basin are used as pastures, and there are well-defined rights and obligations at the community level in relation to the use of these pastures (Odgaard and Maganga, 1995).

According to native law and custom, those who can claim rights to land and other natural resources in a certain area are primarily the indigenous members of the ethnic group residing in the area. Others may be given such rights (ibid.). Thus in the Ruaha River basin it is first and foremost the Hehe, Sangu and Bena who have indigenous rights in the respective parts of the Ruaha River basin where they reside. Members of other ethnic groups, who have moved into the Hehe and Sangu or Bena 'tribal' areas, are not automatically entitled to such rights. Some of those who have lived in the area for a long time, may have gained customary rights to land and water from the indigenous authorities. Others have obtained such rights through formal legislation, as a result of national policies, or through personal informal arrangements with some of the indigenous inhabitants.

Although some aspects of indigenous rules are still strongly reflected in the land management systems existing today, various factors have also implied fundamental changes and given rise to several other forms of customary arrangements in addition to the ones described above, combined with various forms of statutory rights.

Continuous expropriation of land combined with a steady increase in population, due to natural increase and immigration, has meant that there is generally less land and water available for an increasing number of people. Moreover, commercialization of agriculture has helped to individualize rights to land and other resources, which again has implied social stratification and increased inequality between rich and poor, men and women and young and old people.

During the process, some people have lost their customary rights to natural resources, while others have been able to extend such rights or have obtained such rights through the establishment of social ties (marriage ties, for example), the manipulation of customary rules, corruption, and so on. Some of the groups who have, in general, been very hard hit by the historical changes leading to social stratification and the loss of land rights are pastoralists and women (see, for example, Lane, 1993; Mwaikusa 1994; Odgaard and Maganga, 1995; Odgaard, 1995).

The distinction between being indigenous and non-indigenous to a certain area has, it seems, gained increasing importance alongside the increased pressure on resources in various parts of the Ruaha River basin. However, not even members of the indigenous ethnic groups in the area find themselves well placed any more in the socio-political hierarchy to claim and acquire customary rights to land and water in the area (Kiwasila and Odgaard, 1992; Odgaard and Maganga, 1995).

Officially, land can at present be held in one of two ways in Tanzania: either by granted right of occupancy or by customary right of occupancy (deemed right of occupancy). It is noted by Tenga (1992) that while the granted right is issued by the president or his authorized subordinates, the deemed right is held under customary law, where the law deems customary landowners as 'natives or a native community lawfully using or occupying land in accordance with native law and custom'.

In actual practice the following major forms of land tenure were identified by Odgaard and Maganga (1995) in the Ruaha River basin:

○ villagers who hold agricultural land under various indigenous/customary arrangements (*malungulu*);
○ villagers who hold their land in accordance with the regulations established under Operation Vijiji or allocations made by village governments after villagization;
○ villagers who rent or borrow land from those who owned it by the means already described or by means of statutory rights;
○ village/community-owned land (including pastures, forests, etc.);
○ villagers and private enterprises who hold their land under statutory rights of occupancy; and
○ state-owned land (agricultural state enterprises, forest and game reserves and national parks).

The majority of people in the Ruaha River basin hold land for cultivation under various indigenous/customary regulations or renting/borrowing arrangements influenced by customary rules.

People who do not have customary rights or have been granted a right, either during villagization or through formal legislation, depend on other individuals who possess such rights. For them the use of land for cultivation involves a transfer of either labour, services, goods or money to the one recognized as the owner of the land, whether land ownership is under customary or statutory legislation. The amount of labour, money or goods to be 'paid' to the landowner depends on the degree to which land is a scarce resource, and on the type of relationship existing between the landowner and the renter/borrower.

Rules relating to land used as pastures are quite different from those for land used for cultivation. In principle, membership of an indigenous community implies a right to use pastures communally owned by the members of the respective communities, and an obligation to take part in activities related to the protection and conservation of such areas.

However, development and environmental protection measures have meant that the area available for pastures has decreased in Tanzania, and many pastoralists have been forced to move away from their home areas and look for pastures in other parts of the country. Thus the Ruaha River basin has attracted large numbers of pastoralists, some of them with large herds of cattle.

This, combined with the fact that cattle have always been, and still are, important for the indigenous ethnic groups in the Ruaha River basin, and that the question about pastoral land rights in general in Tanzania is completely unresolved, has meant that the situation for pastoralists in many parts of the area has become very difficult, and has resulted in serious conflicts in some parts of the area.

The fact that the question of pastoral landrights has become a 'grey area' of jurisdiction in Tanzania (see Tenga, 1992) has implied that the *de facto* use of pastures in many parts of the Ruaha River basin is in accordance with a kind of open access situation (see Charnley, 1994).

These arrangements reflect a dynamic interplay between customary regulations and the changes brought about by colonial and post-colonial legislation and policies. They also reflect that the reinterpretation and manipulation of the unwritten customary rules in particular are continuously taking place and giving rise to many overlapping forms of those already existing, the *de facto* abolition of some, as well as to new forms of unwritten customary arrangements.

The many co-existing forms of land tenure and land-use also reflect the varying degree to which the exercise of a right is conditioned by the fulfilment of obligations. Such obligations may be *vis-à-vis* family members and related to maintenance, the sharing of work and resources according to sex and age, and so on. There may also be obligations towards the community and related to an obligation to use and treat the resources to which rights are granted in accordance with generally accepted rules, to take part in community activities related to the conservation and protection of the resources.

While a customary or indigenous right is, for example, tied to the fulfilment of such obligations towards family members and/or the community under the supervision of the community and the local authorities, there is now a tendency that right and obligation become separated in connection with individually granted rights under formal legislation (Odgaard and Maganga, 1995).

Turning now to water management systems, it also appears that rights to utilize water from various sources in accordance with customary regulations are tied to various obligations related to the conservation and maintenance of water sources.

Thus, according to such rules, everybody has a right to collect water in streams, rivers and ponds for domestic use and for watering cattle. If, for example, a person digs a well or makes a water hole on communal land, the rights to the use of such structures are given to whoever does the work. In actual practice today, such rights are sometimes lent to, or rented out to, another person in return for the provision of services, goods or money.

Rights to use water for so-called traditional irrigation activities are connected to rights to the land to be irrigated. Access to the water is regulated through canal committees and sub-committees. There are 'provisions' for when and for how long each holder of water rights may make use of the water in the furrow.

According to customary rules, with specified rights go specified duties to take part in protection and maintenance of the water resources, such as the cleaning and repair of irrigation furrows and canals and the protection of springs.

However, state intervention and increased pressure on water resources has implied that, at the same time as customary rights are increasingly threatened by holders of formal water rights obtained by state organizations, private farmers and enterprises, obligations to conserve and protect the water sources are not in the same way an integral part of a formal right. To the extent that duties in connection with the exercise of a formally granted right are defined, the level of enforcement of these duties is not at the community/village level. Moreover, as shown by MWEM(1995), the authority structures which should supervise the duties associated with a granted water right being adhered to, are very weak in Tanzania.

Experience from the Ruaha River basin shows that, first, the formal water rights granted are often very generous, and second, that the amount of water granted is generally fully utilized, whereas there are difficulties in connection with the fulfilment of the attached obligations (Odgaard and Maganga, 1995).

Social groups and organizations

Based on the above discussion of rules in relation to land and water management in the Ruaha River basin, a number of social groups and organizations, within which the rules and norms in relation to land and water management are generated and enforced, can be identified.

Starting from the level of the individual, we can identify at least the following social groups and organizations:

(1) groups of individuals who are involved in patron–client relationships or contracts related to the management of land and water resources;
(2) the family in its various forms (nuclear and extended, for example), within which rights and obligations to land and water resources are distributed between the different members (men and women, young and old people);
(3) councils of elders, who play an important role both in connection with the distribution of rights and in conflict resolution;
(4) clan and sub-clan leaders;
(5) chiefs and sub-chiefs;
(6) various committees—established according to customary rules as well as according to new rules and policies;
(7) village councils and village government;
(8) ward development committees;
(9) district councils and district governments;

(10) regional authorities;

(11) national authorities in the form of ministries of lands and natural resources, agriculture, forestry, etc.; and

(12) the international community and the various forms of organizations related to the use and conservation of natural resources.

In addition to all these groups and organizations, the court system, at the various levels where it operates, also consists of a number of organizations of relevance for rule generation and enforcement.

All of these fora and organizations play various types of roles in relation to both the generation, enforcement and change of the rules and norms related to natural resource management. They are, however, not necessarily autonomous groups or organizations. An individual may be part of several of these groups and organizations at the same time.

To understand the complex interplay between the various law systems in Tanzania, and the role of individuals and groups of individuals in generating, violating, enforcing and changing rules and norms, we have found the concept of semi-autonomous social fields, as used by Sally Falk Moore, very useful (Moore, 1973 and 1989).

Semi-autonomous social fields refer to both formal and informal social units within which rule generation and rule enforcement take place. They are called semi-autonomous, because they are constantly exposed to influence from 'outside', due to the fact that the members may belong to several such social fields at the same time.

An example here could be a village chairman who, in that capacity, is a member of the village government, which is part of the formal government structure. The village chairman may also be a member of the council of elders, clan leader of a specific ethnic group, head of an extended family, or a member of the Catholic church. Thus the same person moves in and out of social units with rules originating from various parts of the plural legal system, and potentially carrying rules and norms from one to the other.

Looking at the concept of rights in relation to this, experience has shown that formal legislation pertaining to rights has been used, especially by members of social power groups, to manipulate customary rules in order to pursue personal interests (Moore, 1989; Odgaard, 1997). Colonial as well as post-colonial history in Tanzania is also rich in examples of governments violating or manipulating customary rules through the enforcement of formal legislation. The examples we have referred to above, in relation to pastoral land rights, are cases in point.

Although we have not yet worked in detail with the notion of semi-autonomous fields, we feel convinced that the concept can enrich further analyses of the role of social actors in changing rules and norms in relation to natural resource management in plural legal systems.

Conflict resolution

Conflict resolution or conflict management is another mechanism which has recently emerged as one of the important themes in natural resources management (see, for instance, Charnley, 1996; Pendzich, 1994; Cousins, 1996).

Cousins' (ibid.) article focuses on conflict management in the context of the utilization of natural resources for multiple purposes, or by more than one user. He argues that disputes or conflicts are common in these situations, and hence the need for appropriate institutional frameworks for resolving or managing these disputes and conflicts. An example of resource utilization for multiple purposes has occurred on the Usangu Plains, where irrigated agriculture has gained at the expense of pastoralism. Agricultural encroachment onto pastoral lands has at times meant that critical dry season pastures have been lost and there are numerous occurrences of herder–farmer conflicts, as documented in Charnley (1994, 1996) and Odgaard and Maganga (1995). Competition for resources is especially pronounced during the dry season, when water and grazing land are very scarce. Large-scale immigration is another process that has exacerbated the problem of resource utilization by more than one user in the Ruaha River basin, especially in the Usangu Plains. From the 1950s until the present time, herders and cultivators from other parts of Tanzania have flocked to the area, attracted by the possibilities of rice irrigation or attractive grazing fields. Charnley (1996) has noted that, although the different ethnic groups have tried to implement customary resource use and management practices, unfortunately the activities of the different groups undermine each other, and no one group is willing to adhere to the cultural practices of another.

Theoretical works on conflict management (e.g., Burton and Dukes, 1990) differentiate between causes, levels and phases of conflict; and make a distinction between management problems, disputes and conflicts. These distinctions have some implications for conflict resolution. Hence, as noted by Cousins (1996), 'management problems' involve arguments or differences over the choice of alternatives among persons having the same goals and interests; 'disputes' involve competing but negotiable interests; while 'conflicts' involve the development and autonomy of the individual or identity group, and are thus bound up with non-negotiable human needs and questions of identity. Still on conflict resolution, Pendzich (1994) writes about procedures and processes which may be used in dispute settlement and conflict resolution, ranging from those which stress collaboration and voluntary efforts towards finding a solution, to those which involve arbitration by a third party. These include negotiation, conciliation and adjudication.

Commenting on the implications of the above distinctions for conflict management, Cousins (op.cit.) writes:

This suggests different approaches to dealing with these situations; the typology proposes matching the problem situation with appropriate processes and procedures. Thus 'management' problems are best dealt with through processes of problem solving, improved communication and improved personal interaction. In the case of disputes, settlement processes such as judicial procedures, negotiations and bargaining will be appropriate. Interest disputes are readily provoked by competition in the use of resources or by broken agreements, and remedies include sanctions and arbitration. In conflicts . . . 'resolution' processes are required which satisfy deep-rooted human needs and questions of identity, and these cannot be addressed through narrowly defined interest-based negotiation or mediation processes. . . Resolution requires in-depth understanding of relationships, and often the assistance of a third party.

Given the above framework, it is sometimes difficult in the Ruaha River basin to determine whether a situation is an argument, a dispute or a conflict. For example, although Charnley (1996) gives great prominence to cultural conflict, Odgaard and Maganga (ibid.) trace the roots of the conflicts to villagization policies clashing with indigenous land tenure systems, state expropriation of land and the heavy influx of immigrants. Odgaard and Maganga (1995) find no evidence of conflicts arising due to cultural differences, although they admit that these differences may exacerbate already existing conflicts. In contrast, Charnley (op.cit.) insists that there is actually a cultural conflict in the Usangu Plains, and she links this conflict to environmental problems caused by irrigation development, land alienation, uncontrolled immigration, demographic pressure, insecure land tenure, and ineffective resource management practices. To illustrate the conflict, she highlights ethnic hostility between the immigrant Sukuma and other ethnic groups:

> . . . conflict between the Sukuma and other herders manifests itself in violent acts; there are a number of cases in which Maasai and Sukuma have attacked one another with knives. More often, herder–herder conflict is expressed in verbal abuse, social isolationism, and non-co-operation. Sukuma-bashing is a matter of daily discourse in Sangu and Maasai households, where the Sukuma are resented, and continuously and tirelessly berated. . . There is little social interaction between the Sukuma and other ethnic groups. And, efforts between the Sukuma and other ethnic groups of herders to co-operate in solving resource-related problems on Usangu's rangelands have gone nowhere (Charnley, 1996:10).

Examples of water resource management functions in the Ruaha River basin

Uphoff (1986) includes in his definition of institutions: '. . . norms and behaviours that persist over time *by serving collectively valued purposes*' (our emphasis). Interestingly, while other authors stress that institutions or organizations are created and changed by people's actions, they do not similarly emphasize the purposes and functions for which they are created and maintained—or changed—as constitutive for them. It seems to us, however, that the stress on the importance of people's actions for changes in rules, norms and organizations should automatically direct attention towards different people's changing interest in, and perception of, the functions of, in this case, different resource management mechanisms.

We would be somewhat hesitant, though, to use Uphoff's term 'collectively valued purposes', if that is taken to imply an idea of social consensus, as we believe change is constantly brought about precisely through clashes between conflicting and differently valued purposes.

In an earlier study of water resource management in Ruaha River basin we found it useful to distinguish between four main categories of resource management functions: the demand for performance which would arise under quite different circumstances, involve different stakeholders and different types of conflicts, and require different management mechanisms.

Conflicts over resource management and subsequent changes in the management mechanisms will take quite different forms according to whether they are concerned with their existing purposes, or emerge out of demands for the creation of new management functions, for example, in response to a new type of pressure on resources. New functions may of course be disguised in, or grafted on to, existing rules, norms and organizations.

While we do not intend here to take up the question of the sustainability of resource management, it is clear that it is highly related to the ways management functions are created and changed in response to changing demands from different stakeholders.

The four basic categories of water resource management functions identified in the Ruaha River basin study were: (1) water resources development; (2) allocation; (3) pollution control; and (4) environment protection. Development here refers to improving water quantity for all its different uses (e.g., temporal and spatial availability and accessibility) through source improvements as well as through the design, construction, operation and maintenance of service delivery systems, i.e., activities aimed at putting the resource to use. Water-quality control concerns the restrictions placed on those uses and activities that have a direct and discernible impact on water quality in the short and medium terms, and the promotion of activities and uses that have a positive impact on water quality. Allocation refers to decisions and rules regarding which resources may be used for which purposes and by whom. Environment protection ensures that uses and impacting activities are done in such as way as to conserve and protect the quality and quantity of the ecosystems on which water resources are dependent, as well as of water-based ecosystems. We expect that the same four categories of management functions will be relevant for land and possibly other natural resources.

In water resource management, river basin management has become almost a panacea for solving all kinds of problems. In the Ruaha River basin, a basin water board and office were established with basin-wide responsibility for water allocation, pollution control and environment protection.

In fact, the basin office was created in response to an emerging conflict over the allocation of water between irrigation in a limited part of the basin and downstream hydropower generation. Our study confirmed that the priority demand for establishing basin-wide management of allocation of water resources concerned only management of the hydropower reservoir itself and of the major water sources in the area of intensive irrigation.

Other management functions are already being executed at lower levels and through different management mechanisms such as:

○ Local allocation:
  – irrigation canals and furrows have irrigation committees or groups which allocate water, and village governments regulate access;
  – access conflicts are mediated by village elders as well as formal law-courts;
  – access to water is often linked to land tenure rules.

○ Quality control:
   – control of 'modern' (meaning chemical) pollution has so far been the responsibility of regional water engineers, who will also in future have the only laboratories that can execute this function;
   – there are examples where village by-laws restrict cultivation close to streams in order to reduce risk of pollution;
   – local communities have rules limiting washing and bathing to down-stream river locations, reserving upstream parts for the collection of water.

○ Environmental protection:
   – no channels exist presently for catchment co-ordination and manage-ment, but co-operation between village governments is being estab-lished at ward and division level or, ultimately, through the district council;
   – district and village by-laws are increasingly being enforced, but with lit-tle consideration of pre-existing customary rules.

The study thus showed how a new resource management organization was established in response to an emerging conflict over water allocation, and started to establish new allocation rules. While formally charged with much broader functions than allocation, it was only in this area that it became effective, leaving other functions to already existing mechanisms. In relation to allocation, there is still a long way (and many conflicts) to go before the basin office and other allocation mechanisms, such as informal canal com-mittees or customary tenure rules, have come in line with each other, for example, by delineating mutually accepted 'spheres of influence'.

Conclusions

The present research on sustainable agriculture in semi-arid Africa is but one small indicator of the growing world-wide concern that agriculture in many developing countries is becoming unsustainable, and the fear that the required future growth in agricultural production cannot be accomplished in a sustain-able manner. Although the concept of sustainability is not static, and the resilience of ecosystems should not be underestimated, it is clear that increas-ing agriculture-related pressure on natural resources, especially land and water, in many developing countries results in both social conflicts (and vice versa) and resource degradation.

People have always invented resource management mechanisms in response to pressure on natural resources to avoid, or reduce, social conflicts and resource degradation. In order to understand contemporary developments and perhaps crises, and even to suggest prescriptions, we must study historic-ally why and how resource management mechanisms develop and change, both generally and in specific local contexts, and what makes them sometimes appear to develop more sustainable responses than at other junctures.

We have discussed the need to study the dynamics of resource management in the form of different resource management mechanisms with different purposes and functions. This must be seen from an actor perspective, in the sense that on the one hand the resource management mechanisms are but one of a multitude of factors that influence people's interactions in relation to natural resources. Yet, on the other hand, the management mechanisms themselves develop and change through people's actions.

In conclusion, we want tentatively to hypothesize that people act to change the way resources are managed in three different contexts, which all appear from the examples given above:

○ Pressure on resources grows with the intensification of a certain type of use, or diversification and proliferation of new uses. Pressure also increases with the emergence of new user groups.

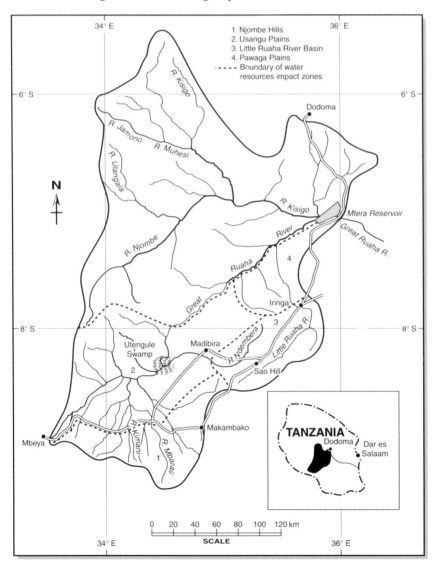

Figure 10. *Map of Ruaha River basin* (from Boesen, 1994)

131

○ Management and sustainability problems arise when the demand for resources is intensified, diversified, or the emergence of new user groups (stakeholders) causes conflicts or resource degradation. These may again lead either to demands for new management functions, which have as yet not been taken care of by any management mechanisms, or vastly intensified execution of existing functions. Under many circumstances, then, existing management mechanisms are adapted or new ones created to perform new functions or existing ones differently, in a sustainable way.

○ Natural resource management mechanisms are continuously being tested and reinterpreted through people's manoeuvring, bargaining and interacting, within and between different sets of rules and organizations. Power relations may refer differently to different sets. But this arena—and its particular power relations—also alters (possibly with completely unintended effects) with changes in power relations, and in economic and social structures in society at large, that may in themselves have no particular reference to natural resources.

○ Technological innovations and change, whether endogenous or exotic, may possibly in their own right instigate demands for management changes. We are, however, still pondering the role of technology as an independent factor in management change, as against a rather Boserupian view, that technology change, like management change, is an effect of social and economic pressures on production and resources.

Sustainable development, industrial metabolism and the process landscape— Reflections on regional material-flow studies

STEFAN ANDERBERG

Introduction

Traditionally, there has been a strong relationship between industrial development, high population density and environmental damage. In densely populated and early industrialized regions of the world, the environment has been put under extreme pressure over a long time period. But during recent decades the local environmental situation in the Western industrialized world has improved considerably as a consequence of decreasing industrial emissions. The environmental threats have become more diffuse and complex, with increasing scales of time and space. To solve problems such as acidification, eutrophication, the diffusion of persistant organic chemicals and climate change requires totally new strategies and efforts that reach far beyond traditional environmental politics, since these problems are linked to the development of relatively rigid societal structures.

The goal 'sustainable development' poses important challenges to both the global society and environmental research. The great challenge is to develop perspectives and methods for analysing society to provide an improved picture of how societal activities, resource use and pollution are linked and change. It concerns the construction of a common frame of reference for studies with different emphasis and direction in such a way that these can be linked and contribute to the development of a more holistic image.

Recent studies of 'industrial metabolism' and 'industrial ecology' (see, for example, Ayres and Simonis, 1994; Socolow et al., 1994; Graedel and Allenby, 1995) have sought to improve the analysis of the linkages between society and the environment. These research efforts have tried not only to improve the analysis of the emissions, but also to offer a more concrete framework for analysing technological change and political strategies for the future. In connection with 'industrial metabolism' studies, the flow perspective has been presented as an integrated approach that is able to improve study methods, as well as our ability to develop sustainable strategies. But critical evaluations of the studies and discussion on the difficulties and limitations of the material-flow perspective are rare.

This chapter makes an attempt to open up a discussion about the role of the flow perspective in linking society and nature in environmental research. The flow perspective is used for an overview of the development of the environmental situation in the industrialized world. Major challenges for environmental management and research are presented. An evaluation of the Rhine Study at IIASA (International Institute for Applied Systems Analysis) is used as a starting point for a general discussion about the flow perspective and industrial metabolism studies in relation to these challenges. Torsten Hägerstrand's time-geographical 'process landscape' is used as source of inspiration for discussing the flow perspective and for suggesting the further development of industrial metabolism studies, such as the Rhine Study.

The development of material-flows in society

For most materials, the flow through society consists of five major steps: the extraction of raw materials, refining, products manufacturing, use and disposal. These steps are shown in Figure 11, with the example of the flows of zinc and cadmium involved in the use of zinc in tyres and galvanized surfaces. Through recycling, loops back to earlier steps can occur. This model is very crude and needs to be adapted to different types of flows, but is often useful for structuring the use of materials and different pollution sources. The extraction step can, for example, be mining or oil production, as well as agriculture and forestry. The refining and products manufacturing are most often connected to industrial activities and usually consist of several steps. The use occurs in, for example, households, industry or agriculture. The disposal stage has traditionally been closely connected to the use, but has become more and more centralized in the industrialized world. In all steps, there are risks for the environment. Losses from the earlier steps in the flow, namely extraction and refining, can be called 'production emissions' and from the latter steps 'consumption emissions' (Anderberg et al., 1989). The transport needed between different steps in the flows is often forgotten, even though

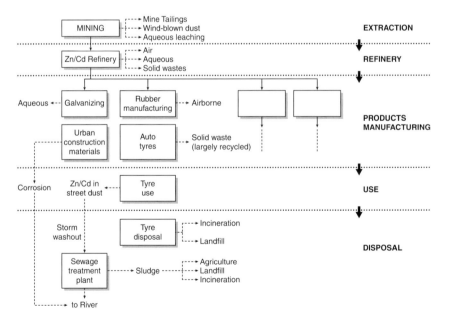

Figure 11. *The flows of zinc and cadmium via use of zinc in tyres and galvanized products* (from Stigliani and Anderberg, 1994)

134

transport emissions may have a significant impact on the environment (e.g. via emissions from fuel combustion, corrosion of vehicles, loading, discharging, cleaning or accidents).

The industrial revolution has brought about dramatic changes in the human use of natural resources and impact on the environment. Population growth, urbanization, increased production and consumption, the intensification of agriculture and accelerated landscape transformation have radically increased the pressure on the natural environment in all parts of the world. Although the physical changes to the landscape have been greater than ever, the most important effect of industrial development is probably the gradual change of the biogeochemical environment, linked to the the enormous growth in the use of materials: especially fossil fuels, metals and chemical products. With industrialization, the intensification of agriculture and forestry and the diffusion of mobile urban lifestyles characterized by high consumption of energy, water and all kinds of goods, material flows have grown and become much more open, with increased losses to the environment. Through the development of transport and trade, the societal flows have expanded geographically. The material flows have also become more complex with the development and increased use of more composite products, perhaps the most important being innumerable synthetic products, which are not easily naturally degradable.

Traditionally, environmental damage has been closely linked to industrial development. The regional economic specialization (type and quantity of industry and agriculture), population density, consumption level and urban development have determined the pollution load. The dominating sources in the traditional emission landscape (Lohm et al., 1994) have been linked to the earlier steps in the material flows: mining, oil exploitation and raw-materials-intensive industries e.g. iron and steel, metal refining, pulp and paper, petrochemical and chemical industry, which process large volumes of impure raw materials using large amounts of energy. The industrial point-source emissions have gradually been complemented by increasing loads from rural and urban areas related to the intensification of agriculture, increasing transport and consumption and the development of sewer systems.

The environment has been put under extreme pressure over a long time period in densely populated and early industrialized regions in Europe, North America and Japan. However, during the last few decades the trend of increasing pollution has been broken in most OECD countries. This development is connected to important industrial and societal change. The increasing environmental awareness, particularly in the most wealthy countries, has led to radical development of regulations and investment in pollution control. The most polluting industries have stagnated, production has in many cases decreased and the efficiency in the use of materials and energy has increased. These trends have often been related to the development of a post-industrial society in material flow terms, characterized by trends of decarbonization and dematerialization (Grübler, 1994; Simonis, 1994).

The Rhine example

The Rhine Basin provides an example of dramatic reduction of many types of pollution as a consequence of such a trend shift. The Rhine Basin Study at

IIASA analysed how the flows of some heavy metals (cadmium, lead and zinc) and nutrients (nitrogen and phosphorus) have changed from the early 1950s to the late 1980s, in what is one of the most densely industrialized regions in the world. The analysis shows dramatic decreases of the emissions to both air and water during the last few decades (Stigliani and Anderberg, 1994; Stigliani et al., 1993). In Figure 12, the heavy metal emissions to water around 1970 and in 1988 are shown, while Figures 13a and 13b show the flows of cadmium in the basin in 1970 and 1980. The reductions are primarily related to improved pollution control of the industrial point sources, but also decreased consumption of the metals for some uses (e.g. lead in gasoline and cadmium for surface treatment), and stagnation and structural change (new processes, and the concentration of production and consumption) in connection with large flows such as coal, iron and steel and phosphates, where heavy metals occur as trace elements, have been important. A large part of the emissions have been connected to such inadvertent flows of the metals. The development of emissions control has led to a redirection of the flows from air and water to solid waste, that is deposited, incinerated or used for construction or in agriculture. Urban air quality improvements have also led to reductions of diffuse emissions, but the diffuse and municipal emissions have not decreased as much as the industrial emissions.

The reduction of heavy metal emissions in the Rhine Basin is relatively extreme, but there are similar findings in several other regions in Western

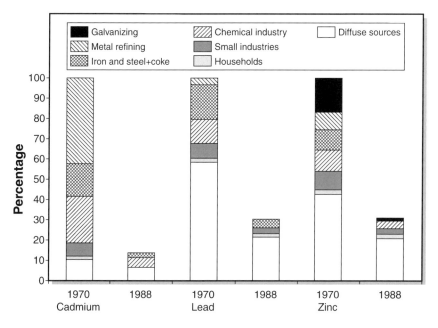

Figure 12. *Comparison of aqueous emissions of cadmium, lead and zinc by point and diffuse sources to the Rhine River around 1970 with emissions in 1988.* (Average yearly emissions in the period 1968–72: 207 t Cd, 1.8 Kt Pb and 12.6 Kt Zn) (Stigliani et al., 1993)

136

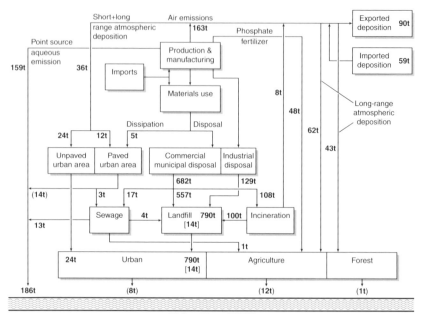

13a

Rhine River (1970)

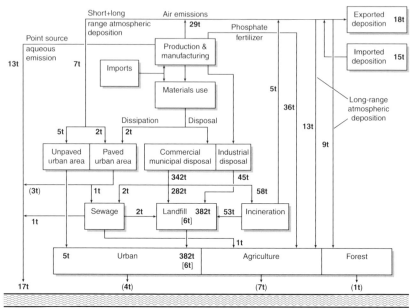

13b

Rhine River (1988)

Figure 13. *Cadmium flows in the Rhine Basin 1970 (13a) and 1988 (13b).* (The parentheses show diffuse water emissions and numbers in brackets show the estimated biological availability.) Source: Stigliani and Jaffe (1993).

Europe and the USA. A common trait is that industrial pollutants have decreased radically, while nutrient loads have only been marginally affected. The result of the industrial clean-up is a shift towards the latter steps of the societal material flows: the relative importance of consumption emissions has increased.

Besides illustrating the dramatic decrease of industrial pollution and the increased importance of emissions from the latter steps of the materials flows, the Rhine example indicates the influence of a dynamic economy and increasing environmental awareness. Behind the pollution reductions lies a strengthening national and regional (in Germany) environmental legislation, which has been used by competent and highly motivated environmental authorities, primarily at the local and regional level. One can also observe the effect of EC legislation, but it is difficult to find any direct influence from the International Commission for the Protection of the Rhine (ICPR), at least until the end of the 1980s, even though this organization is often praised for its achievements (Bernauer and Moser, 1996). The ICPR has primarily been concerned with evaluating the situation, mobilizing public opinion for cleaning up the river and ensuring that representatives from the different countries present plans for improving the situation. But binding agreements were not reached until after the Sandoz accident in 1986, when the Rhine Action Plan (IKSR, 1987) was introduced.

Dynamic industrial development with important structural change, the closing of old, heavily polluting plants and investment in modern technology, and emissions control have definitely been of great importance. An interesting observation is that competitive industries seem to have had similar reductions in emissions, while large differences can be found between France and Germany in the area of municipal wastewater treatment and emissions, as well as in less competitive industries such as the Alsacian potash mines. These mines have large salt emissions that have long posed problems for those using the Rhine water, especially in the Netherlands. This problem must be regarded as a major failure of international co-operation. It led to the creation of the Rhine Convention, but in 1990 the salt emissions were 35–40 per cent higher than in the 1930s, when this problem first received attention. After decades of negotiations an agreement was reached in 1991, which concluded that the other Rhine countries pay the unprofitable French state-owned company half a billion francs to reduce its emissions (Bernauer, 1995).

The importance of an active public opinion and motivation in the administration and the industry cannot be exaggerated. The improvements in Germany can hardly be understood without taking into account the dramatic increase of environmental awareness. Since the 1970s, public authorities and industry have been working under increasing pressure from different environmental organizations that evaluate their activities very critically. In this context, the activities of the Rhine Commission have probably been important. They have helped the Rhine problem to gain a central position in the environmental debate, particularly in Germany. The clean-up of the Rhine has become a key challenge to both environmental politics and industry.

138

The problems of the 1990s

In the most advanced industrial countries, the local environmental situation has improved considerably during recent decades. This improvement, however, which has primarily been caused by the radical reduction of industrial point-source emissions, has been overtaken by new problems. Acidification, eutrophication, the diffusion of persistant chemicals and climate change still persist on a regional and global level, but the pollution sources connected to these problems are not so easy to control. The marginal benefit of further end-of-pipe pollution control has decreased radically. The dominant sources are either widespread and diffuse, connected to different steps in the use of various materials (fossil fuels, metals, organic chemicals) in society and not only in connection with production (even if industry is probably also a major source of diffuse emissions), or they are located in foreign countries, e.g. in Eastern Europe. One can view recent changes in environmental debates and politics in Western Europe in the context of this new situation.

The major aims of environmental politics have traditionally been to discover and to cure (Hägerstrand, 1993). The objective has been to control the negative side effects of societal development. Scientific and technological research have given valuable support to these efforts. This will probably still be important in the future, but it will not be fully adequate; the great challenge that environmental politics and research face today and in the future is to foresee and to prevent, and, via more pre-emptive strategies, to steer society towards a sustainable use of resources. For this, new types of knowledge and understanding are needed. The gap between what politicians and administrators expect from research, and what research is able to give, is increasing. In many countries in Europe (e.g. Germany, the Netherlands and the Nordic countries), this crisis is increasingly visible in politicians' frustration about the 'underdeveloped solution research', decreasing financial support for conventional environmental research and the setting up of new cross-disciplinary research programmes directed towards strategies for sustainable development.

The material-flow perspective has experienced a major breakthrough in countries like Germany, Sweden and the Netherlands. What was recently considered fairly new and radical (e.g. Anderberg et al., 1989) is now conventional wisdom. Goals like 'closing the loops' and minimizing waste with the reuse and recycling of materials, life-cycle analysis and environmental auditing are major themes in environmental management and have also influenced major industries (e.g. Nelson, 1994; Paton, 1994). The importance of the consumer is often stressed in this context. Environmental concern is considered important, not only for indirectly influencing the development of legislation, authorities' or companies' investments in pollution control, but also for active participation in recycling and the conscious choice of environmentally benign products.

Global environmental problems have received growing attention. The goal of sustainable development, which links environmental change to economic development, has become established in wide circles. International environmental co-operation has intensified, but international agreements outside the EU remain fairly weak and unable to control development or implement sanctions against countries that do not comply. Outside OECD countries, pollution loads have generally not decreased. The most environmentally damaging industrial activities are not widespread, but where they occur the local and regional effects are often severe and there is still a distinct relationship between production and pollution. According to an increasingly popular view (Figure 14), pollution increases with industrialization and rising economic wealth up to a certain point, then it starts decreasing as a result of rising environmental awareness, increasing efficiency, the introduction of low-waste technology and the decline in importance of heavy industrial production. The curve is referred to as the environmental Kuznets curve. It has been supported empirically by Grossman and Krueger (1995), who found a turning point for sulphur dioxide emissions at a GNP of about US$5000 per capita. The advanced industrial regions are presently moving downhill, while the poorest OECD countries like Portugal and Greece are close to the summit. Other regions are still on the uphill side, with the Far East moving rapidly upwards, while Eastern Europe has for a long time been stuck close to the summit, and the agrarian regions still climb only slowly.

There is some evidence that supports the basic ideas of this model. Development of industry has generally brought radical increases in pollution. Improvements have only been observed in the richest parts of the world. Socialist Eastern Europe never achieved the economic welfare or level of investment necessary for making a trend-shift in terms of pollution. During the last few years there have been signs that the NICs (e.g. Hong Kong, Taiwan, Singapore and South Korea), where economic welfare has increased

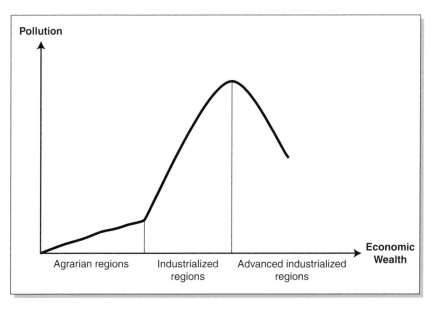

Figure 14. *A tentative illustration of the modern view of the relationship between economic development and pollution* (inspired by Grossman and Krueger, 1995)

radically, also seem to be approaching the turning point, and have begun to develop stricter environmental regulations.

Evidence for the decrease in pollution is limited to crude pollutants such as sulphur dioxide or heavy metals, however, and it does not hold for greenhouse gases, or for transport and energy use. Neither does it take into account important factors like population density, culture and social organization, and its relevance can (and should) of course be questioned. The development of different regions is almost impossible to compare, because of major geographical and historical differences. The industrial revolution in the NICs in Asia is taking place under totally different circumstances in terms of technology and trade than the industrial revolution once did in Europe, Japan and North America. In large parts of the world, radical economic changes associated with industrial growth have occurred without a significant increase of economic wealth, but with increasing pollution.

The generalizing claims, reductionism and implicit determinism of these theories are very questionable. They imply that as long as sufficiently high economic growth is realized, the environmental problems will more or less be solved automatically. This is to overlook other important factors influencing environmental change, such as the associated institutional development which has been a necessary prerequisite for the improvements in Western Europe (where also many environmental problems still persist). It is interesting to note that the research of Grossman and Krueger has been used by GATT-WTO to legitimize liberalization and non-interventionist approaches in relation to environmental issues (Damian et al., 1996). The questions 'Is it really necessary to pass the peak?' or 'Would it not be possible for developing countries to avoid the peak and introduce modern clean technologies directly?', that are raised in connection with this model are also important, even if they often seem based on false premises. Even though modern environmental control is rare in the Third World, industrial technology is hardly totally obsolete and transnational companies particularly have not much incentive to invest in technology on the level of the 1950s or 1960s. It is interesting, nevertheless, that economic development is not only connected to increasing environmental stress, but together with technological and institutional development, it also seems necessary for improving the situation.

The relationship between trade and environmental degradation has also received increasing attention, mostly in connection with the direct influence of international trade and, especially, transnational corporations. The debate on international trade and the environment has so far been rather polarized (Williams, 1993; Söderbaum, 1994) between those (environmentalists) who consider that international trade is inherently bad for the environment and those (liberals) who emphasize the beneficial sides of trade, such as that it encourages efficiency in environmental terms. Research on the relationship between international trade and the environment (e.g. Thomas, 1993; Bengtsson et al., 1994) seems to indicate that this is not an area where one can draw such simplistic conclusions. It is filled with myths like the industrial flight hypothesis (i.e. that polluting production leaves countries with stringent environmental standards for others), that, however, seem to be only marginal phenomena (Williams, 1993). Protectionism seems often to lead to stagnation and very limited environmental improvement. Free trade and competition can have beneficial effects, but these also depend strongly on the institutional setting, and there is certainly very much in the development of Europe and the world, characterized by increasing trade liberalization, that is highly questionable from an environmental point of view.

Research challenges

The goal 'sustainable development' poses important challenges to environmental research. These challenges do not any longer concern the discovery and confirmation of environmental problems, but an improved understanding of society, its change and relation to nature. Research on areas connecting society and nature is fairly undeveloped. This concerns particularly research on society's use of natural resources and how this has changed with the development of consumption, production systems, technology, and political actions. We lack knowledge and understanding of central areas and an ability to handle the complex linkages between society and nature in a changing world. Among the relationships and contexts that are necessary for an environmental analysis of social development, but have so far been hard to grasp, are the linkages between different areas of knowledge and sectors, societal and environmental change, and geographical aspects such as extension, diffusion, spatial flows, the spatial context, and linkages between different scales and management structures. Another problem is the lack of analysis of environmental problems from a power perspective, which often leads to an exaggerated belief in politicians' and consumers' ability to influence.

The great challenge is to develop perspectives and methods that improve the picture of how societal activities and resource use and pollution are linked. A common frame of reference must be constructed for studies with different emphases so that these can be linked and together contribute to the development of a more complete picture. This must be able to handle relationships between emissions and environmental effects, as well as their linkages to political and administrative structures and economic, social, and technological change. Several efforts have been made to develop a common frame of reference for studies of nature and society. It is, however, rare that all desirable aspects are dealt with. Ambitious investigations of different problematic elements that attempt to map use and emissions and analyse different ecological problems and risks can be regarded as one example. Another example is studies of environmental futures, where the scenario often forms a common frame of reference for the analysis of environmental effects and possible political actions. Recent 'industrial metabolism' studies have analysed material flows in society and nature, and can be considered a response to the problems encountered in emission estimations and environmental futures studies.

Can material-flow studies serve as an integrative framework?

The flow perspective has, in connection with 'industrial metabolism' studies, been launched as a useful framework for integrating the analysis of nature and society, analysing technological change and environmental effects and improving the basis for emission estimates, environmental policies and development strategies. The implications of the flow perspective to change and close the flows, minimize the losses and increase efficiency and recycling, have experienced a remarkable breakthrough in environmental political debate. This breakthrough is connected to growing dissatisfaction with conventional environmental protection strategies that have not been successful in handling problems related to, for example, solid waste and diffuse consumer-related emissions. The flow model is an excellent tool for illustrating and summarizing complicated matters coherently (see Figures 11 and 13) and it communicates well with the natural sciences. After a growing stream of studies and initiatives based on a material-flow perspective, the introduction of this perspective seems completed.

Geographical scale, methods, data sources, study objects, and analyses of the flows and emissions vary in the various studies. Most studies have been performed at a national level (e.g. Billen et al., 1983 (Belgium); Bergbäck, 1992 (Sweden); Klepper et al., 1995 (Germany); van der Voet, 1996 (The Netherlands)). This can be explained by the fact that data are most easily accessible at this level. However, there are also many studies for city regions and local areas (e.g. Newcombe et al., 1978), and river basins of different sizes (e.g. Ayres and Rod, 1986; Stigliani and Anderberg, 1994; Brunner et al., 1994). Most studies focus on determining flows of an element (very often heavy metals) in a region in one particular year, but some projects have also tried to reconstruct the historical development and the geographical distribution of the flows and emissions (e.g. Lohm et al., 1994).

The studies are often preliminary and the presentations spend considerable efforts arguing for the advantages, implications, and potential of their approach. Efforts are seldom made to discuss difficulties, uncertainties, and constraints of the studies. The difficulties encountered in these studies are rather obvious. Statistics and other relevant information about different activities do not adapt very well to the needs of this type of study. For developing the approach so that it is able to contribute to current challenges, more critical evaluation of the flow perspective as it is used in different studies is needed. A recent study (Anderberg, 1996) has made an attempt to provide a critical analysis of the Rhine Study as a starting point for a more general assessment of the limitations of the 'industrial metabolism' or societal material flow studies. The results and discussion of this study are summarized below. The discussion considers the work of Torsten Hägerstrand, who has developed an alternative framework.

Evaluation of the Rhine Basin Study
The Rhine Basin Study analysed how the flows and emissions of three heavy metals (cadmium, lead and zinc) changed between the early 1950s and the late 1980s in the River Rhine basin. In this study, as in other industrial metabolism studies, the flow analysis is considered an important instrument for evaluating the environmental impact of social activities. The research placed more emphasis on the location of different activities and emissions than other industrial metabolism studies. The presentation of results focuses on emissions and their development, but attention is also given to environmental effects. Studies of the historical development of uses and emissions have been used as a basis for construction of future scenarios of materials use and emissions

143

and for analysis of risks connected to accumulation in agricultural soils—so called 'chemical time bombs' (see Stigliani et al., 1991). Related studies have analysed the causes behind the emission reductions.

The challenge to find perspectives for a common framework for the study of the interaction between society and the environment is the basis for the evaluation. This analytical framework should be able to consider pollution as well as decision-making processes and different forms of economic, social, and technological change, that are of relevance in this context.

Such a study can contribute to an improved overview of the flows, emissions, and environmental effects of society. The analysis gives a view of the development in time and space of emissions and flows, and provides a basis for assessing the environmental effects of production and consumption, the risks associated with the accumulation of pollutants and the effects of economic and technological change and political actions. But it needs to be emphasized that this study is really only the first step towards such goals.

The most valuable aspect of the study is the testing of the methodology of regional material-flow analysis and the opportunity for evaluating the difficulties that are connected to studies based on the material-flow perspective. The statistics are far from ideal and the available information about emission sources is seldom sufficient for making generalizations. Therefore, the results must be regarded as preliminary. The study is severely limited in its attempt to connect to broad social change related to economic and technological development and decision-making. No attempt has been made to reveal structures that direct and change the flows and emissions. The analysis of heavy metal emissions is isolated and not linked to the total environmental impact of society or the development of different activities, uses, products, infrastructures, and institutions.

These limitations stem from the flow perspective and how it has been used. The analysis of flows is quite limited and intended mostly as a framework for estimating emissions. Conventional flow models focus primarily on the flows as linkages, but do not encourage contextual analysis of different parts of the flows, analysis of flows in time or analysis of the interlinkages of different elements. It is difficult to conduct a broad analysis of the flows and their preconditions in the Rhine Study, because the focus in this study is on single elements and because of the delimitation and treatment of the region. This region is inappropriate for studying international relations. For such an analysis, national boundaries are necessary because of the organization of trade statistics. The region serves primarily as a summary unit and the analysis becomes too one-dimensional, which makes it difficult to connect the analysis to social, political, and economic developments. This also makes the study and its analysis insufficient as a basis for broader future scenarios or historical studies of the social, economic, and political development of the Rhine Basin. For evaluating social change and constructing scenarios that can serve as frameworks for analysing and discussing strategies for societal development, it is insufficient to focus only on a few elements in society.

Difficulties and limitations of the material-flow approach
The flow perspective can definitely contribute to an improved overview of different parts of the societal use of natural resources and improve the analysis

of emissions and other environmental impacts at various scales. Since the flow perspective is established in the natural scientific environmental discipline, this kind of analysis is relatively easy to combine with an assessment of environmental effects. Material-flow studies may also be able to combine with new dimensions in connection with future studies, where the flow approaches can make scenarios more concrete. Related ideal models, such as closed material cycles, may also inspire new ideas in connection with societal planning and environmental policy and strategy contexts.

One should remember, however, that this type of study has its difficulties. The statistics are not very well adapted for this type of study, and the information about different types of emission is not abundant, is relatively uncertain and is hard to generalize. This means that many provisional assumptions have to be made, and this makes the results fairly uncertain. These difficulties vary, of course, for different study substances and regions. The availability of data and emission inventories is best at a national level. Heavy metals and energy are relatively well documented.

In connection with analyses of societal flows, it is necessary to keep the limitations of the flow perspective in mind. The conventional flow model, which primarily builds on abstraction based on similarity criteria, focuses particularly the flows as linkages. It is along these that coherence is sought, while a more contextual analysis of different parts of the flows is not emphasized. Even though the flow perspective may appear fairly holistic in theory, the model is most often used in fairly abstract and reductionistic fashion. Often single elements in a region are focused upon and not the wider context of the flows, the activities that drive them, their technological aspects or how they are shaped and limited by different physical, economic, social and institutional frames. It is therefore difficult to connect the flow analysis of single elements like heavy metals to wider questions regarding the development of the total environmental impact of society, spatial and temporal aspects, economic and technological change and decision-making in politics, administration and industry. While the flow analysis communicates well with environmental impact analysis, it is more problematic to link it to a wider analysis of society. This is particularly so when, as in the Rhine Study, little attention is put on activities, industrial branches and institutional frames, and when the choice of region and study object is also based on natural scientific considerations.

The process landscape

The 'process landscape' framework, developed by Hägerstrand (1993), provides an alternative perspective for the analysis of flows and aims to serve as a basis for a more contextual analysis. The process landscape is a development of the time–geographical perspective and is primarily concerned with how different processes in the landscape occur and interact ultimately with the forces (physical, biological or social, e.g. legislation and other political or administrative initiatives) that form and change these processes. From the point of view of the dominant environmental research, the process landscape approaches environmental problems from an unconventional and very different perspective: its ambition is to develop a dynamic view of how different processes occur and interact in the landscape, and to catch the forces that form and change these processes. The trajectories and flows in the process landscape should be viewed as a 'web caught in a hierarchical network of domains'. This framework has the aim of serving as 'a bridge between the societal actors and institutions, their technical equipment and the terrain, where both the events of nature and the physical actions of humans out of necessity take place' (Hägerstrand, 1993:52 (my translation)).

The starting point is the entirety that is made up of part of a landscape. This entirety provides an overview and a framework that can be used for more detailed studies. It should primarily be viewed as a framework for thought, to help avoid losing sight of the whole when limited detailed studies are undertaken. The important aspect of this approach is that attention is focused on the way things in the process landscape co-exist and compete in a limited area of time, space and energy. The challenge is to observe the relations in time and space around and between different processes in the landscape. When phenomena are placed in their natural context, the analysis can focus on how the processes are linked, interact and are limited by other processes and phenomena. In this analysis it is necessary to clarify the restrictions on different processes. Hägerstrand uses primarily a time–geographical concept apparatus for the analysis of the process landscape. He thinks the existing language, which has been taken from various disciplines, makes it very difficult to treat different process types in the same manner, but through introducing a new frame of concepts this aim can be achieved. He distinguishes between individual corpuscles (i.e. living creatures, natural objects like stones and cultural artefacts like tools and buildings), which move in *trajectories*, and *amounts* (gases, water, grain, etc.), which move in flows. In a time–space perspective everything is always moving. If an object is immobile in space, it is still moving in time. The trajectories are not divisible, an organism or an object cannot be in more than one place at the same time, while the flows are as divisible as their content allows.

It should be emphasized that the process landscape is not connected to a certain scale of time and space and the level of detail and aggregation can be flexible, even though Hägerstrand aims at avoiding conventional simplifications. The approach contains a striving towards seeing phenomena in a concrete setting for making generalizations at high geographical levels. The objective is to be able to make a detailed analysis in the context of a comprehensive perspective, making it possible to maintain an overview and to connect different geographical scales systematically. Hägerstrand also connects the process landscape to an analysis of management, and introduces a conceptual framework for this analysis. The analysis of the management structures of the process landscape starts off from the micro-level and focuses on how this is encapsulated in a hierarchical net of domains, of which some are responsible for the functional and some for the territorial order. Similar to the analysis of the processes in time and space, the goal is to identify the boundaries of the room of action for different actors. Administrative influence is dominantly exerted through definition and change of the boundaries for action. The aim of viewing the trajectories and flows of the process landscape as a web, caught in a network of domains, is to provide a frame of thought that is able to connect the actors and institutions in society, their technical equipment and the terrain, where both the events of nature and the physical actions of people take place.

It should be observed that the flow perspective is not incompatible with the process landscape; the former is, rather, incorporated into the latter. But the view of the flows differs from the conventional flow perspective. Time and space are the basis for the analytical framework, and this gives a different perspective on the flows, which is important for seeing them not only as isolated flows, but as related to other processes, elements and structures of society. The conventional flow model is based on similarity: the emphasis is on adding similar activities without taking into account their diverging contexts. The spatial dimension brings in the nearness aspect and spatial arrangement of activities, while the temporal dimension emphasizes the different time scales of various processes in the landscape. The treatment of the region is also quite different: instead of being a limited summation unit, it is an arena for the study of interaction. The management structure of the process landscape is important to consider from the start. This makes it possible to introduce a power perspective (who can do what and when can they do it?). The objective is to make a detailed analysis of the local context at different steps in a material flow, while maintaining the larger context. It is necessary to know the actors, situations and arrangements involved to be able to identify the constraints (physical, economic, social or legal) for different actions. It is also important to be able to connect flow analysis to human behaviour and decision-making processes.

The process landscape might inspire a way out of some of the major shortcomings of conventional flow studies. There are, however, still very few studies that have been based on this analytical framework. Lenntorp's (1993) analysis of the flows connected to the construction of four small houses in the Nordic countries is one of these few studies. An example from this study is given in Figure 15, which shows the flows in time and space associated with the production of the vacuum cleaner in the Norwegian house. This study can be described as a geographical life-cycle analysis. It shows clearly the necessity of putting flows and life-cycles of products in a time–space context. When only summarized flows in a limited region or in connection with life-cycles are analysed, the spatial arrangement of the flows, which is a very important trait, is absent in the analysis. The aim of getting closer to human actions cannot be clearly recognized in this example, but it is clear that the starting point in a specific house increases the potential to connect this analysis to a study of human actions and the frames of these actions.

To meet the challenges of the modern situation, such as improving the analysis of consumption and trade and being able to get closer to human behaviour and decision-making, it is necessary to have a broader perspective where the context of the flows are focused. Hägerstrand's process landscape provides inspiration and guidance to such efforts.

Conclusion

Challenges for modern social research into environmental problems and sustainable development are many and diverse. The flow perspective is a useful and perhaps indispensable tool in this context. Even if statistics generally

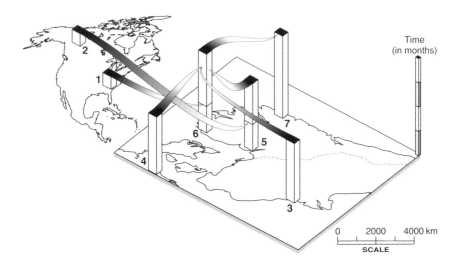

Figure 15. *The deliveries to a central vacuum cleaner in a Norwegian home.* The motor comes from the USA (1). PVC tubes are brought from Canada (2). Metal parts come from Sweden (3). The motor and the ventilation system come from Germany (4). There is a wholesale store in Ski in Norway (5), while the manufacturing of the vacuum cleaner occurs in Sandnes, in another part of Norway (6) and the final destination is the construction site in Volda, still another part of Norway (7). (From Lenntorp, 1993.)

do not adapt very well to this type of study and the information on different types of emissions is limited, relatively uncertain and hard to generalize, conventional flow studies can help to improve the overview of resource flows at various scales of analysis. Since the flow perspective has a long tradition in scientific environmental research, it can easily be combined with an assessment of environmental consequences. Related ideal models such as closed material cycles may also provide new ideas in connection with societal planning and environmental policy and strategy.

For a better understanding of resource flows and how they change, however, it is necessary to develop the studies and to keep the limitations of the flow perspective in mind. Flow analysis communicates well with environmental impact analysis, but its linkage to a wider analysis of society is more problematic. To address this limitation it is not sufficient to focus on flows of single elements and to summarize them at a certain level of aggregation. It is necessary to analyse their context, especially the physical, economic, technological, and social structures that influence, form and limit the flows. To improve the relevance of material-flow studies as a tool for analysis, it is necessary to focus on the broader geographical context of the flows. The analysis should incorporate temporal and spatial aspects of the flows, infrastructures, patterns of industry and settlement and linkages to the institutional framework. Material-flow analysis must be directed towards improving the general understanding and knowledge about the flows of materials in society and their

148

change. The flows must not be cut off from their social context and other flows and processes. To understand the development of products, industries, and transport, the analysis must take place at different levels, for example, the region, industrial branches, enterprises, factories and households. Industrial production and trade enterprises and households should be emphasized as particularly important in such an analysis. Variations in approach, methods and detail are necessary, but it is important that the analysis at different levels is concerned with the framework of the flows and with questions of power (what and who can influence?). The ultimate challenge is to connect the international, even global, level to the local level, where the real action takes place.

To summarize, flow-based perspectives can be used to improve communication and integration between studies with different emphases that increase our knowledge and understanding of relationships between society and nature in a changing world. This potential can hardly be realized with only a conventional flow perspective, however, which often becomes too abstract and narrow and cannot easily be connected to the wider context of the flows. Therefore, additional perspectives must be used to handle the temporal and spatial aspects of the flows and their physical, economic, and social frameworks. By emphasizing the context of flows in time and space, as well as their constraints and their institutional context, the time–geographical process landscape may help to address the limitations of pure material-flow studies in evaluating social development and in creating a basis for analysing development strategies for sustainable environmental management.

Environmental awareness, conflict genesis and governance
GÖRAN HYDÉN

Introduction

We, the Barabaig of Tanzania, are a poor and troubled people. We are a pastoral minority dependent on our livestock for survival. Every day we strive to sustain our herds and secure a better future for ourselves and our children. We are few in number and live in scattered communities. We have little political power. We have struggled against great odds for many years. . . Our herds need forage, water and salt. Our land has all these things. Without them we cannot survive. From as long ago as we can remember our land is being taken from us. People are continually moving in to grow crops on our pastures. . . The growing of wheat on what was once pasture is destroying the environment. By stripping away the vegetation cover with mechanized cultivation, the soil is laid bare to be carried away by flash floods, creating deep gullies and silting up water sources and our sacred Lake Basotu. The area of land we are left with is generally less fertile and too small for our needs. (From an 'Open Letter to the Canadian People' on behalf of the Barabaig people of Hanang District, Tanzania, dated 15 February 1989, published in Canadian journals.)

This now relatively well-known case illustrates starkly the issues that this volume is concerned with in an interdisciplinary and holistic manner. Development—at least the way it has been defined to date—implies the integration of livelihoods into an increasingly global economy where the destinies of people living continents apart are no longer separate. New forms of social consciousness emerge from the effects of these globalized resource flows. More and more, conflicts arise over control of resource flows and the way these resources are conceived, managed and sustained. These, in turn, pose challenges to existing ways of governing our affairs at different levels.

The growing realization that individual livelihoods and the fate of local communities can no longer be viewed in isolation from national or international structures and processes has given rise to new forms of scholarship in which micro and macro considerations are being combined to provide fresh perspectives and insights on issues that previously were studied in isolation from each other. This means that in the same way as we are increasingly interdependent in pursuit of our livelihoods, we are, as scholars, more and more dependent on each others' theoretical and methodological contributions. Interdisciplinarity comes naturally with that recognition.

This chapter focuses on the intellectual concerns associated with the concept of 'security'. This has for a long time occupied a prominent place in the literature on international relations. Debates about security, therefore, have typically been interpreted mainly in terms of what it means to the nation-state. Furthermore, it has usually been seen primarily in terms of military security.

This orientation among international relations scholars was particularly pronounced in the days of the Cold War, when calculations about military security drove state policy, especially among the major powers. The 'realist' school, which argues that states act in the international arena to maximize their own security, was for a long time the trend-setter in the study of international politics.

Realist assumptions continue to influence the field, but they have become increasingly challenged, particularly in recent years, for at least two major reasons. The first is the end of the Cold War, which has allowed scholars to revisit such concepts as security with a view to making it more applicable to a world where bipolar tensions between the East and the West no longer dominate the international arena. The second is the globalization of the capitalist economy and the threats to, as well as opportunities for, human welfare that follow in the wake of this process. Conflicts over resources and their use are now being studied not merely as part of the international political economy, but are increasingly analysed in terms of security. The Gulf War is an obvious case in point, but this is evident also in the way that communities within nation-states, e.g. the Ogoni in Nigeria and the Barabaig in Tanzania, struggle to protect their security in the light of threats posed by international forces. At the heart of many of these conflicts are often different interpretations of the concept of security. The latter is not only a concern for states, but also individuals and communities. Furthermore, threats to states, communities and individuals are no longer seen as only military, but include also economic poverty, political instability and environmental degradation. This new debate also alerts us to the different time horizons that often apply to the notion of security. In thinking about what security means, analysts can no longer escape the differential time horizons that apply to various categories of security. For example, with growing interest in the notion of environmental security has come a recognition of the need for studying the long-term consequences of specific state policies or interventions.

The debates among political scientists, and international relations scholars in particular, therefore, are a fruitful starting-point for a closer examination of how macro and micro sets of issues are increasingly being studied in more holistic terms. The approaches that are evolving in academic circles are of interest not only because of their theoretical or methodological dimensions, but also because they do also serve as the lenses through which eventually policy is likely to be examined and evaluated. Theories typically shape the way we interpret the world around us and they are of interest, therefore, not only because of their analytical, but also their prescriptive, value.

The evolving discourse on security

For the purpose of this volume it may suffice to characterize the emerging debate on the concept of security as taking place in response to two simple, but fundamental, questions: (1) what security? and (2) whose security? The discourse centring on the first of these questions may be seen as a lateral extension of the concept. By emphasizing that threats to states and societies are not only military—as tended to be assumed by realists—but include economic poverty, political instability and environmental degradation, the idea of different categories of security, i.e., political, economic and environmental, has begun to take hold in the literature (e.g. Buzan, 1991). The need for a reconceptualization of security studies is also discussed in a recent review article by Baldwin (1995). A good deal of the academic work along these lines has been funded in the past 10 years by the joint US Social Science Research Council–MacArthur Foundation Program on Peace and Security in a Changing World. Other efforts include an edited volume with special focus on Africa (Hjort-af-Ornäs and Salih, 1989), published under the auspices of the Scandinavian Institute of African Studies (now the Nordic Africa Institute). More recently, Ken Booth and Peter Vale (1995) have advocated the need for a new and critical outlook on security in southern Africa, using a laterally expanded definition of security.

Implied in this and other similar work is the assumption that it is the various spheres of modern life that are the contexts of security, rather than the state (Latham, 1995:44). These spheres, which are variably defined but include the configuration of military power, the dynamics of collective existence, the structuring of the polity, the organization of material life, and the conditions of biological and non-human life on the planet, are not isolated but intertwined, and constitute part of the conceptual apparatus needed for redefining security in the present global setting. Recent trends of events in a number of African countries, e.g. Liberia, Rwanda and Somalia, illustrate the need for studying the interrelationship between these spheres in an integrated fashion, if we want to understand the problems of peace and security in the present global environment. Ethnic conflict fuelled by the supply of arms from other countries in societies where material existence is hazardous and political institutions weak, combine to affect resource flows adversely, which in turn threatens livelihoods. Similarly, a more intensified use of natural resources may pose serious security threats to both state and society, such as the battles for control of water resources in the Middle East and the waters of the Nile.

The ongoing redefinition of security has a simultaneous and complementary vertical dimension. By this is usually meant the inclusion of other units of analysis than the nation-state. 'Whose security?' may refer to specific communities of people within a country, or to regional and other international entities. In this respect, the study of security issues is expanded both upwards and downwards. The important thing is that these levels, like the spheres discussed above, are interrelated. At a practical level, this articulates itself in the motto, often used in NGO circles: 'Think globally, act locally!' For the student interested in the connections between environmental awareness, conflict genesis, and governance, it is important to recognize not only that local values and institutions are often mediated by national, regional and global influences, but also that the opposite may take place.

Some of this literature addresses the question of whether it is possible to have a 'bottom-up' approach to the definition of security or, put in somewhat different terms, whether civil society has a place in defining security concerns in the present era. For example, Fisher (1994) points to the problems for indigenous non-governmental organizations in the Third World caused by the dominance of more powerful international (read: Northern) NGOs. Booth and Vale (1995) discuss the challenges facing South Africa and its neighbours in achieving national reconciliation through a focus on people, justice and change, stressing that regional security is possible only by the building of common identities and the spreading of moral and political obligations to the various state and non-state actors involved. A more broad-based study of environmental activism in the global arena by Wapner (1995) focuses on the new strength of transnational environmental action groups (TEAGs) and the emergence of a civic public realm that transcends national boundaries. The point he is making is that state actors in the international arena are not only influenced by other states or multinational corporations but increasingly also by TEAGs that demand—and often obtain—changes in the behaviour and stance of individual governments.

The idea of expanding the study of security vertically has also gained momentum from the growing recognition among comparative politics students that the state in some parts of the world is weak or even disintegrating. The notion of the state as passive victim rather than active agent features prominently in much of contemporary commentary about the emerging security agenda (Del Rosso Jr., 1995). This is perhaps best exemplified by the journalist Robert Kaplan's article on 'The Coming Anarchy' (Kaplan, 1994). In this article, he paints a ghoulish picture of the assorted demographic, environmental, and societal stresses afflicting states in West Africa, which he holds up as a harbinger of a future world of 'ever-mutating chaos'. Among academics, Robert H. Jackson (1990) describes African states as 'quasi-states', possessing juridical statehood but having only a tenuous empirical claim to such status. In this perspective, it is easy to see that other institutions than the state may be identified as necessary complements to the task of making the world a safer place.

It may be helpful to summarize this emerging debate by dividing the literature with the two cross-cutting lines identified above: (a) the lateral dimension, involving a redefinition of security to include aspects other than the military, and (b) the vertical dimension, extending the concept to involve actors other than the nation-state. The matrix in Figure 16 captures these dimensions and identifies four different schools that participate in the ongoing discourse on security.

The realist school continues to focus on the state and treats the threat of war between nations as the primary focus of its intellectual concerns. The moralist school dwells first and foremost on the breakdown of political order and the threat of civil violence to human security. While focusing on the use of military means, its concern with security extends beyond the state. The liberal school concentrates its intellectual efforts on the implications of a technologically and economically interdependent world and what governance measures need to be instituted in order to promote greater security and co-operation among existing nation-states. The populist school is furthest removed from conventional security studies by accepting an expanded definition of the concept along both a vertical and lateral line. Thus, its main concern is with the effects of resource degradation, not only for the security of states but also for individuals and societies alike. In the remainder of this chapter I shall deal with each of these schools in turn.

153

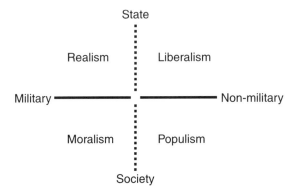

Figure 16. *Four contemporary perspectives on the study of security*

The realist school

In spite of the growing interest, particularly in recent years, in redefining security, it would be wrong to imply that realism is waning as a leading paradigm in the study of international relations. It continues to occupy a hegemonic position, especially among analysts of foreign policy in the United States. The extent to which there are new concepts of security emerging in the literature is more the outcome of new groups of scholars taking an interest in it, than a major upheaval in the study of international relations. Realism is very much alive and kicking, as the saying goes.

This does not mean that all those who may be referred to as realists in their approach to the study of security are of one and the same persuasion. Looking at security studies in international relations over time, it is clear that the interpretation of war and military threat, and their implications for national and collective security, has varied. Going back to the seminal work of Quincy Wright (1942), war was primarily a problem to be solved, a disease to be cured, rather than an instrument of statecraft. Although the preoccupation was with war, it was affecting national security as a malfunction of the international system. Growing out of scholarship in the period between the two World Wars, realism, in that perspective, called for interventions to improve the workings of the international system as a whole. 'National security', however, took on a very different meaning in the Cold War era when the consideration of force, as it relates to policy in conflicts among nations, emerged as the first and foremost concern of realists. Although the initial period after 1945 was characterized by a definite caution with regard to how far to interpret security only in military terms (e.g. Brodie, 1949), the emergence of 'deterrence theory' in the 1950s and 1960s, often hailed as the most impressive intellectual achievement in the history of the study of international relations, initiated a specific focus on nuclear weaponry and related issues such as arms control and limited war. The work of Thomas Schelling (1960) stands out as a good illustration of the orientation of realist scholars of that period. The breakdown of *détente* and the renewal of cold war tensions in the 1980s stimulated further interest in security studies, but the realist's concern tended to remain focused on 'the study of the threat, use, and control of military force'. What was new in this latter period was that perspectives from history, psychology, and organization theory were brought in to enrich security studies. In none of these versions of realism, however, did concern with livelihoods and resource flows feature, with the exception that realists acknowledged that war in the modern era would have a disastrous effect on civilian life.

There is obviously much more that should and could be said about the realist school. It suffices to stress here, though, that realism does not necessarily mean that military force or war is the only variable entering into their equation of what constitutes security. Nor does it have to exclude concerns about the nature of the international system. What is best in the interest of a nation, in other words, may take on varying interpretations in the realist perspective. It is important to take this into consideration in the contemporary setting when other intellectual perspectives are being launched to challenge realism. The latter is likely still to hold its ground and, at least in the United States, foreign policy debates are likely to be pursued on the terms set by realists rather than by other schools. In other words, it is not very likely that Washington security analysts are going to be persuaded to abandon their own realist premises in favour of some other fashionable theory. In this respect, one can reasonably assume that the hard-core realist perspective on security will continue to be significant in the ongoing discourse on security. The challenge, therefore, is how to make environmental and other concerns an integral part of the realist equation.

The moralist school

The fact that the global setting in the 1990s differs from that of the Cold War creates space for alternative views that now compete for attention among scholars. A particularly important driving force for the emergence of rival schools is the tendency for conflicts to be within, rather than between, states. Such conflicts tend to be particularly violent in multi-ethnic states (Carment, 1993). Evans (1994:3) mentions that of the 30 conflicts receiving international attention in 1992, no less than 29 were within state borders. This trend has been exacerbated by the breakdown of empires, notably the Soviet one, but also the collapse of the state in many former colonies in Africa. Bosnia, Rwanda and Somalia, mini-states without their own clout in the global arena, have occupied the attention of policy analysts in recent years, not the military threat of competing global super-powers.

This is to many the essence of what is sometimes referred to as the 'post-imperialist age'. The principle of national self-determination, we have come to assume, is not in question. Interventions are no longer imperial but humanitarian. We prefer to imagine the acts of rescue undertaken in countries like Bosnia, Kurdistan and Somalia since 1989 as exercises in post-imperial disinterestedness, as a form of therapeutics uncontaminated by lust for conquest or imperial rivalry, as Ignatieff (1995:78) argues. Nor is this mere illusion. In the cases mentioned above, the intervening forces have stopped short of occupation. Even if these interventions have been more associated with failure than success, they have changed the parameters of the debate about security in ways that still prevail.

The bottom line of the moralist school is that the international community has a collective responsibility for not only all member states but also for the people living in these member states. Security is no longer possible to define in narrow national terms, but has to be viewed as co-operative, i.e., as involving every member state of the international community in renouncing the use of force among themselves and coming collectively to the aid of any one of them attacked. Co-operative security, then, in the language of one analyst (Evans, 1994:7), means consultation rather than confrontation, reassurance rather than deterrence, transparency rather than secrecy, prevention rather than correction, and interdependence rather than unilateralism. Peace is seen as a necessary condition for development, this school argues, while pointing to the fact that it is no coincidence that those countries whose economies are declining, whose political institutions are failing, and where human rights are not respected, should also be the ones experiencing the greatest amounts of turmoil and violence.

The moralist position favours a stronger role for preventive diplomacy, conducted not unilaterally by the already strong powers but through global or regional mechanisms. Its advocates would point to the fact, for instance, that the UN's peacekeeping budget for 1993 was $3.3 billion while the US-led coalition that defeated Iraq spent more than $70 billion. To enhance the mechanisms available for pursuing collective security, a number of proposals have been made. Some suggest that if member states contributed just 5 per cent of their existing defence budgets to the UN, the world body would have a security budget of some $40 billion a year—more than 10 times what it has available now. Others have suggested a flat levy on international air travel or a 0.1 per cent turnover tax on foreign exchange transactions to boost the ability of the United Nations to engage in preventive diplomacy and peace-keeping.

The moralist position, however, has its own problems, which stem not just from the failures of the global efforts in recent years to ensure collective security or pursue preventive diplomacy. The political will to engage in these ventures understandably slackened in the mid-1990s, even though the real reason for the failures is that there was never enough political backing in the first place. For example, it is hardly reasonable for states to deny the UN desperately needed funds, then turn around and blame it for the failures that lack of resources inevitably generate. Nor is it reasonable to blame the UN as an institution for the failures of member states in the Security Council to provide decisive leadership.

Another problem with the moralist position is the difficulty of knowing where its boundaries go. Morality is often invoked, but seldom delineated. Because objectives and motives are hard to concretize in situations where morality is an important factor, exercises aimed at crisis prevention often create their own backlash (Harff, 1995:36). Humanitarianism is morally seductive, but it also easily leads to hubris of the same kind that characterized the old imperialism. What else but imperial arrogance, asks Ignatieff (1995:79), could have led anyone to assume that an outside power—even one mandated by the international community—could have gone into Somalia, put an end to factional fighting and then exited, all within months?

Our moral reflex—'something must be done!'—has often been sustained by the unexamined assumption that we have the power to do anything. We have taken our technological and logistic might for granted. Now that we are faced with the partial, if not total, failure of almost all interventions attempted in the name of humanitarianism or collective security, the theme of moral disgust is emerging. The thought is not too far away that maybe civil wars must be allowed to burn themselves out of their own accord. Add to that the anguished suspicion that our attempts to stop them either delayed the inevitable, or even prolonged the agony, and we find ourselves adopting the moral reflex of self-exculpation by blaming the victim and thus justifying moral withdrawal.

There is a need for everyone who seriously ponders what we can do in Burundi, in the former Yugoslavia after the Dayton Peace Accord, or in any other place where intra-state violence occurs or is likely to occur, to consider seriously the dilemma that follows from adopting the moralist stand. It is seductive, but it creates its own traps into which we all are prone to fall. The moralist argument, therefore, while important for pointing to the relationship between civil war and the collapse of resource flows and livelihoods, carries its own prescriptive limitations, when it comes to policy, which are not always fully considered. The result is typically disgust, cynicism, and withdrawal, i.e., the opposite of what the school demands of the global community.

The liberal school

The liberal school lays primary emphasis on the growing economic and technological inter-dependence of states and societies in the contemporary world setting. It accepts that security concerns go beyond military aspects. In a liberal international economic system, vulnerability to external economic events and dependence on foreigners are a necessary consequence of immersion in global markets. They are viewed as the source of opportunities for improved living standards, not threats to be avoided. This means that the sense of insecurity for individuals, firms and nations that follows from the uncertainty associated with liberal capitalism is regarded as a necessary evil, if not an outright positive thing (Cable, 1995). Yet, even liberals agree that policies that enhance security, for example, to guarantee resource flows, are necessary. There are different versions of this liberal definition of security.

Robert McNamara (1968) is one of those who most forcefully have argued for a broader definition of security than what was typically inherent in the concept of national security in the Cold War era. His apostasy is particularly interesting, given his role as architect earlier in the decade of America's involvement in the Vietnam War. McNamara, on the eve of becoming President of the World Bank, articulated an expansive notion of security that included the promotion of economic, social and political development in poor nations as a means of preventing conflict and preserving a minimal measure of global order and stability. Contrary to the moralist, who argues that peace is a precondition for development, McNamara argued that development is a precondition for peace. The problem with his expanded notion of security was how to delineate and operationalize it. It was not easy to identify, for example, which specific policies would really promote greater global security. The policy of massive resource transfers in support of the poor that was pursued by the World Bank in the 1970s, under McNamara's leadership, proved quite soon to be inadequate for that purpose. All it did was to leave these poor nations heavily indebted to the West.

Others who tried to articulate a similar non-military definition of security were not more successful. For example, during the 1970s, a growing number of activist scholars began pointing to ecological degradation and population growth as existential threats to human survival. This group, preaching the new gospel of saving the planet, included, as Del Rosso Jr. (1995:185) reminds us, Rachel Carson, Barry Commoner, Jacques Cousteau, Paul Ehrlich, Buckminster Fuller, Garrett Hardin and Margaret Mead. Every one of them emphasized a particular aspect of the problem, but the urgency that drove their separate appeals was enshrined in the 1972 Club of Rome study, *The Limits to Growth*, which painted an unremittingly grim picture in which the world's economic system was destined to collapse as a result of unchecked population and industrial growth. It was ironically the alarmist nature of their warnings of inescapable disaster that in the end undermined the political impact of their calls. At least in the perspective prevailing in policy circles in the 1970s, these 'Jeremiahs' were seen as advocating policies that were totally unfeasible. Whether they should be described as being ahead of their time or not, these advocates of 'saving the planet' had very limited impact on either the 'silent majority' or the policymakers in governments, because the explicit link between non-military phenomena and the prevailing, typically realist notion of security, was not effectively made. This verdict applies also to the effort by Lester Brown (1977), eventually President of the WorldWatch Institute, and Robert Ullman (1983) in redefining national security to include such security threats as climate change, soil erosion, food shortages, and deforestation.

It was only with the dramatic shifts in geopolitical terms after the end of the Cold War that space evolved for considering more seriously the points about security advocated by the liberal school. Gwyn Prins (1992) was one of the first, and more influential, writers in advocating a new field of security in which the key referent object was the entire globe, rather than the state. Global security is about survival. The existential needs of humans—and non-humans, notably animals, trees and plants—were now more readily accepted as part of the security agenda. Building on James Lovelock's 'Gaia Hypothesis', which describes the world in which all elements, including human beings, are inextricably linked by powerful feedback loops that sustain a fragile global equilibrium, this new apostasy of security emphasized the critical interrelationships among some of the most daunting threats to human existence such as poverty, environmental degradation, and rapid demographic change (Myers, 1989).

Much of this was dismissed by conventional security analysts as 'globaloney', but this liberal message had greater impact in the 1990s than it had had two decades earlier. Behind their often inflated rhetoric lay, after all, some important, and underappreciated, dimensions of the evolving international system, which after the liberalization of the world economy in the 1980s had become increasingly apparent. The critique that the liberal definition of security moved the concept away from the fundamental notion of protection from organized violence could no longer be sustained, because it was now more readily recognized than in the 1970s that factors emerging in the non-military realm were capable of causing as much harm to stability and order as the arsenals of the world's armies. For example, Homer-Dixon (1994), drawing on a wide range of cases from around the world, concludes that environmental scarcities definitely contribute to violent conflicts in many parts of the developing world.

The philosophical underpinnings of the liberal gospel of security in the 1990s are not new, but what is new is their pretension for filling the conceptual vacuum left in the wake of the dissolution of the Soviet Empire. 'Geoeconomics' has been emerging as a natural successor to geopolitics in a world in which the force of arms is not only bad for humanity but also bad for business (Del Rosso Jr., 1995).

The liberal definition of security continues to exercise influence in academic circles and there is evidence that these ideas are beginning to permeate policy circles too. For example, in the US State Department, traditionally a fortress of realist thinking, there exists, since President Clinton took office, a special Under-Secretary for Global Affairs. The same kind of office exists also in other countries. We can safely say, therefore, that non-military aspects of security as they affect not only the nation-state but the global community as an integrated whole, are receiving greater recognition today. More and more analysts and policymakers realize that livelihoods and resource flows have to be secured in new and more imaginative ways than in the past.

The populist school

The populist school shares some of the same points as the liberal perspective on development. In particular, it accepts that the security concept needs to be expanded to include non-military aspects. Like the liberal school, it recognizes also that developmentalism must be tempered by a definite dose of environmentalism. It differs from the former, however, in that it recognizes not only states and markets as important actors, but also people. To the populist school, indigenous organizations and civil society are important concepts. Their answer to the question of whose security we are concerned with, is that it is the security of the more marginalized groups and peoples of the globe. The environmental and demographic threats that the liberal school identifies in more generic terms are seen by the populists as applying in differential terms. The poor and the marginalized are more exposed than others. It is their livelihoods that need special protection. It is the way resource flows affect them that should be our priority. The populist school draws considerable inspiration from the Report of the Global Commission on Environment and Development, chaired by Gro Harlem Brundtland (World Commission on Environment and Development 1987). Like the liberal school, there are different shades of this perspective. One noticeable difference is how the populists relate to the question of how large-scale development affects small-scale efforts, and vice versa.

One group starts from the assumption that the principal challenge is to draw the lessons of grassroots development for the purpose of improving national or global development. It presupposes that the foundation for development lies with the people; that they are the best judges of how to use scarce resources judiciously. For them, security lies in the notion that things grounded in society stand a better chance of being protected and promoted. If developmental and environmental factors may pose threats to human survival and security, it is important that we get the equation right by proceeding from the bottom up. Considering the magnitude of the challenge, however, it is important to ask: ultimately how large can small become? Can that which is local build upon itself so that small is institutionalized and widely replicated? Can a species of development flourish that maintains the virtues of smallness, but at the same time reaches large numbers of people, transfers genuine power to the poor, and provides the prospect of sustainable development?

Annis (1987) answers these questions affirmatively with reference to Latin America. He believes that every Latin American country is now permeated with a web of grassroots organizations intertwined with each other and the state, which provide the basis for the scaling up of small-scale development. Friberg and Hettne (1988) agree with Annis, and add that micro processes can produce macro transformation for three reasons. First, the conventional distinctions of levels (local, national, global) are simplifications that distort our understanding of the aggregate effects of dispersed and localized phenomena. Second, there is a dynamic interplay between the functional macro system and the territorial micro system, which has been spurred by local responses to the operation of the world economic system in which those who suffer from unemployment, marginalization, and the destruction of their habitat react and take their future into their own hands. The resulting dialectic between the macro and the micro makes more room for local initiatives. Third, while the issues of local development vary considerably because of contextual differences, they are similar at a deeper level. It is possible, therefore, to speak of a tendency towards convergence.

There certainly appears to be a growing consensus, not only among analysts but also practitioners, that the implementation of most global policies will require acceptance of these policies by most of the people of the world (Alger, 1990). The view of Western moral and technical superiority that was so prevalent some years ago is finally being called into question. For example, the notion that Europeans could succeed where indigenous people had failed can no longer be sustained on the basis of existing performance records, whether the sector is agriculture or health. The re-focus on the poor, therefore, draws attention to the indigenous, often marginalized, groups who in the past were subjected to the experiments of Western 'developmentalism'. In trying to find answers to the questions raised by the interplay of environment, human rights, governance and development, Western models are no longer viewed with the same confidence as before. In fact, it is increasingly recognized, as in the case of the CAMPFIRE project in Zimbabwe (Derman, 1995), that national proprietorship and local ownership must be recognized as fundamental to the success of any effort to combine environmental concerns, in this case wildlife protection, with the development aspirations of indigenous communities. An interesting example of what Brock (1991) calls 'peace through parks', which involves the participation of grassroots communities as well as governmental agencies, is the attempt to establish the world's largest consecutive wildlife corridor in southern Africa, involving South Africa, Mozambique and Zimbabwe. This is a practical example of the efforts in the region to reduce the tensions between South Africa and the member states of

160

the Southern African Development Community (SADC) that Booth and Vale (1995) are advocating in their review of the post-apartheid security concerns in the region.

An opposite approach to dealing with the macro–micro interrelations is to start from the more negative assumption that all macro (or mega) development is harmful to the micro, whether defined in human, institutional or biological terms. Many analysts adopting this particular approach focus their attention on what development does to indigenous communities. Their security is being threatened by the global development forces set in motion by an assertive capitalist economy. Sometimes, these concerns are expanded to include not only human communities but also wildlife, whose existence is being threatened by economic or social forces. 'Parks and people' programmes constitute one practical example of how governments, sometimes non-governmental organizations, have tried to deal with the tensions that exist, e.g., in eastern and southern Africa, between the development needs of human communities and the demands of wildlife protection.

Another example of interest here is the struggle to protect the rain forest in the Amazon. Of particular significance has been the Kayapo Indian protest, which over the years helped galvanize a new environmental consciousness in Brazil and in neighbouring countries. The protest focused on the proposal to build the Kararao Dam, which would have drowned a considerable part of the rain forest and would have displaced members of the local Indian community. With the help of international NGOs, like Friends of the Earth and Survival International, the Kayapo staged a major demonstration in the town of Altamira that eventually had the effect of making the World Bank withdraw its promise of a loan for the project to the Brazilian Government (Fisher, 1994). The Altamira Kayapo protest not only achieved the objective of stemming further destruction of the rain forest, but also profoundly changed the political reality of the indigenous Indian communities and their expectations of what they could do to protect their own livelihoods. In this case, the small managed successfully to defend itself against the large-scale development efforts funded by governments and international finance institutions.

Some of the same concerns have arisen in conjunction with the conservation of biodiversity. Here it is not so much human communities as the biological riches that are at stake, but the two go together in that the best protectors of biodiversity are often local communities who have a stake in the continued existence of certain species. Community management of biodiversity, therefore, has more recently become an interest of scholars and practitioners alike, in Africa, Asia and Latin America, where such diversity is particularly rich. There is also growing realization in the richer parts of the world that these efforts are of value not only to the local communities, but also to the rest of the world. Again, it is the small, by being defended, that can provide benefits to the large.

While the security concept which presupposes that the protection of local communities has a value to the global community at large is still an enigma to most security analysts, the populist school does provide a new dimension to the discourse on security that complements other perspectives in a meaningful manner. Even though it is the polar opposite of realism, and most conventional security analysts would reject it as lying outside their concerns, other groups interested in the concept are seriously grappling with it, not only as an esoteric but a practical phenomenon.

Conclusions

This chapter has traced the evolving discourse on the concept of security in recent years. There are certain important things that emerge from this review. The first is that the vertical and horizontal expansion of the concept has broadened the debate and created at least four different perspectives that compete for attention among academics and policy analysts alike. As a result, the debate is richer and no longer the prerogative of a highly specialized group of international relations experts only. Even though each of these perspectives has its own limitations, especially when it comes to operationalization, they do challenge the hegemonic position of realism in new and interesting ways.

A second point is that the actors participating in the debate about security are no longer only government officials worrying about the security of the nation-state. Increasingly, representatives of civil society participate in the debate with a view to demonstrating how the definition of security bears on their welfare and livelihoods as well. Even though many analysts experience the present situation as disorderly, and dismiss the debate in the post-Cold War era as confusing, the parameters of the debate have changed for good, because the stakeholders are now more of a diverse group than ever. The recognition that civil society is as important an actor as the state, guarantees that the concept of security will be defined in terms that reflect society's interests much more than before.

The third point is that the rise of 'geo-economics' is drawing attention to new dimensions of security that are difficult for governments to ignore in a world where 'everything is related to everything else, only more so now than ever', to quote an American diplomat (Del Rosso Jr., 1995:175). Threats to economic security are potentially as harmful as many military threats might be. For example, disruption of supplies, whether of food, oil, or raw materials needed for production, can cause major damage to a country's economy and potentially spark off political violence. Such threats to resource flows are bound to have implications for people's livelihoods in ways that politicians cannot ignore. They can hit rich countries as well as poor ones.

The fourth point is that human-induced environmental scarcity, such as degradation of land resources and population pressures, helps precipitate agricultural shortfalls, which in turn leads to adverse social and political outcomes. Mexico, for example, is vulnerable to such interactions. People are already reported as leaving the State of Oaxaca because of drought and soil erosion. It is estimated that future global warming could decrease Mexican rain-fed maize production by up to 40 per cent. This change could in turn interact with ongoing land degradation, free trade and the privatization of communal peasant lands to cause grave internal conflict. The potential threat to national security of these processes has already been demonstrated in the State of Chiapas.

The fifth point is that although some may wish to brush off the above scenario as scare tactics, there is a definite need to build into the calculation of security the fact that it is affected by a dual set of variables, one fast-moving,

162

the other operating in the longer haul. The discourse on security in the past has been influenced mainly by consideration of fast-moving variables such as military interventions or economic crashes. Equally important, however, are the processes of land degradation, population growth, and climate change, which, if not considered, may create shocks causing as much long-term damage to resource flows and livelihoods as those that more usually get considered by security analysts.

All the great post-war settlements in the modern era—at Vienna in 1815, at Versailles in 1919, and at San Francisco in 1945—have been accompanied by new principles of international security. The Cold War was also a large international conflict. Like the two World Wars it came to an end with momentous changes in the political configuration of Europe and it, too, has been followed by a new political interest in principles of security, notably how the security of individuals, groups and communities other than the state can be objects of international policy.

This is not a time for celebration of these new concerns, but for recognition that the apparent disorderliness in the debate about security—and, for example, how it relates to resource flows and livelihoods—is a source of strength, and something that should not be shunned as we continue our search for more appropriate mechanisms of governance at the global, as well as national and local, levels of social action. As this chapter has demonstrated, there is convincing evidence for many policy alternatives and it is not clear which is more appropriate or valid in any given situation. Peace makes development as convincing as development makes peace. As we grapple with contemporary situations, we cannot afford to confine ourselves to believing in only one of those equations.

Culture, cultural values, norms and meanings—A framework for environmental understanding

UNO SVEDIN

The culture-nature dichotomy

A RHETORICAL QUESTION can be used as a point of departure for our reflections about cultural values, norms and meanings with regard to the environment: 'What has culture to do with the environment?'

Culture is often seen as the antithesis of the natural world—'nature' being regarded as that state which is independent of human affairs. What is completely natural is, from this viewpoint, that which is not manipulated and interfered with by humans.

It must be evident to everyone today, however, that in practice this is a very problematic position. Not even the ice cap of Antarctica is free from the traces of human activity. This is not an allusion to a few researchers living in huts on the ice, but to the waste products of industrial societies in other parts of the world, which set their chemical fingerprints upon the ice cap.

Even if, by a miracle, some geographical islands of natural independence were found, still it would not be conceptually possible to keep culture and the environment apart. We have to face the analytical use of dichotomization as a debating position, expressing a deeply ingrained Western cultural intellectual habit, which today is imposed on wider and wider segments of the world.

The separation of the phenomena of the world of humans from the world of what is not touched by people, is also deeply problematic because it is humans who:

○ label the natural phenomena in order to approach them;
○ frame their connotations;
○ extract and highlight the intricacies of the causes and effects within the natural world; and
○ attach values to phenomena in the natural world, in providing normative frameworks with regard to human actions aimed at interference with the natural world.

Indeed the framing of the environment in conceptual terms is a deeply human activity.

Just as there are problems separating these two worlds, so there are difficulties dividing the different parts of the knowledge-generating systems that deal with the various parts of the world. One classical analysis of this is of course the separation suggested by C.P. Snow between the 'two cultures' of knowledge.

We know that differences exist, generating many tensions between scientific disciplines which look at the world from a variety of angles. Indeed, the understanding of natural phenomena is channelled through a process of human interpretation. That is why the inclusion of a social science and humanities outlook on environmental issues is so essential.

Having emphasized this point, it is, however, possible to try to impose too strong a 'cultural construction of reality' approach on the causalities in the natural world. After all, water in a river flows progressively down the valley following the gravity gradient to the ocean, and the outcome is the same whatever the intellectual discipline observing the event.

Guiding patterns of human understanding and action

There is both independence and dependence between culture (including the norms, the connotations and the meanings) and the natural world. This is the case even before any human manipulation of the natural world has taken place, whether it be in prehistoric times, for example the digging of a hole in the ground to catch a large animal such as a mammoth, or today in a nuclear power plant the attempt to capture the energy content of the dance of the neutrons.

The cultural framework provides a grid of understanding, covering a vast number of phenomena in nature, and also provides:

○ concepts;
○ normative selection rules for behaviour;
○ institutions encompassing and codifying such rules; and
○ practices in the day-to-day world, for example, shaping life styles, and including the tools developed for these purposes that we normally call 'technologies'.

Cultural values, norms and meanings provide guiding patterns for human actions in general. This also holds true with regard to the environment and the connected livelihoods that provide humans with access to a variety of resource flows. Such values may be explicitly or implicitly expressed in a certain culture. In all cases they provide a guiding force for the direction of practices. However, the relationship between the realm of values and the realm of action is not always a simple one, not least because of the internal tensions between the various components of the normative systems.

The knowledge system that supports the realm of action reflects the interests of the various actors involved. In this way knowledge systems also express cultural preferences of different kinds. This is the case especially with regard to different degrees of emphasis on approaches, varying from the local to the global, and exemplified by the various land-use/land-cover analysis entry points (see Figure 17).

It also holds true with regard to the variation of other types of general actor interests, including different professional ones, stressing, for example, individual or collective entry points. The different views emerging from these knowledge systems may be seen not only as reflecting world views, but also varying political interests in a broad sense. The discussion about sustainable livelihoods is inseparable from this cultural and political framing of what different actors perceive of the world.

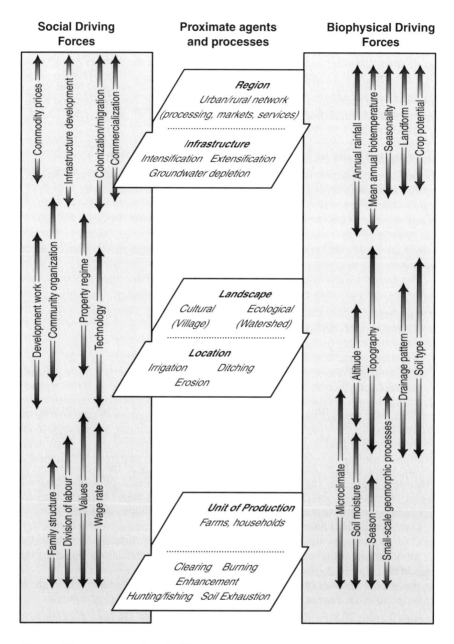

Figure 17. *An example of different approaches on a micro/macro scale: the case of land use/land cover* (from the IGBP/IHDP LUCC project)

Dimensions of sustainable development

There are many entry points to the discussion on paths to sustainable development world-wide, and there is enormous breadth in the aspects that have to be contemplated. Central dimensions of the discourse of such paths must include:

○ *the biophysical dimensions* in terms of the flows, their connections and the processes binding them together;
○ *the socio-economic societal frameworks* within which the flows connect and transform, including the institutional embedding;
○ *the knowledge base* about connections, including the forms of knowledge which are incorporated in 'technologies' in a wide sense; and
○ *the value base* from which the direction of human interference with the natural world is drawn, in terms of cultural preferences, norms and underlying meanings.

Different approaches stress one or the other of these dimensions. The chosen emphasis also expresses the specific interest of a certain knowledge tradition, e.g., in an academic disciplinary sense. However, it is important to stress that the nature of a sustainable world cannot be understood if knowledge is developed without taking into account the full realm spanned by all the dimensions of understandings indicated above.

'Mappa mundi'

A central expression of cultural values, norms and meanings is found in their penetration into world views in operation. In the Western medieval period world views were implicit in, among other things, maps of the world, or *mappa mundae*. Figure 18 illustrates what *mappa mundi* at that time conveyed in terms of understanding. What we see is the expression of a synthesis aspiration aiming at putting as many as possible relevant pieces of knowledge together in order to create a holistic image of the world.

The process in the design includes:

○ choices about components to be included and excluded and why the selections are made in the way they are;
○ choices about scales involved, especially the relationship between the global scale and the local constituencies whose livelihoods build up the world;
○ opinions—implicit or explicit—on philosophical ideas of the time, e.g., in terms of what are considered relevant knowledge and foci of interests.

Following Valerie I.J. Flint in her analysis of *The imaginative landscape of Christopher Columbus* (1992), we find the following aspects involved in the creation of *mappa mundi*:

○ components of the world view:
 – cultural-religious aspects
 – ways of modelling contemporary geographical understanding
 – interplay between craftsmanship and theoretical knowledge
 – personal narratives

Figure 18. Example of a medieval mappa mundi
By permission of The British Library (Mappa mundi, MS Cotton TIN.B.V. Pt. 1. f56v)

○ available technology (e.g., shipbuilding, navigation skills); and
○ the political situation.

The *mappa mundae* of today, although they channel a more updated form of contents, are as necessary to us as for the people in medieval times in order to understand what we still do not see, to handle large systems' complexities and to make it possible for us to act within an expanded time horizon of maybe two to three generations. At the same time we need, as was already true in the medieval period, to keep a relevant political action time-span valid as well.

Cultural aspects of a mappa mundi
When we consider the values appropriate for the build up of a *mappa mundi* of relevance for the environmental challenges of today, what should we remember? We should take note that:

○ values of relevance for the environment have a broader base than the environment itself;
○ values express themselves in many ways, e.g., in terms of laws, administrative practices, choice of technology, and social organization;
○ values appear in different cultural circumstances at different levels of consolidation and force;
○ values often change over time; and
○ values are very important for development in the long term, but may be difficult to use looking into the future for prognostic purposes.

Having said this it might be interesting to dwell on forms in which values may enter into the design of a *mappa mundi*. The values are often made visible through the way by which the domain of interest is expressed, i.e., among other things through the choice of boundary conditions, including preconditions about what is self-evident, for a particular analysis. The selection of causal elements considered as relevant also has a considerable normative content. This also holds true with regard to the style in which the questions are posed within the specific *mappa mundi* framework. Which questions are considered interesting and within which scholarly disciplines are they addressed? The very use of one analytical approach and not another is in itself a normative choice.

A cultural frame of environmental interest

Trying to be more selective and asking ourselves which questions would be culturally interesting with regard to environmentally oriented *mappae mundi*, the following pairs might be useful to contemplate, among others:

○ the small and the large;
○ the complex and the simple;
○ the reducible and the non-reducible; and
○ the visible and the invisible.

Having started to scan these culturally interesting dimensions, we may go on by asking ourselves with special regard to the environment what may, against the background of the history of ideas, be seen as a set of fruitful and as far as possible not directly related (i.e., 'orthogonal') dimensions of analysis. Such a choice is, of course, highly subjective. Only the interest of the outcome of the exercise provides the justification for it.

For the moment disregarding many other dimensions that could have been selected, that the chosen set is probably not entirely independent, that we have a spectrum of positions and not polar pairs, that the chosen concepts are vaguely defined, and so on, we note that:

○ In many environmental discourses and even more in a cross-religious dialogue on environmental affairs it is apparent that there is tension between Nature seen as sacred and Nature seen as *profane*.

○ In studies of the history of ideas, the development of the idea of Nature seen as a *potentiality* (for some other emerging state) in antiquity moved towards a more 'modern' position, emerging more clearly in the seventeenth century with Nature seen as a *thing*.

○ In discussions about the Gaia hypothesis with regard to the biosphere there is sometimes an underlying idea that Nature has a goal. This holds true also for the perspective on the development of the earth system, for example Teilard de Chardin (1940) who saw the planet developing towards a much more complex system, i.e. the 'no-sphere' where immaterial phenomena interplay with the material ones in a coherent fashion. By comparison the much more prevalent natural-science influenced concept of a *non-goal* Nature (the non-acceptance of the fourth category of causality of Aristotle) stands against such types of goal-oriented approaches.

If we combine these three dimensions (Figure 19) we find the contemporary Western science-based culture occupying mainly the upper, right-hand back corner, i.e., that of Nature as *thing*, *non-goal*, *profane*. The conceptual move in Western culture over 200 years corresponds to a move from the front-mid plane to the upper-back right-hand corner. Introducing ideas such as the Gaia hypothesis may shift the emphasis towards the upper, left-hand, back corner, and what could be termed the 'sacredness revival' would move the centre of the cultural perceptual gravity towards the lower plane. Several different scenarios of changes in cultural perception with regard to the environment may thus be contemplated and visualized.

This is not to say in any way that changes in the way people see the environment and nature can be understood in these terms only. To some extent, however, such devices may provide a visual aid for contemplating the dynamics of environmentally oriented, long-term cultural traits.

Regarding broad environmental policy, other aspects may be as important as those covered above, for example, the challenge of the female perspective

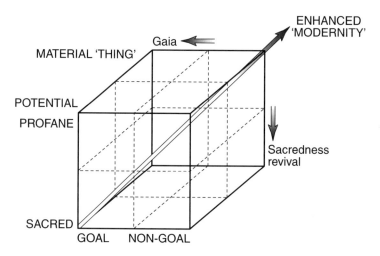

Figure 19. *A cube illustrating cultural perceptions of nature*

170

applied to the environmental–population–society nexus, as demonstrated at the NGO forum associated with the UN Rio Conference on the Environment and Development 1992 and later at the 1994 Cairo Conference on population issues. The North-South political polarity has cultural connotations as well.

Reference for sustainable livelihood outlooks

What is the relevance of these reflections to a discussion of cultural norms with regard to sustainable livelihoods? They provide not only a frame of reference which takes into account strong movements over a very long time in societies influenced by Western culture, but also take note of counter or complementary movements within the present Western cultural ideology.

The normative aspects of livelihoods develop constantly, which should be distinctly considered in the analysis of these phenomena. What should be emphasized is that such studies of livelihoods need to take into consideration the broader framework of comparative cultural contexts.

Contemporary challenges

So what are the challenges we are facing in our contemporary society? What, in other words, is the character of the malaise which has to be recognized and acted upon in our civilization? It is the separation between the different conceptual worlds of phenomena: those in the societal realm and those in the natural world. It is the separation of ideas in the academic world from the thoughts currently informing the world of action. It is the separation of the phenomena of the very micro level from those at the macro level and even at the supra-macro level. It is wrong to say that we now live in a global world, and therefore that everything important is global now and has to be treated in one supra-macro context. But it is equally wrong, in highlighting deeply significant and probably decisive phenomena at the micro level, to let them be the entire focus of interest, disregarding the broader regional and global contexts.

The understanding of macro-world phenomena must constantly be upgraded in order to develop knowledge that provides the contexts for the understanding of the world of micro events. This may not seem new, but what is new is that strategic choices of sets of micro events must be put together in such a pattern that provide *from below* a context, or conditionality, to the understanding of global phenomena. Using such new approaches to the formation of knowledge moving both upwards and downwards in scale, action at the world level can be given a fresh starting point.

The relationships between knowledge and action, the interplay between levels, and their connections to norms, cultural frameworks and ethical considerations, must be scrutinized in view of the environmental societal issues of our day. This has to be done by a scientific constituency which is not afraid of facing new alliances even outside academic confines. The arrogance involved in considering only one type of knowledge, or recognizing only one group of actors as endowed with understanding of environmentally related cultural norms, has to be left behind. It is bridging the gaps that will provide a path for the promotion of real human values such as peace, harmony, human dignity and a sense of sharing.

171

We live in a world where, to quote President Nelson Mandela in his inaugural speech: 'Our deepest fear is not that we are inadequate. Our deepest fear is that we are powerful beyond measure. It is our light, not our darkness that needs to frighten us.' This insight also has significance for us in our attempts to find a better path promoting the development of the normative cultural basis for the sustainable development we may envisage. For this purpose we need to mobilize all our capacities to evolve this framework for the benefit of the future of mankind.

Bibliography

Life, livelihood, resources and security—Links, and a call for a new order

Brown, L. and H. Kane 1994. *Full house: Reassessing the earth's population carrying capacity*. The Worldwatch Environmental Alert Series. New York: W.W. Norton & Co.

Desai, U. 1992. 'Introduction', *Policy Studies Journal*, Vol. 20 No. 4: 621–7.

Fogel, R. 1994. 'The relevance of Malthus for the study of mortality today: Long-run influences on health, mortality, labour force participation and population growth'. In K. Lindahl-Kiessling and H. Landberg (eds.), *Population, economic development and the environment*. Oxford: Oxford University Press, pp. 231–84.

Hjort-af-Ornäs, A. and S. Lodgaard (eds.) 1992. *The environment and international security*. Uppsala: EPOS, Uppsala University (also published at PRIO, the International Peace Research Institute in Oslo).

Homer-Dixon, T.F., J.H. Boutwell and G.W. Rathjens 1993. 'Environmental change and violent conflict. Growing scarcities of renewable resources can contribute to social instability and civil strife', *Scientific American*, February: 38–45.

IFPRI (International Food Policy Research Institute) 1995. *A 2020 vision for food, agriculture, and the environment*. Washington D.C.

Kaplan, R. 1994. 'The coming anarchy', *The Atlantic Monthly*, February: 44–76.

Lindahl-Kiessling, K. and H. Landberg (eds.) 1994. *Population, economic development and the environment*. Oxford: Oxford University Press.

Sen, A.K. 1994. 'Population and reasoned agency: Food, fertility, and economic development'. In Lindahl-Kiessling and H. Landberg (eds.), *Population, economic development and the environment*. Oxford: Oxford University Press, pp. 51–78.

UNDP 1994. *Human development report*. Oxford University Press.

—— 1995. *Human development report*. Oxford University Press.

Vaillancourt, J.-G. 1993. 'Earth summits of 1992 in Rio', *Society and Natural Resources*, Vol. 6: 81–88.

Ogoni—oil, resource flow and conflict in rural Nigeria

Ake, C. 1985. 'The future of the state in Africa'. In *International Political Science Review*, Vol. 6 No. 1.

Ake, C., O. Nnoli and E. Nwokedi (n.d.). 'The causes of conflict in Africa'. A research proposal (mimeo).

Alavi, H. 1972. 'The state in post-colonial societies: Pakistan and Bangladesh'. In *New Left Review*, No. 74.

Amin, S. 1987. 'Preface: The state and the question of development'. In P. Anyang' Nyong'o (ed.), *Popular struggles for democracy in Africa*. London: Zed Press and United Nations University.

Berkowitz, M. and P. Bock 1968. 'National Security'. In *International Encyclopedia of the Social Sciences*, Vol. 11. New York: Macmillan and the Free Press.

Bock, P. and M. Berkowitz 1966. 'The emerging field of national security', *World Politics*, Vol. 19.

Colby, M. 1991. 'Environmental management in development: The evolution of paradigms'. In *Ecological Economics*, Vol. 3.

Earth Action 1994. 'Defend the Ogoni people in Nigeria', *Alert*, No. 3.

Ekekwe, E. 1986. *Class and state in Nigeria.* Lagos: Longman.

Engels, F. 1978. *Origins of the family, private property and the state.* Peking: Foreign Languages Press (originally pub. 1884).

Ezeanozie, I. 1991. 'Environmental degradation and social conflict in Nigeria: A case study of the oil-producing areas of Rivers State'. BSc project, Department of Political Science, University of Nigeria.

Folke, C. and A. Jansson 1992. 'The emergence of an ecological economics paradigm: Examples from fisheries and aquaculture'. In U. Svedin and B. Aniansson (eds.), *Society and the environment: A Swedish research perspective.* London: Kluwer Academic Publishers.

Freedman, L. 1992. 'The concept of security'. In M. Hawkesworth and M. Kogan (eds.), *Encyclopedia of government and politics*, Vol. 2. London: Routledge.

Gramsci, A. 1971. *Selections from the prison notebooks.* London: Lawrence and Wishart.

Gurr, T. 1974. *Why men rebel.* Princeton: Princeton University Press.

Hjort-af-Ornäs, A. 1989. 'Environment and the security of dryland herders in Eastern Africa'. In Hjort-af-Ornäs and Mohamed Salih 1989 op. cit.

—— 1992. 'Local models, global change: community impacts and sustainability visions'. In U. Svedin and B. Aniansson (eds.), *Society and the environment: A Swedish research perspective.* London: Kluwer Academic Publishers.

Hjort-af-Ornäs, A. and M.A. Mohamed Salih 1989. 'Introduction: ecology and politics: environmental stress and security in Africa'. In A. Hjort-af-Ornäs and M.A. Mohamed Salih (eds.), *Ecology and politics: environmental stress and security in Africa.* Uppsala: Scandinavian Institute of African Studies.

Human Rights Watch 1995. 'Nigeria: The Ogoni crisis: A case study of military repression in south-eastern Nigeria', *Human Rights Watch/Africa*, Vol. 7, No. 5.

Hydén, G. 1998. 'Environmental awareness, conflict genesis and governance'. In this volume.

Ibeanu, O. 1992. 'The state and population displacement in Nigeria'. Ph.D. dissertation, University of Nigeria.

—— 1993a. 'The state and the market: Reflections on Ake's analysis of the state in the periphery'. In *Africa Development*, Vol. 18, No. 3.

—— 1993b. 'Ogonis: Oil and environmental conflict in Nigeria'. In *Nigeria Now*, Vol. 2, No. 11 (November).

Joseph, R. 1987. *Democracy and prebendal politics in Nigeria: The rise and fall of the Second Republic.* Cambridge: Cambridge University Press.

Leys, C. 1976. 'The "overdeveloped" post-colonial state: Re-evaluation'. In *Review of African Political Economy*, No. 5.

Movement for the Survival of Ogoni People (MOSOP) 1992. *Ogoni Bill of Rights.* Port Harcourt: Saros International Publishers.

Nwankwo, J. and D. Irrechukwu (n.d.). 'Problems of environmental pollution and control in the Nigerian petroleum industry'. Petroleum Inspectorate, Nigerian National Petroleum Corporation, Lagos (mimeo).

Poulantzas, N. 1978. *Political power and social classes.* London: Verso.

—— 1975. *Classes in contemporary capitalism.* London: New Left Books.

Rodney, W. 1982. *How Europe underdeveloped Africa.* Enugu: Ikenga Publishers.

Rosenau, J. (ed.) 1964. *International aspects of civil strife.* Princeton: Princeton University Press.

Shell 1995. *The Nigeria brief: The Ogoni issue.* Lagos: The Shell Petroleum Development Company of Nigeria Limited.

Stockdale, J. 1989. 'Pro-growth, limits to growth, and a sustainable development synthesis', *Society and Natural Resources*, Vol. 2.

Underwood, D. and P. King 1989. 'On the ideological foundations of environmental policy', *Ecological Economics*, Vol. 1.

Wolfers, A. 1952. '"National Security" as an ambiguous symbol', *Political Science Quarterly*, Vol. 67.

Nigerian newspapers and magazines consulted:

African Concord (94:4:11)
AM News (95:10:12)
Daily Champion (94:8:26)
The Guardian (94:3:28)
The News (93:5:17)

Environmental awareness and conflict genesis—People versus parks in Mkomazi game reserve, Tanzania

Anderson, G.D. 1967. 'A reconnaissance survey of the land use potential of Mkomazi Game Reserve and an appraisal of factors affecting present and potential land use and productivity in its environs'. Unpublished report.

Anderson, D. and R. Grove 1987. 'The scramble for Eden: past, present, and future in African conservation'. In D. Anderson and R. Grove (eds.), *Conservation in Africa: People, policies, and practices*. Cambridge: Cambridge University Press.

Anstey, D. 1955. 'Mkomazi Game Reserve', *Oryx*, Vol. 3:183–5.

Appadurai, A. 1994. 'Disjuncture and difference in the global cultural economy'. In P. Williams and L. Chrisman (eds.), *Colonial discourse and post-colonial theory: A reader.* New York: Columbia University Press.

Arhem, K. 1985. *Pastoral man in the garden of Eden: The Maasai of the Ngorongoro Conservation Area, Tanzania.* Uppsala Research Reports in Cultural Anthropology.

Arusha 1994. 'Policy for Wildlife Conservation and Utilisation'. Unpublished draft.

Bayart, J.-F. 1993. *The state in Africa: The politics of the belly.* London: Longman.

Behnke, R. H. Jr., I. Scoones and C. Kerven (eds.) 1993. *Range ecology at disequilibrium: New models of natural variability and pastoral adaptation in African savannas.* London: Overseas Development Institute.

Bekure, S., P.N. de Leeuw, B.E. Grandin and P.J.H. Neate 1991. *Maasai herding. An analysis of the livestock production system of Maasai pastoralists in eastern Kajiado District, Kenya.* Addis Ababa: International Livestock Centre for Africa.

Berger, P.L. and T. Luckmann 1967. *The social construction of reality.* Garden City, NY: Anchor Books.

Berkes, F. (ed.) 1989. *Common property resources, ecology and community-based sustainable development.* London: Belhaven Press.

Bonner, R. 1993. *At the hand of man: peril and hope for Africa's wildlife.* New York: Alfred A. Knopf.

Brockington, D. 1995. 'Upgrading thesis, UCL'. Unpublished report.

——1998. 'Land loss and livelihoods. The effects of eviction on pastoralists moved from the Mkomazi Game Reserve, Tanzania'. Unpublished PhD thesis, University College, London.

Brockington, D. and K. Homewood 1996. 'Debates concerning Mkomazi Game Reserve, Tanzania'. In M. Leach and R. Mearns (ed.), *The lie of the land: Challenging received wisdom on the African environment.* London: International Africa Institute.

Bromely, D.W. and M.M. Cernea 1989. 'The management of common property natural resources. Some conceptual and operational fallacies'. *World Bank Discussion Paper No. 57.* Washington DC: World Bank.

Business Times 1996. 12–18 April, 9. 'Pastoralists re-endanger Mkomazi Game Reserve'. New report from the Wildlife Department.

Campbell, D.J. 1993. 'Land as Ours, Land as Mine: Economic, political and ideological marginalization in Kajiado District'. In T. Spear and R. Waller (eds.), *Being Maasai: ethnicity and identity in East Africa.* London: James Currey.

Charnley, S. 1994. *Cattle, commons and culture: The political ecology of environmental change on a Tanzanian rangeland.* PhD thesis, Stanford University.

Dryzek, J.S. 1987. *Rational ecology.* Oxford: Oxford University Press.

Evernden, N. 1992. *The social creation of nature*. Baltimore: The Johns Hopkins University Press.

Fatton, R. Jr. 1992. *Predatory rule: State and civil society in Africa*. Boulder: Lynne Rienner.

Fitzjohn, T. 1993. *The Mkomazi Project: Field Director's Report and Trustee's Report of the Friends of Mkomazi Visit*. London: The George Adamson Wildlife Preservation Trust.

—— 1994. 'Speech to the Royal Geographic Society'.

Fitzjohn, T. and K. Ellis 1992a. 'Wild Dog Conference', *The Mkomazi Project Newsletter,* No. 5: 6–7.

—— 1992b. 'Abroad to Fundraise', *The Mkomazi Project Newsletter*, No. 5: 8–11.

Fosbrooke, H.A. 1992. 'Consultant's report to the IIED'. Unpublished report.

Galaty, J.G. 1994. 'Ha(l)ving land in common: The subdivision of Maasai group ranches in Kenya', *Nomadic Peoples*, 34–35:109–22.

George Adamson Wildlife Preservation Trust 1994. *Mkomazi Game Reserve: An appeal by the George Adamson Wildlife Preservation Trust*. London: The George Adamson Wildlife Preservation Trust.

Haas, P.M. 1989. 'Do regimes matter? Epistemic communities and Mediterranean pollution control', *International Organization,* Vol. 43 No. 3: 377–403.

Haas, P.M., R.O. Keohane and M.A. Levy (ed.) 1993. *Institutions for the earth: Sources of effective environmental protection*. Cambridge: The MIT Press.

Harbeson, J.W., D. Rothchild and N. Chazan (eds.) 1994. *Civil society and the state in Africa*. Boulder: Lynne Rienner.

Hartley, D. 1996. 'Why you can't make an omelette without breaking eggs', *Miombo*, Sept. Technical supplement.

Homewood, K.M. and W.A. Rodgers 1991. *Maasailand ecology: Pastoralist development and wildlife conservation in Ngorongoro, Tanzania*. Cambridge: Cambridge University Press.

Huntington, S.P. 1968. *Political order in changing societies*. New Haven: Yale University Press.

Hyden, G. 1980. *Beyond Ujamaa in Tanzania: Underdevelopment and an uncaptured peasantry*. Berkeley: University of California Press.

Ibeun, J.S. 1976. 'A management proposal for Mkomazi Game Reserve'. Unpublished MWEKA College dissertation, Moshi, Tanzania.

IIED 1994. *Whose Eden?* London: International Institute for Environment and Development, IIED.

Juma, I. 1996. 'Pastoralists preserve Mkomazi Game Reserve', *Business Times*, 26 April–3 May, 9.

Kimambo, I.N. 1996. 'Environmental control and hunger in the mountains and plains of North-eastern Tanzania'. In G. Maddox, J. Giblin and I.N. Kimambo (eds.), *Custodians of the land: Ecology and culture in the history of Tanzania*. London: James Currey.

Kiondo, A.S.Z. 1994. 'The new politics of local development in Tanzania'. In P. Gibbon (ed.), *The new local level politics in East Africa: Studies on Uganda, Tanzania and Kenya*. Uppsala: Scandinavian Institute of African Studies.

Kiser, L.L. and E. Ostrom 1982. 'The three worlds of action: A metatheoretical synthesis of institutional approaches'. In E. Ostrom (ed.), *Strategies of political inquiry*. Beverly Hills: Sage Publications.

Kiwasila, H. 1995. 'Upgrading thesis, UCL'. Unpublished report.

—— 1996. 'Mkomazi Game Reserve village profile. A socio-economic study'. Unpublished report.

Lane, C.R. 1991. *Alienation of Barabaig pasture land: Policy implications for pastoral development in Tanzania*. London: International Institute for Environment and Development.

Lemarchand, R. 1972. 'Political clientelism and ethnicity in Tropical Africa', *American Political Science Review*, Vol. 66:68–90.

Lewis, D. and N. Carter (eds.) 1993. *Voices from Africa: Local perspectives on conservation*. Washington, DC: World Wildlife Fund.

Lindsay, W.K. 1987. 'Integrating parks and pastoralists: some lessons from Amboseli'. In D. Anderson and R. Grove (ed.), *Conservation in Africa: People, policies and practice.* Cambridge: Cambridge University Press.

Lutz, C.A. and J.L. Collins 1993. *Reading National Geographic.* Chicago: University of Chicago Press.

Mangubulli, M.J.J. 1992. 'Mkomazi Game Reserve—A recovered pearl', *Kakakuona,* Vol. 4 No. 1:11–13.

March, J.G. and J.P. Olson 1989. *Rediscovering institutions.* New York: The Free Press.

McCormick, J. 1993. 'International nongovernmental organizations: Prospects for a global environmental movement'. In S. Kamieniecki (ed.), *Environmental politics in the international arena: Movements, parties, organizations, and policy.* Albany, NY: State University of New York Press.

Mduma, S.R. 1988. 'Mkomazi Game Reserve: Dangers and recommended measures for its survival', *Miombo,* Vol. 2 (Dec.):17–19.

Migdal, J. 1988. *Strong societies and weak states.* Princeton: Princeton University Press.

MS-Danish Association for International Co-operation 1996. *Annual Report, 1996: MS-Tanzania.* Dar es Salaam, Tanzania: Semezana Production Service.

Msekwa, P. 1977. *Towards party supremacy.* Arusha, Tanzania: Eastern Africa Publications Ltd.

Mustafa, K. 1995. 'Eviction of pastoralists from the Mkomazi Game Reserve. A statement'. Unpublished report, IIED, London.

Mwaikusa, J.T. 1993. 'Community rights and land use policies in Tanzania: The case of pastoralist communities', *Journal of African Law,* Vol. 37 No. 2:144–63.

Neumann, R.P. 1995. 'Local challenges to global agendas: Conservation, economic liberalization and the pastoralist rights movement in Tanzania', *Antipode,* Vol. 27 No. 4: 363–82.

Nordlinger, E. 1987. 'Taking the state seriously'. In M. Weiner and S. Huntington (eds.), *Understanding political development.* Boston: Little, Brown, and Company.

Okumu, J.J. and F. Holmquist 1984. 'Party and party-state relations'. In J.D. Barkan (ed.), *Politics and public policy in Kenya and Tanzania,* revised edition. New York: Praeger Publishers.

Olson, M. 1965. *The logic of collective action.* Cambridge, Mass: Harvard University Press.

Parker, I.S.C. and A.L. Archer 1970. 'The status of elephant, other wildlife and cattle in Mkomazi Game Reserve with management recommendations'. A Wildlife Services Ltd Report to the Tanzanian Government. Unpublished report.

Parkipuny, M.S. 1989. 'Pastoralism, conservation and development in the Greater Serengeti Region'. *Ngorongoro Conservation and Development Project Occasional Paper No. 1.* Nairobi, Kenya: IUCN Eastern Africa Regional Office.

Potnanski, T. 1994. *Property concepts, herding patterns and management of natural resources among the Ngorongoro and Salei Maasai of Tanzania.* London: IIED.

Rosenau, J.N. 1990. *Turbulence in world politics.* Princeton: Princeton University Press.

Rothchild, D. and N. Chazan (ed.) 1988. *The precarious balance: State and society in Africa.* Boulder: Westview Press.

Saning'o, M. and A. Heidenreich 1996. 'Rare land rights victory brings new hope to the Maasai', *EcoNews Africa,* Vol. 7 No. 4:1–2.

Schneider, A. and H. Ingram 1993. 'Social construction of target populations: Implications for politics and policy', *American Political Science Review,* Vol. 87 No. 2:334–47.

Scoones, I. (ed.) 1994. *Living with Uncertainty: New directions in pastoral development in Africa.* London: Intermediate Technology Publications.

Sembony, G. 1988. 'Mkomazi shall not die'. *Malihai Clubs Newsletter.*

Simons, H. and T. Nicolasen 1994. 'Outreach programme for the Mkomazi Project'. In N. Leader-Williams, J.A. Kayera and G.L. Overton (ed.), *Community-based conservation in Tanzania.* PAWM, Department of Wildlife, Dar es Salaam.

Turner, J.B. 1970. 'A discussion of Wildlife Services Ltd'. Report to the Tanzanian Government. Unpublished document.

Watson, R. 1991. 'Mkomazi—restoring Africa', *Swara,* Vol. 14:14–16.

Western, D. and R.M. Wright (eds.) 1994. *Natural connections: Perspectives in community-based conservation.* Washington, DC: Island Press.

Wunsch, J.S. and D. Oluwu (eds.) 1990. *The failure of the centralized state: Institutions and self-governance in Africa.* Boulder: Westview Press.

Young, C. 1986. 'Nationalism, ethnicity and class in Africa: A retrospective', *Cahiers Etudes Africaines,* Vol. 26:421–95.

Ethnic groups and the globalization process—Reflections on the Amazonian groups of Peru from a human ecological perspective

Arévalo, V.G. 1994. *Medicina indigena, las plantas medicinales y su beneficio en la salud, Shipibo-Conibo.* Lima: Edicion AIDESEP.

Aroca, J.W. Ardito and L. Maury. 1993. *Nueva constitucion; el problema de la tierra,* Centro Amazonico de Antropologia y Aplicacion Practica.

Baer, G. 1992. 'The one intoxicated by tobacco, Matsigenka Shamanism', in E. Jean Matteson Langdon and Gerhard Baer (ed.), *Portals of power, Shamanism in South America,* pp. 79–100.

Barth, F. (ed.) 1969. *Ethnic groups and boundaries,* Oslo: Oslo University Press.

—— 1994. 'Enduring and emerging issues in the analysis of ethnicity', in Hans Vermeulen and Cora Govers (ed.), *The anthropology of ethnicity, beyond ethnic groups and boundaries,* Amsterdam: Het Spinhuis.

Boischio, A.D. Henshel 1996. 'Methylmercury exposure and fish lore among an indigenous population along the Madeira River, Amazon', in M. Follér, L.O. Hansson (ed.), *Human ecology and health: Adaptation to a changing world,* Göteborg: Göteborg University, pp. 118–34.

Boyden, S. 1987. *Western civilization in biological perspective.* Oxford,Clarendon Press.

—— 1993. 'Human ecology and biohistory: Conceptual approaches to understanding human situations in the biosphere', in D. Steiner and M. Nauser (ed.), *Human ecology, fragments of anti-fragmentary views of the world,* London: Routledge, pp. 31–46.

Buzan, B. 1991. *People, states and fear: An agenda for international security studies in the post-Cold War era.* New York: Harvester Wheatsheaf.

Chirif, T.A.C. and B. Mora 1976. *Atlas de Comunidades Nativas,* SINAMOS Peru.

Commission on Developing Countries and Global Change, 1992. *For Earth's Sake,* Ottawa: IDRC.

Crosby, A.W. 1986. *Ecological imperialism: The biological expansion of Europe, 900–1900.* Cambridge: Cambridge University Press.

DeBoer, W.R. 1981. 'Buffer zones in the cultural ecology of aboriginal Amazonia: An ethnohistorical approach'. *American Antiquity* Vol. 46 No. 2: 364–77.

Elsass, P. 1992. *Strategies for survival: The psychology of cultural resilience in ethnic minorities,* New York: New York University Press.

Field, L.W. 1994. 'Who are the Indians? Reconceptualizing indigenous identity, resistance, and the role of social science in Latin America', *Latin American Research Review* Vol. 29 No. 3: 237–48.

Follér, M. 1990. *Environmental changes and human health: A study of the Shipibo-Conibo in Eastern Peru.* Humanekologiska Skrifter 8, Göteborg University.

—— 1995. 'Future health of indigenous peoples: A human ecology view and the case of the Amazonian Shipibo-Conibo', *Futures,* Vol. 27, No. 9/10, pp. 1005–23.

—— 1997, 'Protecting nature in Amazonia. Local knowledge as a counterpoint to globalization'. *Cross-cultural protection of nature and the environment,* F. Arler and I. Svennevig (ed.), Odense University Press, Denmark, pp. 134–47.

Follér, M. and M.J. Garrett. 1996. 'Modernization, health and local knowledge: The case of the cholera epidemic among the Shipibo-Conibo'. In M. Follér and L.O. Hansson (ed.), *Human ecology and health: Adaptation to a changing world,* Göteborg: Göteborg University, pp. 135–66.

178

Gray, A. 1986. '*And after the gold rush? Human rights and self development among the Amarakaeri of Southeastern Peru*, IWGIA Document 55.

—— 1994. 'Territorial defence as the basis for indigenous self development' (editorial) *Indigenous Affairs/International Work Group for Indigenous Affairs* 4: 2–3.

Hames, R.B. and W.T. Vickers (ed.) 1983. *Adaptive responses of native Amazonians*, Studies in Anthropology, New York: Academic Press.

Heras, J. 1975. *Historia de las misiones del convento de Santa Rosa de Ocopa*, Editorial Milla Batres.

Hettne, B. 1992. *Etniska konflikter och internationella relationer*, Lund: Studentlitteratur.

Hylland Eriksen, T. 1993. *Ethnicity and nationalism, anthropological perspectives*, London: Pluto Press.

—— 1994. *Kulturelle Veikryss: Essays om kreolisering*, Oslo: Universitetsforlaget.

INEI.1992–3. *Region Ucayali Compendio Estadistico*, Table 2.6.

Langlais, R. 1995. *Reformulating security: A case study from Arctic Canada* Human-ekologiska Skrifter 13, Göteborg University.

Lawrence, R.1993. 'Can human ecology provide an integrative framework? The contribution of structuration theory to contemporary debate', In D.Steiner and M. Nauser (ed.), *Human ecology, fragments of anti-fragmentary views of the world*, pp. 213–28.

Matteson Langdon, J. and G. Baer (ed.) 1992. *Portals of power: Shamanism in South America*, Albuquerque: University of New Mexico Press.

Maybury-Lewis, D. 1992. *Millenium, tribal wisdom and the modern world*, New York.

McNeill, W. 1976. *Plagues and peoples*, Middlesex: Penguin.

Moran, E.F. 1979. *Human adaptability: An introduction to ecological anthropology*, North Scituate, Massachusetts: Duxbury Press.

—— 1993. *Through Amazonian eyes: the human ecology of Amazonian populations*, Iowa City: University of Iowa Press.

Regan, J. 1983. *Hacia la Tierra sin Mal: Estudio de la religión del pueblo en la Amazonza.* Iquitos: Tomo I. CETA.

Ribeiro, D. 1971. *The Americas and civilization*, London.

Rosengren, D. 1987. *In the eyes of the beholder: Leadership and the docial construction of power and dominance among the Matsigenka of the Peruvian Amazon.* Etnologiska studier 39, Göteborg.

Santos, R, C. Coimbra, N. Flowers and S. Gugelmin. 1996, 'Human Ecology and Health in the Context of Change: the Xavante Indians of Mato Grosso, Brazil'. In M. Follér, L.O. Hansson (ed.), *Human ecology and health: Adaptation to a changing world*, Göteborg: Göteborg University, pp. 94–117.

Sponsel, L. 1986, 'Amazon ecology and adaptation', *Annual Review of Anthropology*, Vol. 15: pp. 67–97.

Steiner, D. and M. Nauser (ed.) 1993. *Human ecology; Fragments of anti-fragmentary views of the world*, London: Routledge.

Stern-Pettersson, M. 1993, 'Reading the project, "Global Civilization: Challenges for sovereignty, democracy, and security"' *Futures*, Vol. 25 No 2.

Todorov, T. 1982, *The conquest of America: The question of the other*. New York: Harper Colophon Books.

Tournon, J. 1994a. 'Como los Shipibo-Conibo nombran y clasifican los animales'. *Anthropologica*, Vol. 11: 93–108.

—— 1994b. 'Los Shipibo-Conibo y la fauna acuática'. *Anthropologica*, Vol. 12: 29–61.

Urban, G. and J. Sherzer (ed.) 1991. *Nation states and Indians in Latin America.* Austin: University of Texas Press.

Viveiro de Castro, E. 1996, 'Images of nature and society in Amazonian ethnology', *Annual Review of Anthropology*, vol. 25: 179–200.

Waters, M. 1995. *Globalization*, London: Routledge.

World Resources Institute with UNEP and UNDP. 1990. *World Resources 1990–91.* Oxford: Oxford University Press.

Increasing competition, expanding strategies—Wage work and resource utilization among the Paliyans of South India

Barnard, A. 1983. 'Contemporary hunter-gatherers: Current theoretical issues in ecology and social organisation', *Annual Review of Anthropology*, Vol. 12:193–214.

—— 1992. *The Kalahari debate: A bibliographical essay*. Edinburgh: Centre for African Studies, Edinburgh University.

Baxter, P.T.W. 1972. 'Absence makes the heart grow fonder. Some suggestions why witchcraft accusations are rare among East African pastoralists'. In M. Gluckman (ed.), *The allocation of responsibility*. Manchester: Manchester University Press, pp. 163–91.

Bender, B. and B. Morris 1988. 'Twenty years of history, evolution and social change in gatherer-hunter studies'. In T. Ingold, D. Riches and J. Woodburn (eds.), *Hunters and gatherers 1: History, evolution and social change*. Oxford Publishers Ltd., pp. 4–14.

Bharati, S. 1993. 'Spirit possession and healing practices in a South Indian fishing community', *Man In India*, Vol. 73 No. 4:343–52.

Bird, N. 1983a. *Conjugal families and single persons: An analysis of the Naiken social system*. PhD thesis, University of Cambridge.

—— 1983b. 'Wage-gathering: Socio-economic changes and the case of the food-gathering Naikens of South India'. In P. Robb (ed.), *Rural South Asia: Linkages, change and development*. Collected papers on South Asia, No. 5. London: Curzon Press, pp. 57–88.

Bird-David, N. 1988. 'Hunters-gatherers and other people—a re-examination'. In T. Ingold, D. Riches and J. Woodburn (eds.), *Hunters and gatherers 1: History, evolution and social change*. Oxford Publishers Ltd., pp. 17–30.

—— 1992. 'Beyond "the hunting and gathering mode of subsistence": Culture-sensitive observations on the Nayaka and other modern hunter-gatherers', *Man*, (N.S.) 27:19–44.

Bourdieu, P. 1977. *Outline of a theory of practice*. Cambridge: Cambridge University Press.

Burch, E. S. Jr. 1994. 'The future of hunter-gatherer research'. In E.S. Burch Jr. and L.J. Ellanna (ed.), *Key issues in hunter-gatherer research*. Oxford Publishers Ltd., pp. 441–55.

D'Andrade, R.G. 1992. 'Schemas and motivation'. In R.G. D'Andrade and C. Strauss (eds.), *Human motives and cultural models*. Cambridge: Cambridge University Press, pp. 23–44.

D'Andrade, R.G. and C. Strauss (eds.) 1992. *Human motives and cultural models*. Cambridge: Cambridge University Press.

Dahmen, F. Rev. 1908. 'The Paliyans, a hill-tribe of the Palni Hills (South India)', *Anthropos,* Vol. 3:19–31.

Dumont, L. 1986. *A South Indian subcaste: Social organization and religion of the Pramalai Kallar*. Delhi: Oxford University Press.

Fawcett, W.B. Jr. 1991. 'Comments to P.M. Gardner "Foragers' Pursuit of Individual Autonomy"', *Current Anthropology*, Vol. 32 No. 5:562–3.

Fuller, C.J. 1992. *The camphor flame: Popular Hinduism and society in India*. New Delhi: Viking Penguin India.

Gardner, P.M. 1965. *Ecology and social structure in refugee populations: The Paliyans of South India*. PhD thesis, University of Pennsylvania.

—— 1966. 'Symmetric respect and memorate knowledge: The structure and ecology of individualistic culture', *Southwestern Journal of Anthropology*, Vol. 22:389–415.

—— 1969. 'Paliyan social structure'. In D. Damas (ed.), *Contributions to anthropology: Band societies*. National Museums of Canada Bulletin 228. Ottawa, pp. 153–63.

—— 1972. 'The Paliyans'. In M.G. Bicchieri (ed.), *Hunters and gatherers today*. New York: Holt, Rinehart & Wilson, pp. 404–47.

—— 1985. 'Bicultural oscillation as a long-term adaptation to cultural frontiers: Cases and questions', *Human Ecology*, Vol. 13 No. 4:411–32.

—— 1988. 'Pressures for Tamil propriety in Paliyan social organization'. In T. Ingold, D. Riches and J. Woodburn (eds.), *Hunters and gatherers*, Vol. 1:91–106.

—— 1991a. 'Foragers' pursuit of individual autonomy' with Comments, *Current Anthropology*, Vol. 32 No. 5:543–72.

—— 1991b. 'Pragmatic meanings of possession in Paliyan shamanism', *Anthropos*, Vol. 86:367–84.

—— 1993. 'Dimensions of subsistence foraging in South India', *Ethnology*, Vol. 32 No. 2:109–44.

Geertz, C. 1973. *The interpretation of culture*. New York: Basic Books.

Grinker, R.R. 1991. 'Comments to P.M. Gardner "Foragers' pursuit of individual autonomy"', *Current Anthropology*, Vol. 32 No. 5:563.

Gudeman, S. and A. Rivera 1990. *Conversations in Colombia: The domestic economy in life and text*. Cambridge: Cambridge University Press.

Guenther, M. 1991. 'Comments to P.M. Gardner "Foragers' pursuit of individual autonomy"', *Current Anthropology*, Vol. 32 No. 5:563–4.

Harper, E. 1957. 'Shamanism in South India', *Southwestern Journal of Anthropology*, Vol. 13:267–87.

Kooiman, D. 1992. 'Plantations in Southern Asia: Indigenous plants and foreign implantations', *South Asia*, Vol. 9 No. 1:53–79.

Larsson, M. and C. Norström 1993. *Central decisions—local activities: Historical factors behind deforestation in Western Ghats, Tamil Nadu, India*. Stockholm: Stockholm University, Department of Social Anthropology.

Lee, R.B. 1992. 'Art, science, or politics? The crisis in hunter-gatherer studies', *American Anthropologist*, Vol. 94:31–54.

Lee, R.B. and M. Guenther 1991. 'Oxen or onions? The search for trade (and truth) in the Kalahari', *Current Anthropology*, Vol. 32 No. 5:592–601.

Long, N. 1989. 'Conclusion: Theoretical reflections on actor, structure and interface'. In N. Long (ed.), *Encounters at the interface: A perspective on social discontinuities in rural development*. Wageningse Sociologische Studies 27. Wageningen: Agriculture University, pp. 221–43.

Manndorff, H. 1960. 'Notes on some primitive hunting tribes of southern and central India', *Bulletin of the international committee on urgent anthropological and ethnological research*, No. 3.

Milner, M. Jr. 1994. *Status and sacredness: A general theory of status relations and an analysis of Indian culture*. New York: Oxford University Press.

Moffat, M. 1979. *An untouchable community in South India: Structure and continuity*. Princeton: Princeton University Press.

Morris, B. 1982a. *Forest traders: A socio-economic study of the Hill Pandaram*. New Jersey: Athlone Press.

—— 1982b. 'The family, group structuring and trade among South Indian hunter-gatherers'. In E. Leacock and R. Lee (eds.), *Politics and history in band societies*. Cambridge: Cambridge University Press, pp. 171–87.

Nelson, J.H. 1989 (1868). *The Madura country. A manual*, Part I–V. Delhi: Asian Educational Service.

Östör, Á., L. Fruzzetti and S. Barnett (eds.) 1992. *Concepts of person: Kinship, caste and marriage in India*. Delhi: Oxford University Press.

Palni Hills Conservation Council 1986. *Palni Hills National Park*. Kodaikanal.

Pruthi, J.S. 1992 (1976). *Spices and condiments*. New Delhi: National Book Trust.

Ricoeur, P. 1979. 'The model of the text: Meaningful action considered as text'. In P. Rabinow and W.M. Sullivan (ed.), *Interpretive social science: A reader*. Berkeley: University of California.

Scott, J.C. 1985. *Weapons of the weak: Everyday forms of peasant resistance*. New Haven: Yale University Press.

Sherring, M.A. 1975. (1909). *The tribes and castes of the Madras Presidency*. Delhi: Cosmo Publications.

Solway, J.S. and R.B. Lee 1990. 'Foragers, genuine or spurious?', *Current Anthropology*, Vol. 31 No. 2:109–46.

Strauss, C. 1992. 'Models and motives'. In R.G. D'Andrade and C. Strauss (ed.), *Human motives and cultural models*. Cambridge: Cambridge University Press, pp. 1–20.

181

Tamil Nadu Forest Department 1994. *Report of the committee on the formation of a wildlife sanctuary at Kodaikanal.* Madras.

Thurston, E. 1909. 'Paliyans'. In *Castes and tribes of Southern India*, Vol. 5. Madras: Government Press, pp. 461–72.

Uberoi, P. (ed.) 1993. *Family, kinship, and marriage in India.* Delhi: Oxford University Press.

Wilmsen, N.W. and J.R. Denbow 1990. 'Paradigmatic history of San-speaking peoples and current attempts at revision', *Current Anthropology*, Vol. 31 No. 5:489–524.

Winterhalder, B. and E.A. Smith (eds.) 1981. *Hunter-gatherer foraging strategies.* Chicago: University of Chicago Press.

Agroforestry intensification in the Amazon estuary

Altieri, M.A. and S.B. Hecht 1990. *Agroecology and small farm development.* Boston: CRC Press.

Anderson, A.B. 1987. 'Use and management of native palm forest'. In H.L. Gholz (ed.), *Agroforestry: Realities, possibilities and potentials.* Dordrecht: Martinus Nijhoff Publisher.

Anderson, A. 1988. 'Use and management of native forests dominated by *açaí* palm (*Euterpe oleracea*) in the Amazon estuary', *Advances in Economic Botany*, Vol. 6:144–54.

Anderson, A.B. (ed.) 1990. *Alternatives to deforestation: Steps toward sustainable use of the Amazon rain forest.* New York: Columbia University Press.

Anderson, A.B. 1991. 'Forest management strategies by rural inhabitants in the Amazon estuary'. In A. Gomez-Pompa, T.C. Whitmore and M. Hadley (eds.), *Rain forest regeneration and management.* Paris: MAB, Vol. 6, pp. 157–68.

Anderson, A.B. 1992. 'Land-use strategies for successful extractive economies in Amazonia'. In D.C. Nepstad and S. Schwartzman (eds.), *Non-timber products from tropical forests—Evaluation of a conservation and development strategy.* Advances in Economic Botany Vol. 9. New York: New York Botanical Garden.

Anderson, A. et al. 1985. 'Um sistema agroforestal na varzea do estuario Amazonico (Ilha das Oncas, Municipio de Barcarena, Estado do Para)', *Acta Amazonica*, Vol. 15:195–224.

Anderson, A. and E. Iorys 1992. 'The logic of extraction: Resource management and income generation by extractive producers in the Amazon Estuary'. In R. Kent and C. Padoch, *Conservation of neotropical forests.* New York: Columbia University Press.

Anderson, A.B. and M.A.G. Jardim 1989. 'Costs and benefits of floodplain forest management by rural inhabitants in the Amazon estuary: A case study of *açaí* palm production'. In J.O. Browder (ed.), *Fragile lands of Latin America.* Boulder: Westview Press.

Ayres, D.M. 1992. 'History, social organization, identity and outsiders' social classification of the rural population of Amazonian region'. Unpublished PhD dissertation, King's College, Cambridge.

Balle, W. and A. Gely 1989. 'Managed forest succession in Amazonia: The Ka'apor case', *Advances in Economic Botany*, Vol. 7:129–58.

Bates, H.W. 1988. *The naturalist on the River Amazon.* New York: Penguin Books.

Beckerman, S. 1979. 'The abundance of protein in Amazonia: A reply to Gross', *American Anthropologist*, Vol. 81:533–60.

Behrens, C.A. et al. 1994. 'A regional analysis of Bari land-use intensification and its impact on landscape heterogeneity', *Human Ecology*, Vol. 22 No. 3:279–316.

Boserup, E. 1965. *The conditions of agricultural growth: The economics of agrarian change under population pressure.* Chicago: Aldine.

Brondízio E.S. 1996. *Forest farmers: Human and landscape ecology of caboclo populations in the Amazon estuary.* PhD dissertation, School of Public and Environmental Affairs, Indiana University, Bloomington.

Brondízio E.S., E.F. Moran, P. Mausel and Wu Y. 1996. 'Changes in land cover in the Amazon estuary: Integration of thematic mapping with botanical and historical data', *Photogrammetric Engineering and Remote Sensing*, Vol. 62 No. 8:921–29.

Brondízio, E.S. and W.A. Neves 1992. 'A percepcao do ambiente natural por parte de populacoes Caboclas do estuario do Amazonas: uma experiencia piloto atravez do metodo de trilhas pre-fixadas'. In C. Pavan (ed.) *'Uma Estrategia Latino Americana para Amazonia'*, Sao Paulo: Editora Unesp, pp. 167–82.

Brondízio, E.S. and A.D. Siqueira 1997. 'From extractivists to forestry farmers: Changing concepts of caboclo agroforestry in the Amazon estuary', *Research in Economic Anthropology*. Vol. 18:233–279.

Brondízio, E.S., E.F. Moran, P. Mausel and You W. 1993a. 'Dinamica da vegetacao no Baixo Amazonas: Analise temporal do uso da terra integrando imagens Landsat TM, levantamento floristico e dados etnograficos', *Proceedings of the 7th Brazilian Symposium of Remote Sensing*, Vol. II: 38–46, Curitiba, PR.

Brondízio, E.S., E.F. Moran, P. Mausel and You W. 1993b. 'Padroes de assentamento caboclo no baixo Amazonas: Analise temporal de imagens Landsat TM como suporte aos estudos de Ecologia Humana na Amazonia'. *Proceedings of the 7th Brazilian Symposium of Remote Sensing*. Curitiba, May 1993.

Brondízio, E.S., E.F. Moran, P. Mausel and Wu Y. 1994a. 'Land-use change in the Amazon estuary: Patterns of caboclo settlement and landscape management', *Human Ecology*, Vol. 22 No. 3:249–78.

Brondízio, E.S., E.F. Moran, A.D. Siqueira, P. Mausel, Wu Y. and Li Y. 1994b. 'Mapping anthropogenic forest: Using remote sensing in a multi-level approach to estimate production and distribution of managed palm forest (*Euterpe oleracea*) in the Amazon estuary', *International Archives of Photogrammetry and Remote Sensing*, Vol. 30 No. 7a:184–91.

Brookfield, H.C. 1962. 'Local study and comparative method: An example from central New Guinea', *Annals of the Association of American Geographers*, Vol. 52:242–54.

Brush, S.B. 1975. 'Concept of carrying capacity for systems of shifting cultivation', American Anthropologist, Vol. 77:799–811.

Bunker, S.G. 1985. *Underdeveloping the Amazon: Extraction, unequal exchange, and the failure of the modern state*. Chicago: The Chicago University Press.

Calzavara, B.B.G. 1972. 'As possibilidades do açaízeiro no estuario Amazonico', *Boletim da Fundacao de Ciencias Agrarias do Para*, Vol. 5:1–103.

Carneiro, R. 1961. 'Slash-and-burn cultivation among the Kuikuru and its implications for cultural development in the Amazon basin'. In J. Wilbert (ed.), *The evolution of horticultural systems in native South America*. Caracas.

Chibnik, M. 1991. 'Quasi-ethnic groups in Amazonia', *Ethnology*, Vol. 30:167–82.

—— 1994. *Risky Rivers*. Tucson: The University of Arizona Press.

Clarke, W.C. 1966. 'From extensive to intensive shifting cultivation: A succession from New Guinea', *Ethnology*, Vol. 5 No. 4:347–59.

—— 1976. 'Maintenance of agriculture and human habitats within the tropical forest ecosystem', *Human Ecology*, Vol. 4 No. 3:247–59.

Conant, F. 1990. '1990 and beyond: Satellite remote sensing and ecological anthropology'. In E. Moran (ed.), *The ecosystem approach in anthropology. From concept to practice*. Ann Arbor: The University of Michigan Press.

Conklin, H.C. 1957. *Hanunoo agriculture: A report of an integral system of shifting cultivation in the Philippines*. Rome: FAO.

Cunha, E. 1941. *A Margem da Historia*. Porto: Lello e Irmao.

Dale, V. et al. 1993. 'Cause and effects of land-use change in central Rondonia, Brazil', *Photogrammetric engineering and remote sensing*, June (6):997–1005.

Denevan, W. 1984. 'Ecological heterogeneity and horizontal zonation of agriculture in the Amazon floodplain'. In M. Schimink and C.H. Wood (ed.), *Frontiers expansion in Amazonia*. Gainsville: University of Florida Press.

183

Denevan, W. and C. Padoch (eds.) 1987. 'Swidden-fallow agroforestry in the Peruvian Amazon', *Advances in Economic Botany*, Vol. 5. New York: The New York Botanical Garden.

Ellen, R. 1982. *Environment subsistence and system*. Cambridge: Cambridge University Press.

FIBGE 1988, 1990, 1991. *Producao da estracao vegetal e da silvicultura*. Depto. Agropecuario, Diretoria de Pesquisas.

Geertz, C. 1963. *Agricultural involution: The process of ecological change in Indonesia*. Berkeley: University of California Press.

Guillet, D. 1987. 'Agricultural intensification and deintensification in Lari, Colca Valley, Southern Peru', *Research in Economic Anthropology*, Vol. 8:201–24.

Hecht, S.B. 1992. 'Valuing land-uses in Amazonia: colonist agriculture, cattle and petty extraction in comparative perspective'. In K.H. Redford and C. Padoch (ed.), *Conservation of neotropical forests*. New York: Columbia University Press, pp. 379–99.

—— 1993. 'The logic of livestock and deforestation in Amazonia', *BioScience*, Vol. 43 No. 10:687–95.

Hecht, S.B., A.B. Anderson and P. May 1988. 'The subsidy from nature: shifting cultivation, successional palm forests, and rural development', *Human Organization*, Vol. 47 No. 1:25–35.

Hiraoka, M. 1985. 'Zonation of mestizo riverine farming systems in north-east Peru', *National Geographic Research*, Vol. 2 No. 3:354–71.

—— 1989. 'Agricultural systems on the floodplains of the Peruvian Amazon'. In J.O. Browder (ed.), *Fragile lands of Latin America*. Boulder: Westview Press.

—— 1992. 'Caboclo and ribereno resource management in Amazonia: A review'. In R. Kent and C. Padoch (ed.), *Conservation of neotropical forests*. New York: Columbia University Press.

—— 1994. 'The use and management of 'Miriti' (*Mauritia flexuosa*): Palms among the ribeirinhos along the Amazon estuary'. Paper presented at *Diversity, Development and Conservation of Amazonian Floodplain*, Dec. 12–14, Macapa, Amapa, Brazil.

Homma, A. 1993. *Extrativismo vegetal na Amazonia: Limites e oportunidades*. Brasilia, D.F.: Embrapa.

Jardim, M.A.G. 1991. 'Aspectos da biologia reprodutiva de uma populacao natural de açaízeiro (*Euterpe oleracea*) no estuario Amazonico'. Unpublished Master Dissertation, Escola Superior de Agricultura 'Luiz de Queiroz', University of Sao Paulo, S.P., Brazil.

Jardim, M. and A. Anderson 1987. 'Manejo de populacoes nativas de Açaízeiro no estuario Amazonico–Resultados preliminares', *Boletim de Pesquisa Florestal*, Vol. 15:1–18.

Jardim, M.A.G. and P.Y. Kageyama 1994. 'Fenologia de floração e frutificação em população natural de açaizeiro (*Euterpe oleracea*) no estuário Amazônico' ('Flowering and fruiting phenology of a natural population of *açaí* palm in the Amazon estuary'), *IPEF*, Vol. 47:62–5.

Lathrap, D. 1970. *The upper Amazon*. London: Thames and Hudson.

Lima, R.R. 1956. 'Agricultura nas varzea do estuario do Amazonas', *Boletim Tecnico do Instituto Agronomico do Norte*, Vol. 33:1–164.

Lopes, A.V.F. J.M.S. Souza and B.B.G. Calvazara 1982. *Aspectos economicos do açaízeiro*. Belem: Sudam.

LUCC 1996. 'Land-use and land cover change. Science/research plan'. IGBP Report No. 35, HDP Report 7, Stockholm.

Mausel P., Wu Y., Li Y., E. Moran and E.S. Brondízio 1993. 'Spectral identification of successional stages following deforestation in the Amazon', *Geocarto International*, Vol. 8 No. 4, 10pp.

McGrath, D. 1987. 'The role of biomass in shifting cultivation', *Human Ecology*, Vol. 15 No. 2:221–42.

Meggers, B. 1954. 'Environment limitations on the development of culture', *American Anthropology*, Vol. 56:801–24.

—— 1971. *Amazonia: man and culture in a counterfeit paradise*. Chicago: Aldine.

Meggers, B. and C. Evans 1957. *Archeological investigations at the mouth of the Amazon*. Bureau of American Ethnology, Bulletin 167.

Moran, E. 1974. 'The adaptive system of the Amazonian caboclo'. In C. Wagley (ed.), *Man in the Amazon*. Gainesville: The University of Florida Press.

—— 1989. 'Models of native and folk adaptation in the Amazonia'. In D. Posey and W. Balee (eds.), *Resources management in Amazonia: Indigenous and folk strategies. Advances in Economic Botany*, Vol. 7, pp. 22–9.

—— 1993. 'Deforestation and land-use in the Brazilian Amazon', *Human Ecology*, Vol. 21 No. 1:1–21.

—— (ed.) 1995. *The comparative analysis of human societies: Toward common standards for data collection and reporting*. Boulder: Lynne Rienner Publishers.

Moran, E.F., E.S. Brondízio and P. Mausel 1994. 'Secondary succession and land-use in the Amazon', *National Geographic Research & Exploration*, Vol. 10 No. 4:456–76.

Moran, E.F., E.S. Brondízio, P. Mausel and Li H.Y. 1993. 'Assinaturas espectrais diferenciando etapas de sucessao secundaria no leste Amazonico', *Anais do 7@ Simposio Brasileiro de Sensoriamento Remoto*, Vol. II: 202–9, Curitiba, PR.

Moran, E.F., E.S. Brondízio, P. Mausel and You W. 1994. 'Deforestation in Amazonia: Land-use change from ground and space level perspective', *Bioscience*, Vol. 44 No. 5: 329–39.

Murrieta, R.S. 1994. 'Diet and subsistence: Changes in three caboclo populations on Marajo Island, Amazonia, Brazil'. Unpublished Master Dissertation, University of Colorado, Boulder.

Murrieta, R.S.S., E.S. Brondízio, A.D. Siqueira and E. Moran 1989. 'Estrategias de Subsistencia de Uma Populacao Ribeirinha da Ilha de Marajo, Brasil', *Boletim do Museu Paraense Emilio Goeldi, Serie Antropologia*, Vol. 5 No. 2:147–63.

—— 1992. 'Estrategias de Subsistencia da Comunidade de Praia Grande, Ilha de Marajo, Brasil', *Boletim do Museu Paraense Emilio Goeldi, Serie Antropologia*, Vol. 8 No. 2:185–201.

NASA 1990. *Applications of space-age technology in anthropology*. Conference Proceedings, Nov. 28, John C. Stennis Space Center, Mississippi.

National Research Council 1992. *Global environmental change: understanding the human dimension*. Edited by P.C. Stern, O. Young and D. Druckman. Washington, D.C.: National Academic Press.

Nepstad, D.C. and S. Schwartzman (eds.) 1992. *Non-timber products from tropical forests—Evaluation of a conservation and development strategy*. Advances in Economic Botany, Vol. 9. New York: New York Botanical Garden.

Netting, R.M. 1963. *Kofyar agriculture: A study in the cultural ecology of a West African people*. PhD dissertation, University of Chicago.

—— 1965. 'Household organization and intensive agriculture: The Kofyar case', *Africa*, Vol. 35:422–9.

—— 1993. *Smallholders, householders—Farm families and the ecology of intensive, sustainable agriculture*. Stanford: Stanford University Press.

Neves, W.A. 1992. 'Antropologia ecologica de populacoes ribeirinhas do estuario do Amazonas: Subsistencia e adapatacao', *Relatorio Cientifico*, CNPq, Brazil.

Nugent, S. 1993. *Amazonian caboclo society. An essay on invisibility and peasant economy*. Oxford: BERG, Province.

Nye, P.H. and D.J. Greenland 1960. 'The soil under shifting cultivation', *Commonwealth Bureau of Soils*, Harpendern, Technical Communication 51:1–156.

O'Neill, R.V., D.L. DeAngelis, J.B. Waide and T.F.H. Allen 1986. *The hierarchical concept of ecosystems*. Monographs in Population Biology 23. Princeton: Princeton University Press.

Padoch, C.1989. 'Production and profit in agroforestry practices of native and riberено farmers in the lowland Peruvian Amazon'. In J.O. Browder (ed.), *Fragile lands of Latin America*. Boulder: Westview Press.

—— 1992. 'Marketing of non-timber forest products in western Amazonia: General observations and research priorities'. In D.C. Nepstad and S. Schwartzman (eds.), op.cit.

185

Parker, E. 1985. 'Caboclization: The transformation of the Amerindian in Amazonia, 1615–1800', *Studies in Third World Societies*, Vol. 29.

Peters, C. 1992. 'The ecology and economics of oligarchic Amazonian forests', *Advances in Economic Botany*, Vol. 9:15–22.

Peters, C., A. Gentry and R. Mendelsohn 1989. 'Valuation of an Amazon rainforest', *Nature*, No. 339:656–7.

Pires, J.M. 1973. *Tipos de vegetacao da Amazonia*. Belem: Museu Paraense Emilio Goeldi.

Plotkin, M. and L. Famolare (ed.) 1992. *Sustainable harvest and marketing of rain forest products*. Washington, D.C.: Island Press.

Posey, D.A. 1985. 'Indigeneous management of tropical forest ecosystems: The case of the Kayapo Indians of the Brazilian Amazon', *Agroforestry System*, Vol. 3:139–58.

Prance, G.T. 1980. 'A terminologia dos tipos de florestas Amazonicas sujeitas a inundacoes', *Acta Amazonica*, Vol. 10:495–504.

RADAM 1974. *Levantamento de recursos naturais*. Rio de Janeiro.

Roosevelt, A.C. 1989. 'Resource management in Amazonia before the conquest: Beyond ethnographic projection', *Advances in Economic Botany*, Vol. 7:30–62.

——— 1991. *Moundbuilders of the Amazon: The geophysical archeology on Marajo Island, Brazil*. New York: Academic Press.

Ross, E. 1978. 'The evolution of the Amazon peasantry', *Journal of Latin American Studies*, Vol. 10 No. 2:193–218.

Shukla, J., C. Nobre and P. Sellers 1990. 'Amazon deforestation and climate change', *Science*, No. 247:1322–5.

Siqueira, A.D., E.S. Brondízio, R.S.S. Murrieta, H.P. Silva, W.A. Neves and R.B. Vietler (in press), 'Estrategias de subsistencia da populacao ribeirinha do igarape do paricatuba, Ilha de Marajo, Brasil', *Boletim do Museu Paraense Emilio Goeldi, Serie Antropologia*.

Skole, D. and C.J. Tucker 1993. 'Tropical deforestation and habitat fragmentation in the Amazon: Satellite data from 1978 to 1988', *Science*, No. 260:1905–10.

Slobodkin, L.B., D.B. Botkin, B. Maguire, B. Moore and H. Morowitz 1980. 'On the epistemiology of ecosystem analysis', *Estuarine Perspectives*.

Spruce, R. 1908. *Notes of a botanist on the Amazon and Andes*, edited and condensed by Alfred Russel Wallace. London: Macmillan.

Strudwick, J. and G.L. Sobel 1988. 'Uses of *Euterpe oleracea* in the Amazon estuary, Brazil', *Advances in Economic Botany*, Vol. 6:225–53.

Turner, B.L. and S.B. Brush (ed.) 1987. *Comparative farming systems*. New York: The Guildford Press.

Turner, B.L. and W.E. Doolittle 1978. 'The concept and measure of agricultural intensity', *Professional Geographer*, Vol. 30 No. 3:297–301.

Turner, B.L., R.Q. Hanham and A.V. Portararo 1977. 'Population pressure and agricultural intensity', *Annals of the Association of American Geographers*, Vol. 67 No. 3:384–96.

Vasey, D.E. 1979. 'Population and agricultural intensity in the humid Tropics', *Human Ecology*, Vol. 7 No. 3:269–83.

Vayda, A.P. 1983. 'Progressive contextualization: Methods for research in human ecology', *Human Ecology*, Vol. 11 No. 3:265–81.

Wagley, C. 1953. *Amazon town*. New York: Macmillan.

Wallace, A.R. 1853. *Palm trees of the Amazon and their uses*. London: J.van Voorst.

Weinstein, B. 1983. *The Amazon rubber boom, 1850–1920*. Stanford: Stanford University Press.

Wilken, G.C. 1987. *Good farmers. Traditional agricultural resource management in Mexico and Central America*. Berkeley: University of California Press.

Wilkie, D. 1990. Protecting rain forests and foragers' rights using Landsat imagery. In *Applications of Space-Age Technology in Anthropology*. Conference Proceedings, Nov. 28, John C. Stennis Space Center, NASA, Mississippi.

Rules, norms, organizations and actual practices—Land and water management in the Ruaha River basin, Tanzania

Agrawal, A. 1995. 'Dismantling the divide between indigenous and scientific knowledge', *Development and Change*, Vol. 26:413–39.

Armstrong, A. 1992. *Struggling over scarce resources. Women and maintenance in Southern Africa*. University of Zimbabwe.

Askvik, S. 1993. 'Institutional-building and planned organisational change in development assistance', *Forum for Development Studies*, Vol. 2:149–65.

Berry, S. 1993. *No condition is permanent: The social dynamics of agrarian change in Sub-Saharan Africa*. Madison: University of Wisconsin Press.

Boesen, J. 1994. 'Local level participation in land and water resources management in Rufiji River basin, Tanzania'. In J. Lundqvist and T. Jønch-Clausen (eds.), *Putting Dublin/Agenda 21 into Practice. Lessons and new approaches in water and land management*. Produced for the Special Session at VIIIth IWRA World Congress in Cairo, Nov. 21–25, 1994. Linköping: Linköping University, Department of Water and Environmental Studies, pp. 17–31.

Bradbury, M. et al. 1995. *Working with pastoralist NGOs and land conflict in Tanzania*. IIED (London: International Institute for Environment and Development.)

Burton, J. and F. Dukes 1990. *Conflict: practices in management, settlement and resolution*. New York: St. Martin's Press.

Chanock, M. 1982. 'Making customary law: Men, women and courts in colonial Northern Rhodesia'. In M.J. Hay and M. Wright (eds.), *African women and the law: Historical perspectives*. Boston University. Papers on Africa, VII, pp. 53–67.

Charnley, S. 1994. 'Cattle, commons and culture: The political ecology of environmental change on a Tanzania rangeland'. Unpublished doctoral dissertation, Stanford University.

—— 1996. 'Environmental problems and cultural conflict: A Tanzanian case study'. Draft. Energy and Resources Group, University of California, Berkeley.

Ciriacy-Wantrup, S. and R. Bishop 1975. '"Common Property" as a concept in natural resources policy', *Natural Resources Journal*, No. 15 (Oct.):715–27.

Cousins, B. 1996. 'Conflict management for multiple resource users in pastoralist and agro-pastoralist contexts'. *Programme for Land and Agrarian Studies*, School of Government, University of Western Cape.

Gulliver, P.H. 1957. 'Land tenure and social change among the Nyakyusa. An essay in applied anthropology in South-West Tanganyika'. *East African Studies*, No. 11.

—— 1961. 'Land shortage, social change, and social conflict in East Africa', *The Journal of Conflict Resolution*, Vol. 5 No. 1.

Gunnarsson, C. 1991. 'What is new and what is institutional in the new institutional economics? An essay on old and new institutionalism and the role of the state in developing countries', *Scandinavian Economic History Review*, Vol. 39 No. 1.

Kiwasila, H. and R. Odgaard 1992. 'Socio-cultural aspects of forest management in the Udzungwa'. Prepared for Danida. Centre for Development Research, Copenhagen.

Knudsen, A.J. 1995. 'Living with the commons: Local institutions for natural resource management'. Bergen: *Chr. Michelsen Institute Report R: 1995:2*

Koponen, J. 1988. *People and production in late pre-colonial Tanzania*. Helsinki.

—— 1995. *Development for exploitation. German colonial policies in mainland Tanzania 1884–1914*. Pieksämäki: Raamattutalo.

Lane, C. 1990. 'Barabaig natural resource management: Sustainable land use under threat of destruction'. *UNRISD Discussion Paper 12*. Geneva: United Nations Research Institute for Social Development.

—— 1993. 'The state strikes back: Extinguishing customary rights to land in Tanzania'. Unpublished.

Long, N. 1992. 'Introduction'. In N. Long and A. Long (eds.) *Battlefields of knowledge. The interlocking of theory and practice in social research and development*. London: Routledge.

187

——— 1992. 'From paradigm lost to paradigm regained? The case for an actor-oriented sociology of development'. In N. Long and A. Long (eds.) *Battlefields of knowledge.* London: Routledge.

Maganga, F. 1995. *Local institutions and sustainable resource management: The case of Babati District, Tanzania.* PhD dissertation. Centre for Development Research and Roskilde University Centre.

Moore, S.F. 1973. *Law as process.* London: Routledge.

——— 1986. *Social facts and fabrications. 'Customary' law on Kilimanjaro, 1880–1980.* Cambridge University Press.

——— 1989. 'History and the redefinition of custom on Kilimanjaro'. In J.F. Collier et al. (eds.), *History and power in the study of law.* Cornell University Press.

Mumford, W.B. 1934. 'The Hehe-Bena-Sangu peoples of East Africa', *American Anthropologist*, Vol. 36 No. 2.

Mustafa, K. 1993. 'Eviction of pastoralists from the Mkomazi Game Reserve in Tanzania: A statement'. *Pastoral Land Tenure series.* London: IIED.

Mwaikusa, J.T. 1994. 'Community rights and state control in Tanzania'. In *Never drink from the same cup.* Proceedings from the conference on Indigenous Peoples in Africa, Copenhagen 1993.

MWEM (Ministry of Water, Energy & Minerals, United Republic of Tanzania) 1995. 'Water resources management in the Great Ruaha basin'. Prepared for the Rufiji Basin Water Office, by Joint Danida/World Bank Study of Integrated Water and Land Management.

North, D.C. 1990. *Institutions, institutional change and economic performance.* Cambridge University Press.

Nuijten, M. 1992. 'Local organisation as organising practices. Rethinking rural institutions'. In N. Long and A. Long (ed.) *Battlefields of knowledge.* London: Routledge.

Odgaard, R. 1995. 'Specific examples of general living conditions in a rural community in South Western Tanzania: A gender perspective'. In *Report from seminar on development aspects of the 4th UN Women's World Conference, 8 May.* The Ministry of Foreign Affairs, Copenhagen, Denmark.

——— 1997. 'The gender dimension of Nyakyusa rural–rural migration in Mbeya Region'. In Ngware, Odgaard, Shayo and Wilson (eds.), *Gender and agrarian change in Tanzania.* DUP publications, University of Dar es Salaam.

——— and F. Maganga 1995. 'Local informal land and water management systems in the Ruaha River basin.' In MWEM.

Ostrom, E. 1990. *Governing the commons: The evolution of institutions for collective action.* Cambridge: Cambridge University Press.

——— 1992. *Crafting institutions for self-governing irrigation systems.* San Francisco: ICS Press.

Pendzich, C. 1994. 'Conflict management and forest disputes—A path out of the woods?' *Forests, trees and people newsletter,* No. 20.

Richards, P. 1985. *Indigenous agricultural revolution.* London: Hutchinson.

Shivji, I.G. 1994. 'A legal quagmire: Tanzania's regulation of land tenure (Establishment of Villages Act, 1992)'. IIED Drylands Programme, *Pastoral Land Tenure Series No. 5.* London: IIED.

Tenga, R. 1992. 'Pastoral land rights in Tanzania. A review'. IIED Drylands Programme, *Pastoral Land Tenure Series.* London: IIED.

Thebaud, B. 1995. 'Land tenure, environmental degradation and desertification in Africa: Some thoughts based on the Sahelian example'. IIED *Drylands Programme Paper No. 57.* London: IIED.

TNA (Tanzania National Archives). 'Mbeya District Handbook and Iringa District Handbook'. Dar es Salaam.

Uphoff, N. 1986. *Local institutional development.* Hartford, Conn.: Kumarian.

——— 1992. 'Local institutions and participation for sustainable development'. London, International Institute for Environment and Development, IIED *Gatekeeper Series,* No. 31.

URT (United Republic of Tanzania) 1994. *Report of the presidential commission of enquiry into land matters: Land policy and land tenure structure.* Uppsala: SIAS (Scandinavian Institute of African Studies).

Sustainable development, industrial metabolism and the process landscape—Reflections on regional material-flow studies

Anderberg, S. 1996. *Flödesanalys i den hållbara utvecklingens tjänst—Reflektioner kring en 'metabolism'-studie kring Rhenområdets utveckling.* Meddelanden från Lunds Universitets geografiska institutioner, avhandlingar 128. Lund University Press Studies, Studentlitteratur, Lund.

Anderberg, S., B. Bergbäck and U. Lohm 1989. 'Flow and distribution of chromium in the Swedish environment: A new approach to studying environmental pollution'. *Ambio*, No. 18:216–20.

Ayres, R.U. and S. Rod 1986. 'An historical reconstruction of pollutant levels in the Hudson-Raritan Basin.' *Environment*, Vol. 28 No. 4:14–20, 39–43.

Ayres, R.U. and U.E. Simonis (eds.) 1994. *Industrial metabolism: Restructuring for sustainable development.* United Nations University Press, Tokyo.

Bengtsson, A.-M., A. Hjort-af-Ornäs, J. Lundqvist and J. Rudengren (eds.) 1994. *The environment and free trade.* EPOS, Uppsala.

Bergbäck, B. 1992. *Industrial metabolism. The emerging immission landscape of heavy metal immissions in Sweden.* Linköping Studies in Arts and Science 76.

Bernauer, T. 1995. 'The international financing of environmental protection: Lessons from efforts to protect the River Rhine against chloride pollution.' *Environmental Politics*, Vol. 4 No. 3:369–90

Bernauer, T. and P. Moser 1996. 'Reducing pollution of the Rhine River: The influence of international co-operation.' Working Paper WP-96–7, International Institute for Applied Systems Analysis, Laxenburg, Austria.

Billen G., F. Toussaint, P. Peeters, P. Sapir, A. Steenhout and A. Vanderborght 1983. *L'écosystème belgique—Essai d'ecologie industrielle.* Editions du Centre de Recherche et d'information socio-politiques, Brüssel.

Brunner P.H., H. Daxbeck, P. Baccini 1994. 'Industrial metabolism at the regional and local level: A case-study on a Swiss region.' In R.U. Ayres and U.E. Simonis (eds.): *Industrial metabolism: Restructuring for sustainable development.* United Nations University Press, Tokyo, 163–93.

Damian, M., B. Chauduri, P. Berthaud and F. Catz 1996. 'Commerce international, environnement et développement durable. Sur quelque débats en cours'. Paper presented at the conference 'Ecologie-Société-Economie', Saint-Quentin-en-Yvelines, March 1996.

Graedel, T.E. and B.R. Allenby 1995. *Industrial ecology.* AT&T-Prentice Hall, Englewood Cliffs, N.J.

Grossman, G.M. and A.B. Krueger 1995. 'Economic growth and the environment.' *The Quarterly Journal of Economics*, No. 110:353–78.

Grübler, A. 1994. 'Industrialization as a historical phenomenon.' In R. Socolow, C. Andrews, F. Berkhout and V. Thomas (eds.): *Industrial ecology and global change.* Cambridge University Press, pp. 43–68.

Hägerstrand, T. 1993. 'Samhälle och natur'. In *Region och miljö—ekologiska perspektiv på den rumsliga närings—och bosättningsstrukturen.* NordREFO 1993:1, pp. 14–59.

IKSR 1987. *Tätigkeitsbericht 1987.* Internationale Kommission zum Schutze des Rheins gegen Verunreinigung, Koblenz.

Klepper, G., P. Michaelis and G. Mahlau 1995. *Industrial metabolism—A case study of the economics of cadmium control.* Mohr, Tübingen.

Lenntorp, B. 1993. De fyra nordiska husen. In *Region och miljö—ekologiska perspektiv på den rumsliga närings- och bosättningsstrukturen.* NordREFO 1993:1, pp. 76–111.

Lohm, U., S. Anderberg and B. Bergbäck 1994. 'Industrial metabolism at the national level: A case study on chromium and lead pollution in Sweden, 1880–1980'. In R.U.

Ayres and U.E. Simonis (eds.) *Industrial metabolism: Restructuring for sustainable development*. United Nations University Press, Tokyo, pp. 103–18.

Nelson, K. 1994. 'Finding and implementing projects to reduce waste'. In R. Socolow, C. Andrews, F. Berkhout and V. Thomas (eds.): *Industrial ecology and global change*. Cambridge University Press, pp. 371–82.

Newcombe, K., J.D. Kalma and A. Aston 1978. 'The metabolism of a city: The case of Hong Kong.' *Ambio*, Vol. 7 No. 1:3–15.

Paton, B. 1994. 'Design for environment: A management perspective.' In R. Socolow, C. Andrews, F. Berkhout and V. Thomas (eds.): *Industrial ecology and global change*. Cambridge University Press, pp.349–57.

Simonis, U.E.1994. 'Industrial restructuring in industrial countries'. In R.U. Ayres and U.E. Simonis (eds.): *Industrial metabolism: Restructuring for sustainable development*. United Nations University Press, Tokyo, pp. 31–54.

Socolow R., C. Andrews, F. Berkhout and V. Thomas (ed.) 1994. *Industrial ecology and global change*. Cambridge University Press.

Söderbaum, P. 1994. 'Ecology, economics and markets: internationalisation and self-reliance as two competing ideologies.' In A.-M. Bengtsson, A. Hjort-af-Ornäs, J. Lundquist and J. Rudengren (ed.): *The Environment and Free Trade*. EPOS, Uppsala, pp. 35–54.

Stigliani, W.M. 1995. 'Global perspectives and risk assessment.' In W. Salomons and W.M. Stigliani: *Biogeodynamics of pollutants in soils and sediments—Risk assessment of delayed and non-linear responses*. Springer Verlag, pp. 331–43.

Stigliani, W.M. and S. Anderberg 1994. 'Industrial metabolism at the regional level: The Rhine Basin'. In R.U. Ayres and U.E. Simonis: *Industrial metabolism: restructuring for sustainable development*. United Nations University Press, Tokyo, pp. 119–62.

Stigliani, W.M., P. Doelman, W. Salomons, R. Schulin, G.R.B. Smidt and S.E.A.T.M. van der Zee 1991. 'Chemical time bombs: predicting the unpredictable.' *Environment* Vol. 33:4–9, 26–30.

Stigliani, W.M. and P.R. Jaffé 1993. *Industrial metabolism: a new approach for analysis of chemical pollution and its potential applications*. Research report 93–6, International Institute for Applied Systems Analysis, Laxenburg, Austria, p. 23.

Stigliani, W.M., P.R. Jaffé and S. Anderberg 1993. 'Heavy metal pollution in the Rhine Basin'. *Environmental Science and Technology*, Vol. 27 No. 5: 786–92.

Thomas, C. (ed.) 1993. *Rio—Unravelling the consequences*. Frank Cass, Ilford, U.K.

van der Voet, E. 1996. *Substances from cradle to grave—Development of a methodology for the analysis of substance flows through the economy and the environment of a region with case studies on cadmium and nitrogen compounds*. Doctoral thesis, Centre of Environmental Studies, Leiden University.

Williams, M. 1993. 'International trade and the environment: Issues, perspectives and challenges. In C. Thomas (ed.): *Rio—Unravelling the consequences*. Frank Cass, Ilford, U.K., pp. 80–97.

Environmental awareness, conflict genesis and governance

Alger, C. F. 1990. 'Grassroots perspectives on global policies for development'. *Journal of Peace Research*, Vol. 27 No. 2: 155–68.

Annis, S. 1987. 'Can small-scale development be a large-scale policy? The case of Latin America'. *World Development*, Vol. 15 (Suppl.): 129–34.

Baldwin, D.A. 1995. 'Security studies and the end of the Cold War'. Review article, *World Politics*, Vol. 48 (1, Oct.): 117–41.

Booth, K. and P. Vale 1995. 'Security in Southern Africa: After apartheid, beyond realism'. *International Affairs*, Vol. 71 No. 2: 285–304.

Brock, L. 1991. 'Peace through parks: The environment on the peace research agenda'. *Journal of Peace Research*, Vol. 28 No. 4: 407–23.

Brodie, B. 1949. 'Strategy as a science'. *World Politics*, Vol. 1 (3, July): 462–80.

Brown, L. 1977. 'Redefining national security'. WorldWatch Institute Paper No. 14, Washington D.C. (Oct.).

Buzan, B. 1991. *Peoples, states and fears: An agenda for international security studies in the post-Cold War era*, 2nd edition. Boulder CO: Lynne Rienner Publishers.

Cable, V. 1995. 'What is international economic security?'. *International Affairs*, Vol. 71 No. 2: 305–24.

Carment, D. 1993. 'The international dimensions of ethnic conflict: Concepts, indicators, and theory', *Journal of Peace Research*, Vol. 30 No. 2: 137–50.

Del Rosso Jr, S. J. 1995. 'The insecure state: Reflections on "the state" and "security" in a changing world', *Daedalus*, Vol. 124 No. 2 (Spring): 175–207.

Derman, B. 1995. 'Environmental NGOs, dispossession, and the state: The ideology and praxis of African nature and development'. *Human Ecology*, Vol. 23 No. 2: 199–215.

Evans, G. 1994. 'Cooperative security and intra-state conflict'. *Foreign Policy*, No. 96 (Fall): 3–20.

Fisher, W.H. 1994. 'Megadevelopment, environmentalism, and resistance: The institutional context of Kayapo indigenous politics in central Brazil'. *Human Organization*, Vol. 53 No. 3: 220–32.

Friberg, M. and B. Hettne 1988. 'Local mobilization and world system politics'. *International Social Science Journal*, Vol. 40 No. 3: 341–60.

Harff, B. 1995. 'Rescuing endangered peoples: Missed opportunities'. *Social Research*, Vol. 62 No. 1 (Spring): 23–40.

Hjort-af-Ornäs, A. and M. A. Mohamed Salih (ed.) 1989. *Ecology and politics: Environmental stress and security in Africa*. Uppsala: Scandinavian Institute of African Studies.

Homer-Dixon, T.E. 1994. 'Environmental scarcities and violent conflict'. *International Security*, Vol. 19 No. 1 (Summer): 5–40.

Ignatieff, M. 1995. 'The seductiveness of moral disgust'. *Social Research*, Vol. 62 No. 1 (Spring): 77–97.

Jackson, R.H. 1990. *Quasi-states: Sovereignty, international relations, and the Third World*. Cambridge Studies in International Relations 12. Cambridge: Cambridge University Press.

Kaplan, R. 1994. 'The coming anarchy'. *The Atlantic Monthly* (February): 44–76.

Latham, R. 1995. 'Knowledge and security in a post-Cold War world'. *Items*, Vol. 49 No. 2/3 (June–September): 43–8.

McNamara, R. 1968. *The essence of security: Reflections in office*. New York: Harper & Row.

Myers, N. 1989. 'Environment and security'. *Foreign Policy*, No. 74 (Spring): 23–41.

Prins, G. 1992. 'The global security programme: A key emerging initiative in the campaign for Cambridge'. Cambridge University Global Security Programme Document.

Schelling, T. 1960. *The strategy of conflict*. Cambridge, Mass: Harvard University Press.

Ullman, R. H. 1983. 'Redefining security'. *International Security* (Summer): 123–29.

Wapner, P. 1995. 'Politics beyond the state: Environmental activism and world civic politics'. *World Politics*, Vol. 47 No. 3 (April): 311–40.

World Commission on Environment and Development 1987. *Our common future*. New York: Oxford University Press.

Wright, Q. 1942. *Study of war*, cited in Baldwin, 1995.

Culture, cultural values, norms and meanings—A framework for environmental understanding

Flint, V.I.J. 1992. *The imaginative landscape of Christopher Columbus*. Princeton University Press.

Hjort, A. and U. Svedin 1992. 'Cultural variation in concepts of Nature', *Geojournal*, Vol. 26 No. 2.

Kates, R.W. 1988. 'Theories of Nature, Society and Technology'. In E. Baark and U. Svedin (ed.), *Man, nature and technology. Essays on the role of ideological perceptions*. London: Macmillan, pp. 7–36.

Svedin, U. 1992. 'The challenge of the societal dimension to environmental issues: A Swedish research response'. In U. Svedin and B. Hägerhäll Aniansson (eds.), *Society and the environment: A Swedish research perspective*. Dordrecht, the Netherlands: Kluwer Academic Publishers.

Teilhard de Chardin, P. 1940. *Le phénomène humain*. Editions du Seuil.